Women
for
President

University of
Illinois Press
Urbana
and Chicago

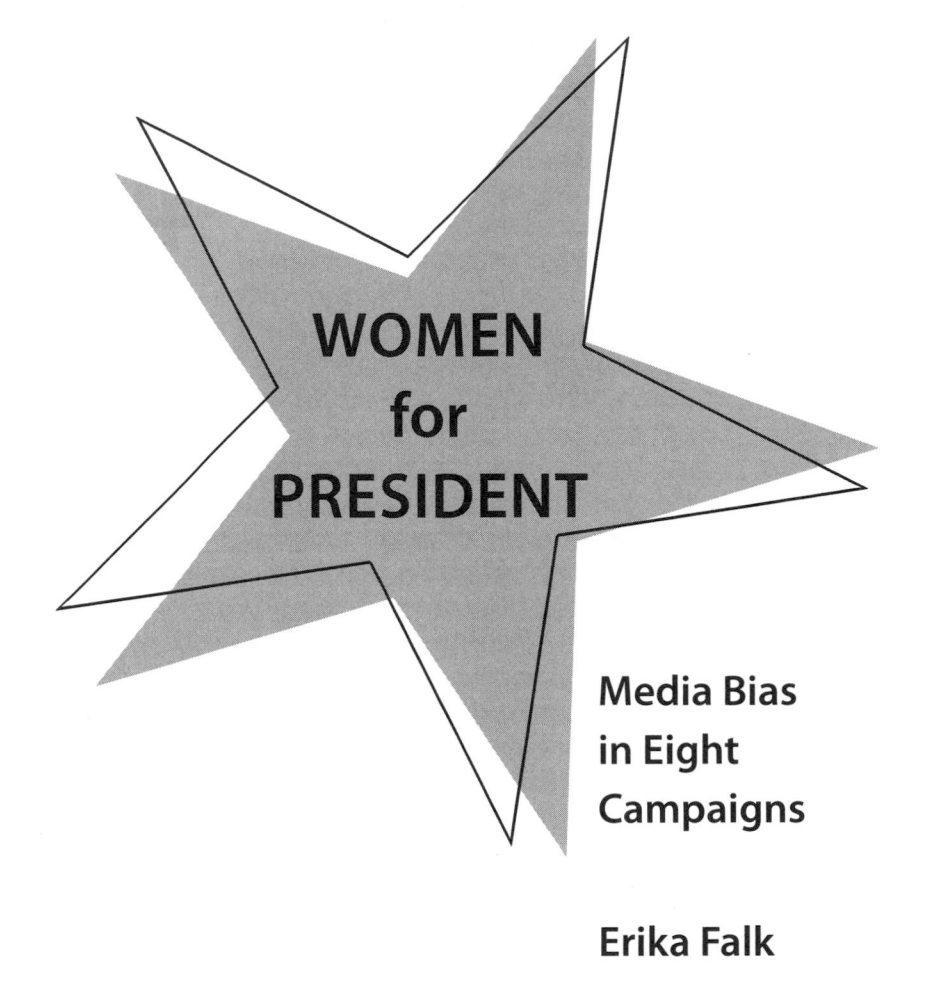

WOMEN
for
PRESIDENT

Media Bias
in Eight
Campaigns

Erika Falk

Library of Congress Cataloging-
in-Publication Data
Falk, Erika.
Women for president : media bias
in eight campaigns / Erika Falk.
p.   cm.
Includes bibliographical references
and index.
ISBN-13 978-0-252-03311-7 (cloth : alk. paper)
ISBN-10 0-252-03311-6 (cloth : alk. paper)
ISBN-13 978-0-252-07511-7 (pbk. : alk. paper)
ISBN-10 0-252-07511-0 (pbk. : alk. paper)
1. Women presidential candidates—
United States. 2. Journalism—Objectivity—
United States. 3. Sex role—Political
aspects—United States.
I. Title
HQ1391.U5F35   2008
324.9730082—dc22   2007030326

Portions of this book previously appeared
in E. Falk and K. H. Jamieson, "Changing the
Climate of Expectations," in *Anticipating
Madam President,* edited by Robert P.
Watson and Ann Gordon, 43–51; copyright
© 2003 Lynne Rienner Publishers; used
with permission. K. Kenski and E. Falk,
"Of What Is That Glass Ceiling Made? A
Study of Attitudes about Women and the
Oval Office," *Women and Politics* 26 (4):
57–80 (2004). E. Falk and K. Kenski, "Issue
Saliency and Gender Stereotypes: Support
for Women as Presidents in Times of War
and Terrorism," *Social Science Quarterly*
87 (1): 1–18 (2006). E. Falk and K. Kenski,
"Sexism and Partisanship: A New Look at
the Question of Whether America Is Ready
for a Woman President," *Sex Roles* 54 (7/8):
413–28 (2006); used with kind permission
of Springer Science and Business Media,
Klewer Academic Publishers.

To the women
who will run
and win

CONTENTS

Illustrations follow page 82.

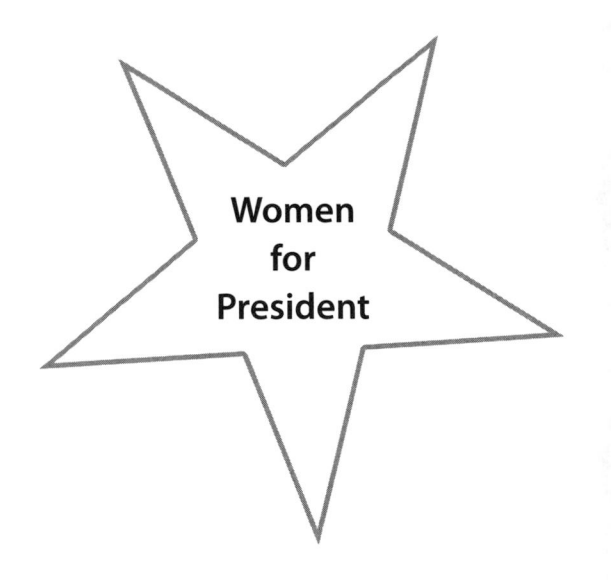

Women
for
President

INTRODUCTION

In January 2007 Senator Hillary Clinton declared her intention to seek the White House and in doing so became the first woman to enter the race as a front-runner for the Democratic Party nomination. A December 2006 poll by the Gallup Organization reported that respondents named Senator Clinton most often (33 percent) as their choice for the Democratic nomination. Senator Barack Obama, who entered the race four days before Clinton, was named second (20 percent). Even though Clinton polled better than Obama, in the month in which both candidates announced they would run for president the top six circulating papers in the United States ran fifty-nine stories that mentioned Obama in the headline and just thirty-six that mentioned Clinton.

That the press seemed biased against a woman running for president was not surprising. In fact, historical trends show that women candidates for president consistently receive less press coverage than equivalent men running in the same race. What was surprising was that such a disparity was present when the woman was the front-runner, and that such a pattern, which had been manifest in press coverage since 1884, still held in 2007. Of course, this was not the first time a prominent and qualified woman had run for president and been treated badly by the press.

In May 1999, Robert Dole, the husband of the Republican presidential candidate Elizabeth Dole, was interviewed in the *New York Times* (Berke 1999). In the course of that now famous interview, Bob Dole told the reporter he "wanted to contribute to the campaign of [rival Republican candidate] Senator John McCain." When given the opportunity to predict that his wife and not the front-runner, George W. Bush, was going to win, he instead said of Bush, "He's in a strong position, no question about it." In response to a question about why, when he was a candidate, he had "never memorized his speeches" as Elizabeth Dole did, he noted that "given his decades in the Senate and service as majority leader he had always felt comfortable discussing issues," implying that his wife did not. If such a dismal portrayal by a spouse of a presidential candidate was ever previously printed in the press, it is not widely known.

In presidential campaigns, media portrayals are particularly important. Unlike lower-level races where interpersonal contact plays a central role, in presidential contests most of what constituents know about any candidate is learned from the media. The press plays an integral role in the campaign by framing, shaping, ignoring, or presenting the candidates to the public. More important, how the press portrays and treats candidates may affect who later decides to be a candidate. Although media reports about a candidate vary, and people draw upon very different experiences and ideas in interpreting them, consistencies and patterns can have important effects. One of the most important potential effects of media coverage of campaigns may be its influence on political participation. Depending on the content, the media can encourage people to participate, engage, and become interested in the political process, or instead determine that the political sphere is not for them.

The early data on press coverage of Clinton's announcement is a single example of press bias against a woman candidate, and the *New York Times* article on Bob Dole's feelings about Elizabeth Dole's candidacy is a single example in which a candidate was portrayed as not very viable. When multiple reports and papers consistently shortchange women or invite the same negative inferences, the candidate and her supporters may be justifiably concerned. Being ignored by the press or being portrayed as a loser almost certainly becomes prophecy. However, when those media patterns involve classes of people and persist across time, the concern is not only for a particular candidate but also for society at large. If we find that women in general, and not just Hillary Clinton and Elizabeth Dole, tend to be treated by the press less seriously than similar men, then the pattern undermines the chances of individuals and also deters women from believing they will be successful should they run. More important, it calls into question the modern democratic assumption that men and women have comparable access to positions of power.

The idea that almost everything known about national candidates is imparted through the media and that systematic bias can have important social effects led me to conduct this study of how newspapers portray women who run for president. In conducting this research, I asked three questions. First, Is there evidence of subtle or overt ways in which the press may have advantaged men or women candidates? Second, Does the press mitigate or perpetrate existing stereotypes and gender roles, particularly about political women? Third, Could the way the press covers women candidates affect women's decision to run for office? Answering these questions is important to understanding how the press may affect women who run for president or other offices (or who decide not to).

The first woman to run for U.S. president was Victoria Woodhull. She ran in 1872 on the Equal Rights Party ticket. Since that time about fifteen American women have gained the nomination of their party. Many more (about one hundred) have sought but not obtained their party's nomination, including approximately fifty who have sought nomination from the Republican or Democratic Parties (Havel 1996). Most of these women did little to advance their cases; they were unknown and received no press coverage. However, among them were women who, given different circumstances, might have become president. These include multiterm members of Congress, cabinet members, ambassadors, women on the ballot in all of the states, and women receiving Federal Primary Matching Funds (FPMF). These are the women selected for this study. Despite the fact that these women campaigned and received press coverage, they are like most losing candidates—lost to history.

The absence of widespread political knowledge about the impressive and capable women who have lived political lives is not without consequence. As I will document in this book, some of the resistance to women's full political integration has grown out of a misconception that women are novel and unnatural in the political sphere. Moreover, the feminist historian Gerda Lerner (1993) argued that the absence of women in official and academic histories has resulted in the retardation of women's intellectual (and I would add political) advancement. Such an absence of historical awareness has meant that women have been denied the opportunity to stand on the shoulders of their predecessors. Thus, although many women have run for president, lackluster press coverage of their campaigns has contributed to the fact that few women are aware of these candidacies, making a female presidential candidacy seem less normative and more difficult. Moreover, as I will discuss in this book, the way the press portrays (and ignores) women who run also makes women appear novel and awkward in the political sphere. This may deter women from having their own political aspirations.

Women have headed nations throughout the world, including in unexpected places such as Turkey, Ireland, Pakistan, and Sri Lanka, not to mention Canada, France, and England. Yet in the United States, which considers itself the most advanced democracy in the world, no woman has ever held the presidency or the vice presidency. Only once has an American woman even been selected as a vice presidential candidate on a major party ticket. That was Geraldine Ferraro in 1984. Some people say the reason there has not been a woman on a major party ticket since Ferraro's defeat is because that ticket fared so badly that the Democratic National Committee (DNC) determined it would never put another woman on the ballot. However, Walter Mondale, the 1984 presidential candidate, was already down nineteen points when Ferraro was nominated. Pat Schroeder, then a U.S. representative, pointed out that given Mondale's showing, it is surprising that the DNC would ever put another man on the ticket. After the 1984 election the *New York Times* estimated that Ferraro had given the Democrats a small net gain in that race (Zipp and Plutzer 1985).

It is remarkable that women have never held the presidency in the United States, given that studies have consistently shown that women who run for lower political office win just as often as men do (Seltzer, Newman, and Leighton 1997). This is despite the fact that bias in the press against women has been shown to exist in congressional and gubernatorial races. Since there is considerable social pressure against women's running for public office, the women who do choose to pursue it may be more driven and competent than the average male candidate. Thus the women compensate for bias in the press. If women tend to succeed despite such prejudice, why should we be concerned about biased and sterotypical press coverage of women at all political levels? As a free and democratic country that prides itself on creating a fair and level political playing field, in which any citizen has the theoretical right to pursue public office, we should be concerned if the press is biased in favor of one class of people over another. This remains true, even if women can compensate for the inequity.

Another reason for us to be concerned is that the press coverage (or lack thereof) may have a chilling effect on women's desire run. That is to say, the press, which tends to ignore women candidates and paints them in stereotypical ways, may deter women from running, and this may be the most significant problem in making gains for women in office. In fact, just 8 percent of candidates for Congress are women, and the percentage of candidates is much lower when it comes to the presidency. Many scholars of women's political participation note that a major reason women are underrepresented in public office is that they run much less frequently than men do.

What might be the most significant effect of lack of coverage, stereotypical coverage, and coverage that makes women appear less likely to win than they actually are? These conditions may suppress women's political engagement and interest and minimize the role-modeling benefits that political women can provide to other women; as a result fewer women are likely to pursue political office. Of course, when women don't run, they don't win. Since the presidency is not considered an entry-level position, a female presidential candidate would have to have run for and won a lower political office; but if few women run, there are few women in the feeder positions that lead to the presidency.

Since the presidency of Eisenhower, all of the candidates that won the office have previously been governor of a state, served in both the House and the Senate, served as vice president, or held the rank of five-star general. However, there have been only thirty-five women in the history of the United States with that kind of experience. There is a strikingly small pool from which to draw female presidential candidates.

There are other reasons for women's slow integration into the political system. About 95 percent of incumbents in the U.S. Congress win reelection, and most incumbents are men. Challengers win only about 5 percent of the time. Even if all challengers were women, the rate at which they would integrate the U.S. Congress would be slow. However, as noted above, just 8 percent of candidates for the U.S. Congress are women, which slows their advancement through the political system and minimizes the likelihood that a woman will seek the presidency.

This process is in many ways self-perpetuating. The relative scarcity of women in higher offices combined with the press's propensity to ignore women who do run means that women are less likely to have role models and mentors. Moreover, Ruth Mandel, a political researcher, found that women were more likely than men to "attribute inspiration or assistance with their political careers to female role models, mentors, and the campaigns of other female candidates" (1993, 46). The importance of role models to political ambition was aptly demonstrated in a political cartoon that appeared during Prime Minister Margaret Thatcher's incumbency. In it a boy and a girl discussed what they would like to be when they grow up. The boy said, "I want to be Prime Minister," but the girl retorted, "You can't be Prime Minister. You are a boy." One of the findings of my research is that women receive less media coverage than men, even when we compare losing candidates. Thus, by ignoring women candidates and painting them in stereotypical ways, the press may amplify the impression that women do not belong in the political sphere and it may minimize the potential effects of women as role models.

Not all of the encumbrances are external. Many researchers point to "role conflict" as a major contributor to women's low rates of candidacy. Traditional social mores have assigned the task of child rearing and housekeeping to women and to some extent this holds true in society today. At the same time, over the last century, women have become increasingly integrated into the workforce. This has created what some feminists have identified as the double burden. Women are not only expected to work as men do; in many families they are also primarily responsible for child care and housekeeping duties. This added burden may deter or delay women's political involvement. Press coverage may present female candidates in traditional roles, highlighting their personal lives and family responsibilities rather than their political accomplishments. Women who read such coverage are reminded that their primary duties and responsibilities lie in the domestic and not the political sphere.

This point is amplified by the fact that women are more likely to run for office after their family responsibilities have diminished. Mandel wrote, "Elected women are more likely than elected men to be widowed, separated, or divorced, and they are less likely to have young children at home. Furthermore, elected women are more likely than elected men to report that the age of their children was an important factor in their decision to run for office" (1993, 46). The fact that women are more likely to feel free to run after children are grown or a husband has left means a later entry into elected office, which leaves them less time to reach the highest political ranks.

Another factor that discourages women from running may be the persistence of the erroneous belief that women have less chance of winning office than do men. As noted earlier, studies show that when women run they win just as often as men do (Seltzer, Newman, and Leighton 1997). However, most people don't believe it. A survey conducted by the National Women's Political Caucus found that two-thirds of a national sample thought it was harder for women than men to get elected (Newman 1994). This belief may be fostered predominantly by the press, which tends to portray women as less viable than men and to cover them less often, making them seem less normative.

As this book will demonstrate, if the press fails to cover women candidates it may exaggerate the impression that women are unusual or risky as office holders, and it may also minimize the opportunity for women to see other women as role models. If the press portrays women as less likely to win, women may resist running. If the press perpetuates anachronistic stereotypes, women may feel less comfortable entering the traditionally male sphere of politics, and if the press trivializes and ridicules women who do run, women may be less likely to hold themselves up for such treatment. There is very good reason to be worried if the press treats women candidates differently than men, because this bias would threaten the very heart of the American dream of equality. However, the more insidious problem with the press treatment of women may be that it makes public office seem less attractive to potential women candidates, resulting in fewer women running.

To reach these conclusions, I analyzed the press coverage of the eight most prominent women who have run for president of the United States: Victoria Claflin Woodhull (candidate in 1872), Belva Bennett Lockwood (1884), Margaret Chase Smith (1964), Shirley St. Hill Chisholm (1972), Patricia Scott Schroeder (1987), Lenora Branch Fulani (1988), Elizabeth Dole (2000), and Carol Moseley Braun (2004). Through the use of content analysis, I also compared the press coverage of each of these women to that of the most equivalent man who sought the same office in the same year, and I examined polling data on attitudes about women and the presidency.

According to the historian James Havel (1996), more than one hundred women have run for president but few of them had any legislative or electoral experience; most did not conduct formal campaigns and few received any press coverage. In this study I selected the women in each decade that were most likely to gain press attention. In choosing these women, I used several criteria. First, I looked for availability of information, since very little is known about most women who ran. The women about whom the most is known were the ones with historical significance as well as those with more successful and well-organized campaigns. I assessed viability, selecting women whose biographies suggested they had presidential character or pertinent experience. In determining viability, I took into account the amount of money raised, the number of states in which the candidate was on the ballot, and the legislative or electoral experience of the candidate. I also selected women from different periods so as to be able to make historical comparisons. Finally, I chose women who represent important milestones in the development of credentials.

From the earliest period in which women ran for president (the late 1800s), I selected two women—Victoria Woodhull and Belva Lockwood. Both ran as Equal Rights Party candidates (different parties of the same name) before universal suffrage. As these two were the first women to run, more than one hundred years ago and twelve years apart, they provided an interesting opportunity for historical comparison. Both women ran during a period of intense social dialogue about the role of women, and their cases thus provided ample and interesting data for examination. Each of these women had the endorsement of her party, and each had a career and experiences that provided suitable qualification for holding the highest executive office. Woodhull ran in 1872. She owned her own newspaper, was the first woman stockbroker on Wall Street, and presided over and supported her extended family. As such, Woodhull had the character and experience necessary for executive office.

Belva Lockwood was the second woman to run for president. She sought the presidency in 1884. As an attorney and partner in her own firm, and as the first woman to practice law before the United States Supreme Court, she had a profession consistent with those of other presidential candidates. She also had campaigned for Horace Greeley and drafted a piece of legislation that was passed by Congress. As the owner and administrator of her own private school, she also had executive experience.

Margaret Chase Smith was the first woman to seek the presidential nomination of the Republican Party and the first woman holding federal office to run; she ran in 1964 after serving nine years in the House and twenty-four years in the Senate. She placed third in popular votes in the Republican primary, but she received only twenty-seven delegate votes at the convention that ultimately nominated Barry Goldwater.

In the following decade (1972), Shirley Chisholm sought the nomination of the Democratic Party after serving two terms in the House of Representatives. Before entering the House she had a long history of political involvement at the local level, and she served two terms in the New York State legislature. With a master's degree in education, she also worked as a school supervisor and for the New York City Board of Education. She was the first woman with national legislative experience to seek the Democratic nomination.

Lenora Fulani ran for president in 1988 and received the nomination of the New Alliance Party. Though Fulani had no legal or legislative experience and had not been previously elected to office, that year she became the first woman to be on the ballot in all fifty states and the District of Columbia. She also became the second third-party candidate to receive Federal Primary Matching Funds (FPMF) (Salit 1999). Fulani was a psychologist by training and had extensive experience in grassroots organizing. Unfortunately, after conducting some research on Fulani I found very few articles about her. Therefore, I decided to add another race from the 1980s.

The woman with the most information available about her was Patricia Schroeder, a Harvard-educated attorney who had served in Congress for eight terms. At the time she ran, she was a senior member of the House Armed Services Committee. Unlike the candidates who preceded her, Schroeder never formally declared her intention to run. I included her, however, because for the four months of her "testing-the-waters campaign" during summer 1987 she acted like a candidate for the Democratic

Party nomination—giving speeches, traveling to New Hampshire and Iowa, and raising money. She also raised enough money to qualify for Federal Primary Matching Funds (Brozan 1987) and during her campaign consistently received about 8 percent of the projected vote in polls.

Elizabeth Dole considered running for the Republican nomination in 2000. Though she too never "officially" declared her candidacy, Dole did campaign for the nomination. Her campaign consisted of a formal announcement, travel, fund raising, stump-speeches, regular news releases about foreign and domestic policy, and ultimately a formal withdrawal. A Harvard-educated lawyer, Dole had served in the cabinet of two different presidential administrations (as secretary of transportation and secretary of labor, respectively). She also had executive experience as president of the American Red Cross and, like Fulani and Schroeder, qualified for Federal Primary Matching Funds (Salant 1999).

Until Hillary Clinton declared, the woman who ran most recently was Carol Moseley Braun in 2004. A Chicago native, Moseley Braun had served six years as an assistant U.S. attorney, ten years in the Illinois House of Representatives, and one term as U.S. senator. She was the ambassador to New Zealand during the administration of President William J. Clinton. In January 2003 Moseley Braun announced she would run for president (though it was not made official until September). She left the race in January 2004, before the first primaries were held.

These eight candidates represent seven different decades and three centuries. Of the eight, five ran for the nomination of one of the two major parties (Chase Smith, Chisholm, Schroeder, Dole, and Moseley Braun) and three ran with the nomination of a minor party (Woodhull, Lockwood, and Fulani). Of the five who ran for major party nominations, three sought the Democratic (Chisholm, Schroeder, and Moseley Braun) and two the Republican nomination (Chase Smith and Dole). Of the eight, five had significant national political experience (Smith, Chisholm, Schroeder, Dole, and Moseley Braun), six had earned graduate degrees (Lockwood, Chisholm, Schroeder, Fulani, Dole, and Moseley Braun), and three had qualified for Federal Primary Matching Funds (FPMF) (Schroeder, Fulani, and Dole).

In order to assess the way in which gender affected the portrayal of these candidates, I also studied a comparable man candidate from each of the respective elections. This enabled me to identify characteristics of the portrayals that were related to gender. For example, without comparisons with men, what may appear to be characteristic of women candidates may in fact characterize losing or third-party candidates. In selecting man candidates I tried to use quantitative criteria by selecting the candidate with the closest number of votes or percentage of projected votes in polls as the woman candidate. In no case was there a perfect match available; rather, I selected the most comparable candidate. Below I detail why each candidate was considered the "most equivalent" and highlight some similarities and differences that may have affected the press coverage.

In the first two elections I studied, the comparison candidates were selected because, like the women in those races, they had the endorsement of a third party and received very few votes. In 1872, when Victoria Woodhull ran for the presidency, the third-party candidate with the second-to-lowest number of votes was James Black, who ran with the Prohibition Party's nomination (Havel 1996). The candidate with the lowest number of votes after Woodhull was William Groesbeck, but as he had previously held political office, I felt that Black was a better match; like Woodhull, Black had never held elected office. On the other hand, Black had studied law whereas Woodhull had only three years of formal schooling; and although Woodhull actively campaigned, Black did not.

In 1884, when Belva Lockwood ran with the nomination of the Equal Rights Party, Benjamin Butler ran as the nominee of the Greenback Party. Butler was the third-party candidate receiving the fewest votes (who remained in the election). Like Lockwood, he was an attorney, but unlike Lockwood, he had held previous elected offices, including several terms in the U.S. House (Havel 1996).

In 1964 and 1972 the women candidates studied were running in primary elections, and the comparable men were selected because they were running in the same primary and party and had the next closest number of primary votes. In 1964, when Margaret Chase Smith ran for the Republican nomination, Nelson Rockefeller also sought the nomination of the Republican Party and was the next closest candidate to Chase Smith in his primary vote total (Havel 1996). Both Rockefeller and Chase Smith had previous political experience and were on the liberal end of the Republican Party. Whereas Chase Smith had served in the U.S. House and Senate, Rockefeller was governor of New York. Rockefeller had a bachelor's degree; Chase Smith had a high-school diploma (Havel 1996). In 1972, when Shirley Chisholm sought the Democratic Party nomination, the next closest primary vote-getter was Henry Jackson (Havel 1996). Both had held national office; Chisholm was a representative in the U.S. House, and Jackson served in both the House and Senate (Havel 1996).

Detailed information about how much money Woodhull, Lockwood, Chase Smith, and Chisholm raised was difficult to obtain since they ran before federal election reform legislation of 1974 that established the Federal Election Commission. However, it is reasonable to assume that all may have raised less money than their counterparts. Woodhull's biographers note that she had trouble raising money after she began taking up the cause of working people. Lockwood ran a very short campaign, and both Chase Smith and Chisholm had built reputations on running and winning office on very low budgets, relying on volunteers and not a paid staff. According to Nichola Gutgold (2006), during Chase Smith's presidential campaign the candidate refused to accept contributions and "anyone who sent her money soon received their donation back with a kind note that she simply could not accept it" (39).

In 1987, when Representative Pat Schroeder considered running for president, Representative Richard Gephardt was the closest in poll results (Schroeder did not stay in long enough to enter any primaries). In July, soon after the press began reporting that Schroeder was considering entering the race, a CBS News and *New York Times* survey gave Schroeder 5 percent and Gephardt 3 percent of the vote (Roper Poll 1987b). At the end of September, right before Schroeder dropped out, ABC News and the *Washington Post* published a poll showing that of the Democratic candidates Schroeder polled 8 percent and Gephardt 9 percent of the Democratic vote (Roper Poll 1987a). Gephardt's record of experience was similar to Schroeder's. He had entered the House in 1976; she had entered in 1972. Both were attorneys, and both had qualified for Federal Primary Matching Funds. Gephardt, by the end of his campaign, had raised more money than Schroeder overall (about nine million dollars compared to about a million), though he had campaigned for much longer. Whereas Schroeder "explored" for just four months, Gephardt officially ran for thirteen months and unofficially for much longer.

In 1988, Lenora Fulani ran with the endorsement of the New Alliance Party. The third-party candidate to receive the closest number of votes to that of Fulani was Ron Paul, who ran as the nominee of the Libertarian Party. As of October 1997 Fulani had raised about one million dollars and received about one million dollars in matching funds (Federal Election Commission 1997). It is believed that Paul could have qualified for matching funds but since the Libertarian Party philosophically opposed the program, he did not apply (Holman 1988). Press reports described his raising about two million dollars, giving both candidates budgets of about the same size. Fulani was on the ballot in all fifty states and the District of Columbia; Paul, in forty-seven states and the District of Columbia ("Here Is the Final Vote Count" 1988). Fulani has a Ph.D. whereas Paul has an M.D. degree. Though Fulani never held elected office, Paul had served four terms in the U.S. House as a Texas representative.

Elizabeth Dole ran in the 2000 campaign. In January 1999, when Dole began campaigning, she was polling 26 percent of the vote. The next closest was Dan Quayle at 7 percent, and Steve Forbes was at 5 percent, according to a Roper Poll report (1999b). Just before she dropped out in August, Dole was polling 14 percent, whereas Forbes then polled 6 percent and Quayle was at 5 percent of the vote, according to a Roper Poll (1999a). Quayle had electoral experience, whereas Forbes, like Dole, had never held elected office, making Forbes a better comparison candidate for my purposes. Dole qualified for FPMF; Forbes chose not to accept the funds and instead used his vast personal resources to fund his campaign. They both raised about the same amount of money (Dole $5.1 million and Forbes $5.7 million; Federal Election Commission 2000). Though neither had held elected positions before, Dole had held cabinet positions whereas Forbes had not. Both had extensive executive experience, Forbes running his family business and Dole as president of the American Red Cross.

Between March 2003 and January 2004, when polling organizations were asking regularly who supported Carol Moseley Braun, she polled on average 4.1 percent of voters. From March through September, when Bob Graham was running, he polled about 4.2 percent of the vote, making him the primary contender with a similar level of support. These candidates had other similarities as well. Both Graham and Moseley Braun had sat in the U.S. Senate. However, Graham was still sitting at the time of his candidacy whereas Moseley Braun was out of office. She had just served one term, whereas Graham had served three. Graham had also served two terms as governor of Florida; Moseley Braun had served as ambassador to New Zealand and Samoa during the Clinton administration. She had a J.D. and had worked as an attorney and prosecutor in the United States Attorney's office in Chicago. Graham had just an LL.B. Both candidates had significant state-level electoral experience. Graham had also served two terms in the Florida House of Representatives and two terms in the Florida State Senate. Similarly, Moseley Braun served in the Illinois House of Representatives for eight years, including service as the assistant majority leader. She was elected Cook County recorder of deeds and held that position for four years. Despite their similarity in background and level of support, Graham had raised much more money, over five million dollars, whereas Moseley Braun had raised just over six hundred thousand.

Of course, no two candidates are equal in all areas (qualifications, ability, support, and money), and trying to match candidates from limited possibilities is an inexact science. I tried to defer to more objective measures, such as poll and vote totals, when comparing candidates, and I then took experience into account. However, using vote totals has an inherent problem. The vote or poll results are often affected by the press coverage that the candidates received. If, for example, the press were biased against women, that bias, rather than comparative merit, may have affected the results of the race. In other words, my selections may have minimized the probability of finding differences in the way gender affects press coverage. The actual disparity may be much greater.

As I explain in the appendix to this book, data for all campaigns were drawn from the *New York Times* from the first day of the first month that the first candidate entered the race in each year studied to the day the last candidate withdrew or the election was held, whichever came first. I also searched the largest circulating newspaper in the home state of each candidate, from the first day of the first month when each entered the race until the election or the date the candidate exited the race. I collected, read, and analyzed more than 1,240 articles that mentioned the candidates.

★ ★ ★

Over the 130-year period in which American women have been running for president, attitudes about women's roles and potentials have changed. In February 1937 a Gallup poll asked respondents, "Would you vote for a woman for president if she were qualified in every *other* respect?" [emphasis added]. Perhaps the respondents were influenced by the thinking of the times or perhaps they were affected by the wording of the question, which supposed that being a woman disqualified one for the job, but only 33 percent of respondents said they would vote for a woman. Through the ensuing years, pollsters continued to ask the same question with minor variations (they dropped the phrase "every other respect" after 1939). Favorable responses rose steadily, roughly keeping pace with the year. By 1955 about half said they would vote for a woman (Gallup 1955), and by 1977 it was 77 percent (General Social Survey 1977). In 1996, 91 percent said they would vote for a woman for president if she were qualified and "if your party nominated [her]" (General Social Survey 1996). One might expect that the dramatic change in the answers over the last fifty years would indicate a shift in conceptions about women and their role in politics, particularly as candidates, and that such a shift would be strongly reflected in the press coverage.

Attitudes about women in office are not the only things that have changed over the last 130 years. Women's involvement in the public sphere itself has been radically transformed. In 1872, when the first woman ran for president, no women held political office and women were not allowed to vote. In many states when a woman got married she suffered a "civil death" and became the property of her husband. Women were very rare in the media world as well. Aside from a few notable exceptions, women did not own, produce, or write the news.

The essential finding of this book is that despite striking and important changes over the last century in women's social and political rights and in attitudes about women and politics, the press has not changed how it covers women candidates. Press coverage is often biased and prejudiced, and it is not much better today than it was in 1872. The most important consequence of this is not what most people would expect: that should a woman run, the press would make it less likely for her to win. The most important consequence is that the press coverage may make women less likely to run.

This conclusion becomes clear over the course of the following chapters. In the first chapter, "Why Worry about the Press?" I present studies from social science that show that language and media affect what people know, what they think about, and how people think. This chapter argues that how the press covers candidates and the language used to do so are important.

In chapter 2, "Unnatural, Incapable, and Unviable," I analyze explicit arguments for and against women candidates for president that appeared in the press between 1872 and 2004. Most press accounts argued that women are "unnatural" in the political sphere and "incompetent" as leaders. They also portrayed women as "unviable" as candidates. Unlike most other aspects of the coverage, explicit arguments have changed over time, and press accounts about the advantages and capabilities of women are more common today than in the past.

Chapter 3, "Baking Muffins and Bombing Countries," notes that compared to equivalent men, women candidates were more likely to be described by their emotions, to have their families mentioned, to be referred to by their first names, and to be framed as aspiring to the vice presidency rather than the presidency, even when they had explicitly said they were not interested in that job. This chapter concludes that stereotypes dominate coverage of women candidates.

Chapter 4, "High-Heeled Boots and Violet Suits," shows that women candidates are more likely than men to be described by how they look. Even when the press gives a physical description of men, such accounts are more likely to mention age, whereas women are most frequently characterized by what they wear. The sad conclusion of this chapter is that even though the number of women in public office may have changed in the past 130 years, the propensity of the press to comment on clothing has not.

In chapter 5, "Do Newspapers Give Equal Coverage to Men and Women Presidential Candidates?" I look at the number of articles written about men and women candidates and conclude that when equivalent candidates are compared, the press writes less about women. Women are less likely to be the subject of articles, but when they are, the articles are shorter than those written about similar men. This chapter also demonstrates that sexism and not viability is behind the lack of coverage.

Chapter 6, "Issues, Biography, and Chaff," concludes that the coverage of women candidates focuses on fewer issues than coverage of male candidates. The press is less likely to describe a woman as having a chance of winning even when the men and women are equally likely to win. Overall, the press portrays women as losers and novelties and not serious candidates.

The final chapter asks the question "Is America Ready?" There I note that press accounts regularly describe America as not ready for a woman president despite the fact that polling on this issue is dramatically at odds with that conclusion. Who supports women candidates and who does not? The interesting results indicate that should a woman run today, she would have no trouble getting elected despite the biased press coverage. The real problem may be that the biased press dissuades women from running.

Finally, in the conclusion, I summarize the findings from the previous chapters and note that although women have made tremendous gains in rights and attitudes about their capacities, there is no clear trend showing improvement in the press's coverage of women candidates. This portion of the book explains why the press is biased and gives tactical suggestions for overcoming the challenges the press presents for women running for the Oval Office. The appendix offers a detailed explanation about how the data for this study were collected and analyzed.

References

Berke, R. L. 1999. "As Political Spouse, Bob Dole Strays from Campaign Script." *New York Times,* May 17, A1.

Brozan, N. 1987. "Woman in the News; NOW Leader: Born Feminist—Molly Yard." *New York Times,* July 20, A1.

Federal Election Commission. 1997. *The Commission's Comprehensive Examinations of the Presidential Public Funding Program.* October 9. Available through LexisNexis.

Federal Election Commission. 2000. *Receipts of 1999–2000 Presidential Campaigns through July 31, 2000.* July 31. Retrieved October 5, 2006, from http://www.fec.gov/finance/precm8.htm.

Gallup. 1937. "Would You Vote for a Woman for President If She Were Qualified in Every Other Respect?" Question 28. ID# USGALLUP.37-66. *Roper online.* Available through LexisNexis.

———. 1955. "If the Party Whose Candidate You Most Often Support Nominated a Woman for President of the United States, Would You Vote for Her If She Seemed Best Qualified for the Job?" Question 3. ID# USGALLUP.55-543. *Roper online.* Available through LexisNexis.

———. 2006. Question 311. ID# 1674733. December 20. Available through LexisNexis.

General Social Survey. 1977. "If Your Party Nominated a Woman for President, Would You Vote for Her If She Were Qualified for the Job?" Question 120. ID# USNORC.GSS77. *Roper online.* Available through LexisNexis.

———. 1996. "If Your Party Nominated a Woman for President, Would You Vote for Her If She Were Qualified for the Job?" Question 125. ID# USNORC. GSS96. *Roper online.* Available through LexisNexis.

Gutgold, N. 2006. *Paving the Way for Madam President.* Boulder, Colo.: Lexington Books.

Havel, J. T. 1996. *U.S. Presidential Candidates and the Elections: A Biographical and Historical Guide.* New York: Simon and Schuster Macmillan.

"Here Is the Final Vote Count." 1988. *U.P.I.* December 19. Available through LexisNexis.

Holman, K. 1988. "Newsmaker—'88—Campaign." *MacNeil/Leherer News Hour,* October 24

Lerner, G. 1993. *The Creation of Feminist Consciousness: From the Middle Ages to Eighteen-seventy.* New York: Oxford University Press.

Mandel, R. 1993. "The Political Woman." In *American Women in the Nineties: Today's Critical Issues,* ed. S. Matteo, 34–65. Boston: Northeastern University Press.

Newman, J. 1994. *Perception and Reality: A Study Comparing the Success of Men and Women Candidates.* Washington, D.C.: National Women's Political Caucus.

Roper Poll. 1987a. Question 23. Accession #0006558. *Washington Post and ABC News.* September 17. Available through LexisNexis.

———. 1987b. Question 28. Accession #0017751. *New York Times and CBS News.* July 22. Available through LexisNexis.

———. 1999a. Question 2. Accession #0336675. *ABC News.* August 22. Available through LexisNexis.

———. 1999b. Question 54. Accession #0319608. *Time and CNN.* January. Available through LexisNexis.

Salant, J. 1999. "Decision by Bush on Funds Aids Rivals: Bigger U.S. Match Available Earlier." *Washington Post,* August 24, A4.

Salit, J. 1999. "Reform Party: Shows Us the Campaign Money." *The Hill,* July 21, 30.

Seltzer, R., J. Newman, and M. V. Leighton. 1997. *Sex as a Political Variable: Women as Candidates and Voters in U.S. Elections.* Boulder, Colo.: Lynne Rienner.

Zipp, J. F., and E. Plutzer. 1985. "Gender Differences in Voting for Female Candidates: Evidence from the 1982 Election." *Public Opinion Quarterly* 49 (2): 179–97.

Why Worry about the Press?

The notion of politically correct speech has been soundly condemned in the popular press, radio talk shows, and informal gatherings. The idea that the words we choose and the language we use might have a substantial impact on the way we perceive the world, think, and even act is often rejected as a ludicrous proposition that any thinking person can easily dismiss. There is, however, a large body of evidence from social science demonstrating that, counter to popular conception, the world we live in is created by the language we use to describe it. Language is important and the words we use and hear (especially those in the mass media) affect not only how we perceive the world but also how we judge, remember, and act in it.

Whereas any individual choice of language in any specific instance may have very limited impact, the social patterns of communication have stronger potential effects. To describe an individual woman as aspiring to the vice presidency and not the presidency is unnotable, but when women who run for the presidency are persistently framed in mass media accounts as though their real ambitions are for the vice presidency, then the potential for language to have an impact is greater. Studies in social science show, counter to the protests about political correctness, that language affects how we perceive and think about the world and that the mass media help create our society. Together these ideas suggest that women candidates should be concerned about how the media portray them, and that we as a society should be interested as well.

Language Affects Perception and Thought

The linguistic anthropologist Edward Sapir and his student Benjamin Lee Whorf are two of the early theorists who studied the role that language plays in the social construction of reality. Their theory that people speaking different languages have different conceptions of reality is commonly referred to as the Sapir-Whorf hypothesis. Sapir wrote,

> Human beings do not live in the objective world alone, nor alone in the world of social activity as ordinarily understood, but are very much at the mercy of the particular language which has become the medium of expression for their society. . . . The fact of the matter is that the "real world" is to a large extent unconsciously built upon the language habits of the group. No two languages are ever sufficiently similar to be considered as representing the same social reality. The worlds in which different societies live are distinct worlds, not merely the same world with different labels attached. . . . We see and hear and otherwise experience very largely as we do because the language habits of our community predispose us to certain choices of interpretation. (Sapir 1929, 209–10)

People experience the world through their senses. As we interact with others, we learn language, and that language provides us with categories and stereotypes that make sense of life and facilitate the conception of the environment. The anthropologist Edmond Leach (1964) described the process this way: "The physical and social environment of a young child is perceived as a continuum. It does not contain any intrinsically separate 'things.' The child, in due course, is taught to impose upon this environment a kind of discriminating grid which serves to distinguish the world as being composed of a large number of separate things, each labeled with a name" (34).

Words form the foundations that hold up our social edifices. The sociologists Peter Berger and Thomas Luckmann (1966) wrote, "As a sign system, language has the quality of objectivity. I encounter language as a facticity external to myself and it is coercive in its effect on me. Language forces me into its patterns" (1966, 38). We then become accustomed to seeing life in the categories given to us by our language. We are, for the most part, unaware that these categories have been imposed and inherited. Rather we believe that the divisions and boundaries in language only reflect the true nature of our environment.

The fluidity of categories and perception is perhaps best described by Lev Vgotsky (1962), a linguist who conducted a series of experiments with children. He found that children do not see categories in the same way as adults do. In his experiment, children were presented with blocks of differing shapes, sizes, and colors and instructed to form a "set"; they were given a particular block with which to start. Given this scenario, a preadolescent child may add one block to the set because it is the same color as the first block, and another because it is similar in shape. The added blocks have no apparent connection, but for whatever reasons they are connected in the mind of the child. Adults will create sets of quadrilaterals, or red blocks, or triangles. These experiments show that "the child's thinking is not hemmed in by word meanings" and "demonstrate that if it were not for the prevalence of pseudo-concepts the child's complexes would develop along different lines from adult concepts" (68).

This is somewhat intuitive for anyone who has seen a child develop language. Take, for example, a child who notices the moon. Her observation might be met with the word "moon" from the parent. The next day the child might notice a street lamp and say "moon." The parent corrects the child and says "lamp." Thus, the child learns that moons and lamps are in different categories (see Carmichael 1964). Yet clearly the tendency to put moons and lamps in the same category is defensible. After all, they are both bright, round objects that shine above at night. Focusing on specific characteristics of the moon and a light enables us to put them in different categories.

Another linguist, Roger Fowler (1991), provided a similar example, noting that the difference between "plants" and "weeds" is not botanical but cultural and linguistic. We are taught to divide linguistically and then believe that these are objective distinctions. Similarly, Fowler argued that language can play a role in creating and maintaining discrimination against groups in society by providing names for categories and thus allowing these names to be spoken and written frequently. He wrote, "Vocabulary divides 'actress' from 'actor,' the '-ess' ending marking 'actress' as a special and unusual case; classifies 'immigrant' as a special and deviant group, just by providing a word for it (what is the opposite term, for the 'normal' case of being a citizen?); awkwardly lexicalizes 'lady doctor,' making overt, in the awkwardness of the term, society's prejudicial sense of the irregularity of a woman practicing a profession" (Fowler 1991, 94). Once a category has found its way into language, it can be spoken and written more easily and frequently, thus contributing to the apparent reality of the category. We can say that "language users are predisposed to categorize their experience according to the mental map engraved in the semantic structure of their habitual linguistic usage: language helps people to sort things, encourages them to think of the world in terms of certain artificial categories tacitly felt to be 'common sense'" (30).

Once we are committed to the parlance of a particular culture, the language affects how we perceive. Ambiguities in the language can translate into ambiguities in thought; similarly, distinctions in language can create distinctions in thought. When Whorf (1956) worked for a fire insurance company, he noticed that "around a storage of what are called 'gasoline drums,' behavior will tend to a certain type, that is, great care will be exercised; while around a storage of what are called 'empty gasoline drums,' it will tend to be different—careless, with little repression of smoking or of tossing cigarette stubs about. Yet the 'empty' drums are perhaps the more dangerous, since they contain explosive vapor" (135). In this example, the word "empty" denotes the absence of the liquid intended for the container. These containers are, in fact, empty under the common usage. Empty of a dangerous substance also may be construed to mean "safe," causing people who use the word "empty" to think "safe." In the case of gasoline, however, "empty" is imprecise, because although the drums are empty of liquid they are not empty of residual gas and are therefore not safe. This example indicates how language can affect perception and behaviors. We have no single word for "empty of a flammable liquid but still likely to contain flammable gas." As numerous insurance cases attest, we often act in the world as though unnamed hazards do not exist. In this example the ambiguity in language elicited behavior that was ultimately problematic, but language can also create distinctions that affect how we perceive and act. Several experiments vividly demonstrate this principle.

Leonard Carmichael, H. Hogan, and A. A. Walter (1932) found that the labeling of ambiguous shapes affected how subjects reproduced them. For example, when an ambiguous sickle shape was shown and a subject was told that it was the letter "C," the subjects were more likely to draw it rounder than the initial object, that is, more like the letter "C," when asked to reproduce the drawing. However, when the same shape was shown and the subjects were told it was a "crescent moon" they were more likely to draw it flatter (like a crescent moon). Clearly, the label affected the perception and/or the recall of the object as well as its reproduction.

Similarly, Phyllis Katz (1963), a psychologist, trained children to identify nonsense syllables with abstract shapes. One set of subjects was taught a group label for all four abstract shapes, while the other was taught an individual label for each shape. The group that learned the common label had greater difficulty distinguishing the stimuli than did the subjects who had labels for each stimulus. In a later experiment Katz (1973) used pictures of a mulatto face adorned in four ways (for example, with eyeglasses).

Some children were taught distinct labels for each picture while others were given none. The subjects who learned the labels for each face were more likely to see a higher degree of difference among the faces than were those in the control (no-label) group.

Such labeling can affect perception in others ways as well. Glen Foster, Carl Schmidt, and David Sabatino (1976) showed two different groups of subjects (teachers) a videotape of a normal fourth-grade child. One group was told that the child was "normal" while the other group was told that the child was "learning disabled." The subjects were asked to rate the observed child in terms of academic skill areas. The results indicated that the teachers who thought the child was learning disabled rated the child as less academically competent than the child with the normal label. The researchers concluded that different labels can generate biases sufficient to alter teachers' perceptions. A similar study by John Darley and Paget Gross (1983) found that when a child was characterized as being from a "high socioeconomic background," subjects rated her abilities above grade level. However, when the same child was identified as being from a "lower-class background" her abilities were rated below grade level.

A cross-cultural study conducted by Paul Kay and Willett Kempton compared color differentiation of English speakers with that of the speakers of Tarahumara (an Uto-Aztecan language of Mexico). Tarahumara docs not have separate words for green and blue. The experimenters placed three color chips on a board. One was green, another, blue; between the two was a chip blending blue and green. The middle chip was slightly more green or blue to make an answer correct when asked about the color of the chip, but the difference was sufficiently small to make the task difficult. Kay and Kempton found that "English speakers showed systematic distortion at the blue-green boundary—'pushing' colors on the blue side more toward blue and colors on the green side more toward green. This systematic distortion took place in 29 out of 30 cases. With the Tarahumara speakers, the distinction was random—almost a perfect 50-50 split" (quoted in Lakoff 1987, 332). These experiments show how language categories affect our perceptions and conceptions of the world. In these cases language created distinctions, drew disparate things together, or changed the evaluation of something.

From these examples we can expect that when reporters use certain words, categories, or labels rather than others they affect the associations or distinctions that may be drawn by the receiver. By featuring gender or by differentiating between men and women, reporters will affect the thoughts of the reader. The reporters' discourse will be a factor in building the receivers' mental representations of the world and therefore their understanding of the world. These cognitive constructs can become habitual; they are employed by individuals in language and in actions, creating a web of linguistically driven social creation. Of course, language is not the only unit by which to understand social creation. The mass media also affect our understanding of the world in ways that go beyond the use of language.

Mass Media Affect Society

The notion that the media affect society is more commonplace than the idea that language affects how we think. Many people accept the idea that the media may affect voter turnout by reporting exit polls or by painting a candidate as unviable. Consonant with these lay conceptions, social scientists have identified many ways in which the media affect society.

In an early landmark study on the effect of the media on political attitudes and behaviors, Mathews and Prothro (cited in St. George and Robinson-Weber 1983) found that when blacks had greater exposure to the media they were more likely to participate and have interest in politics, regardless of education level. Newspaper reading had more of an effect than did television watching. That said, the researchers found that when blacks saw other blacks on television their interest in world affairs increased. It was not just media exposure but the exposure to similar people that affected political engagement. This finding is particularly important when considering how women who read newspaper coverage of elections may be affected by the lack of women candidates covered in the press. The failure of the press to cover equitably the women who run may actually dissuade women from being engaged in the political process.

Paul Lazarsfeld and Robert Merton were the first to name the phenomenon they called "status conferral." They argued that the mass media confer status on issues, people, organizations, and social movements simply by covering them. "The mass media bestow prestige and enhance the authority of individuals and groups *by legitimizing their status*. Recognition by the press or radio or magazines or newsreels testifies that one has arrived, that one is important enough to have been singled out from the large anonymous masses, and that one's behavior and opinions are significant enough to require public notice" (1948, 101).

Joshua Meyrowitz's (1995) work on the media coverage of Larry Agran, a presidential candidate, provided a vivid example of status conferral and the power of media to determine collective conception by creating a persona in social reality. Meyrowitz argued that Agran was a legitimate contender for the Democratic Party nomination for president, having graduated from Harvard Law School and served twelve years as an elected public official (Agran had been mayor of a city in California). In addition, Agran had "measurable showings in some early polls," had the endorsement of some newspapers, qualified for Federal Primary Matching Funds, and "won a few delegates at the Democratic convention" (36).

Although Agran did receive a "fair amount" of local media coverage, he received very little national coverage. He was not invited to participate in the televised debates, and even when invited to attend forums with the other "major" candidates, he was treated by the press as though he were not there. This had two effects. It deprived Agran of the status conferred by the media simply by appearing in it, and it precluded his being important by denying him the means of informing the public of his existence. Meyrowitz argued that it was the failure of the press to cover Agran's campaign—in fact, its deliberate decision not to (and not anything intrinsic to Agran)—that made it impossible for him to be elected.

This case study demonstrates that if a politician is to be elected to a national office, she must be covered by the national press. Although it is possible in local elections for interpersonal contacts to create sufficient awareness of a candidate, in national races such interpersonal contact can never be sufficient. Candidates must exist in the minds of many people simultaneously in order to win office. In national elections only the national media have the power to achieve this. When candidates are overlooked by the media, for whatever reason, we can say they do not exist as a national common conception. In fact, reviews of political-science literature do show that "increased levels of media exposure are associated with increased levels of candidate recognition" (Goldenberg and Traugott 1987, 332).

In other words, the press plays a role in determining which candidates will be viable. If the press never covers a candidate, the public at large cannot know of her and therefore cannot support her. Individuals not covered will not be elected. In addition, individuals who are not given an opportunity to take their message to the electorate through the national media cannot amass the political power needed to implement their policies. The national media help shape the national personae for individuals who affect our national policies and condition.

Stephen Hilgartner and Charles Bosk (1988) made a similar argument with regard to social problems. They asserted that the conception of a social problem in no way corresponds to the objective existence of a problem. Instead it is the media (and other actors) that create the idea of a problem in the mind of the public. Thus, some social problems gain public attention and then fade from the public view, although a new so-cial problem takes the spotlight. When the public does not hear about a social problem, it believes it to be no longer a concern. As Fowler (1991) argued, events or situations are not inherently newsworthy; news does not exist out in the ether ready to be discovered. Something becomes news only when it is selected and transformed by people. The vast majority of events are never mentioned in the news.

The media's ability to establish a social problem as a common con-ception can have important consequences. Solutions to social problems require some kind of collective action. Collective action can take the form of grassroots social protests, as was the case in the anti–nuclear weapons movements of the 1980s; the form of policies sponsored and supported by the government, as in the initiative to put more police on the streets in the 1990s; or even the form of national support for a particular candidate. However, none of these is likely to be accomplished without some kind of civic consensus (even if not universal and not uniform among those who hold the concept). Social movements cannot mobilize the public to action until the individuals are convinced a problem exists.

Nuclear disarmament represents a good example of this. Though there are still enough working nuclear weapons to destroy the planet, the media rarely cover nuclear weapons as a social problem anymore. Moreover, some social scientists would argue that the absence of Soviet domination has resulted in an increased threat of nuclear holocaust. Yet such a threat is rarely covered in the news (or treated in other mediated programs such as the apocalyptic, fictional accounts that appeared as dramatic specials on television, such as *The Day After*), especially in contrast to practices two decades ago. As such, nuclear holocaust is not widely perceived as a pressing social problem. This means that organizations such as Beyond War, which was dedicated to eradicating nuclear weapons, have disbanded because they were unable to mobilize citizens. We can thus say that in the minds of the populace, media coverage both creates and eliminates social problems. Not only does the press construct the existence of people and problems, but it also conveys how important they are.

It was Bernard Cohen who first theorized, "If we do not see a story in the newspaper . . . it effectively has not happened as far as we are con-cerned. . . . [T]he press . . . may not be successful much of the time in telling people what to think, but it is stunningly successful in telling its readers what to think *about*" (1963, 13). Maxwell McCombs and Donald Shaw (1972) wrote the first widely cited study documenting this agenda-setting function of the mass media. They found that the issues that were most heavily covered in the mass media were the ones that individuals identified as the most important of the day. They wrote, "The media appear to have exerted a considerable impact on voters' judgments of what they considered the major issues of the campaign" (180). Many studies that followed have confirmed the mass media's ability to affect what people believe is important or pressing. Studies typically ask what respondents believed was the most important problem facing America and usually found that there was a high correlation between what people identified as America's greatest problem and the issue most often covered in the news.

One of the more extensive experimental tests of this effect was conducted by two political scientists, Shanto Iyengar and Donald Kinder (1987). Their study was more powerful than the correlational surveys in that they actually manipulated the media exposure of subjects and found that what subjects identified as the country's most important problem changed with their media exposure. Not only were these manipulations successful, but Iyengar and Kinder also conducted survey research that included measurements of real-world problems. For example, when they tested whether the media's coverage of inflation created the perception that it was the country's most pressing problem, they added the inflation rate to their regression. They found media effects beyond these real-world effects, thus supporting the hypothesis that the media determine what the public believes to be the most pressing problems.

One real-life anecdote artfully captures the ability of the press to affect the public's perceptions of the world. According to Stephens (1988), in the late 1890s a reporter for the *New York Evening Post* was relaxing with some police officers when they began to talk about a crime that had not been included in their official crime report. After the conversation, the reporter went back to the paper to write the story. Since he had broken an exclusive story, competing newspapers encouraged their reporters not to be undone. Reporters on the crime beat began aggressively seeking out crime stories. One reporter found the place where the list of all crimes in the city was kept and began to raid the location for stories daily. To keep pace, others began eavesdropping through a hole in the wall at police headquarters. Stephens picks up the story:

> Suddenly the newspapers were filled with news of burglaries supplied by their newly bestirred police reporters. It was "one of the worst crime waves that I ever witnessed" Steffens [one of the reporters] writes in his autobiography. Editorial writers began pointing fingers; sociologists set to work; those with possessions presumably took steps to protect them; and the city's reformers, who had recently gained control of the police department, came under attack.

Lost in the rush to purchase additional locks and assign blame was the fact that the rate of crime in the city had not budged" (263).

The "crime wave" ended in a similar way. Once Theodore Roosevelt, then president of New York City's police board, learned the origin of the crime wave, he called in the reporters and asked them to cool it. They did, and the crime wave was ended.

In addition to affecting what and who people see as important, studies on framing reveal that the way the mass media portray issues affects how we understand social reality. Robert Entman (1993), a communications scholar, defined framing as selecting "some aspects of a perceived reality and mak[ing] them more salient in a communicating text, in such a way as to promote a particular problem definition, causal interpretation, moral evaluation, and/or treatment recommendation" (52). In short, a frame provides a way to understand a set of events.

Daniel Kahneman and Amos Tversky (1984) found that by slightly altering word choices they could change people's understandings of the topic. Specifically, they had people read about an outbreak of a disease and framed the consequences of the disease in terms of either how many people would live or how many people would die. Even though the same number of people would live or die regardless of the wording, people were more likely to prefer the scenarios that emphasized the number of people who would live. In other words, the wording and framing had an effect above and beyond the objective content.

Iyengar (1991) also found empirical evidence of framing effects. He concluded that the structure of the story—that is, the way the story was told—affected how the audience perceived the causes of a problem. For example, when a story focused on a specific unwed mother, the readers were more likely to blame the problem of poverty on the characteristics of the poor and not on the systemic factors that produce poverty. The converse was true when the story cited statistics.

What is important here is that small differences in presentation that are probably not conscious on the part of reporters and editors can affect how people understand and therefore act in their world. These effects can have national consequences since there are widely accepted news norms regarding not only who should be covered but also how they should be covered, and because national news reaches wide audiences.

Whereas the power of the press to create candidates, issues, and the public agenda are all important pieces of evidence of media effects, cultivation theory may be most relevant to the issue of coverage of women candidates. Although cultivation theory is based in the power of television, it aptly conveys the power of any mass media to shape our collective reality. Cultivation is a theory of mass-media effects originally posited by two communication scholars, George Gerbner and Larry Gross (1976). This theory suggests that individuals who watch a lot of television use what they see on TV as data in understanding social reality. As Gerbner and Gross argued, "Television is likely to remain for a long time the chief source of repetitive and ritualized symbol systems cultivating the common consciousness of the most far flung and heterogeneous mass publics in history" (174). They posited that television acculturates the public not with specific beliefs but with the basic assumptions about society. Cultivation researchers have found that, among other effects, frequent television watchers were more likely to believe the world was more violent and to have a distorted view of the number of people in various professions. Since some professionals are overrepresented on TV, and since most populations see more violence on TV than they personally experience, people who watch TV confuse their mediated experiences with their actual ones. This occurs despite the fact that people can clearly identify which shows are fiction and which are nonfiction.

Researchers such as Marie-Louise Mares (1996) and Larry Shrum (1995) have tried to identify why television causes distortions in perception to occur. Mares argued that once memories are stored they may be separated from their source and "source confusion" results. Even though people know the difference between reality and fiction, over time they forget where they encountered certain information. Similarly, Shrum explained the cultivation hypothesis with what he calls the "availability heuristic." People believe that whatever is easily accessible from memory occurs frequently. When searching quickly for "violent incidents" it will be quite easy for heavy viewers to recall one, even though the most recent incident a person can recall was probably viewed on television. The cultivation hypothesis suggests that the mass media are part of how we construct our images of our society. These images are created in many people at the same time and affect not only their views of reality but also how they react to the environment.

If cultivation effects occur, media consumers take their cue about social roles from what they see on television. If the media rarely cover women candidates, the public is likely to respond by underestimating how many women candidates there are. When the public does this it makes women leaders seem less normative and more risky. Cultivation theory suggests that the more the media cover women leaders (both in fictional accounts and in the news), the more comfortable the public will be with the idea of a woman president and the more likely they would be to see women leaders as a natural part of their social and political world. The important point here is that the more women leaders are covered, the more women would be likely to see themselves as politicians.

Conclusion

The media not only tell us who our national candidates are, but they are also instrumental in creating our common conceptions of them. Only a candidate who appears in the national media can be a national candidate; the appearance has the ability to create the image of candidacy in enough people's minds to make the collective action of voting successful enough for election. Moreover, the way these individuals are portrayed in the national media helps create the political attributes of the candidates in the common conceptions. If they are framed as viable, the public will be more likely to view them as viable. If they are framed as normative, more people will view them as normative.

Certain ideas about our society—who we are, what is a woman, what is a political woman, and who can solve our problems—can be construed as common conceptions in part by the mass media. This is not to suggest that a person's individual or even collective experiences do not also contribute to our thinking about our society. One's personal experiences with women, politicians, or social problems serve as data in the structuring of an individual's reality. However, what we watch on TV and read in the newspaper also count as experiences, but unlike individual experiences these are collectively shared and therefore have the power to structure reality en masse. Since reality is ultimately shaped by a subjective worldview that is sufficiently similar among enough individuals to make widespread coordination possible, such widespread experiences are important, powerful, and influential.

Clearly not everyone embraces the media's agenda or portrayals. Many people have low or non-mainstream exposure to the mass media, bring a variety of individual experiences and therefore interpretations to mediated experiences, or are skeptical or resistant to the particular version of reality portrayed in the media. Yet, depending on the medium, thousands or millions of individuals can be exposed to the same or similar messages, the interpretation of which is constrained by the message itself.

What is powerful about our mediated experiences is that they are uniform in a way that personal experiences are not. When someone personally experiences violence, that person may share many feelings with other victims of violence and yet may still have personal interpretations or culturally specific reactions. However, although there still may be unique or culturally specific reactions when violence is portrayed on television, thousands will have witnessed exactly the same stimulus, a situation that is unlike the personal experience. Similarly, despite the variety of media and programs available to the public, there are similarities across channels in the topics, the individuals covered, the gender roles portrayed, and the ways issues are framed. These commonalities are what create the shared experiences in the audience. What is simultaneously experienced by the many affects our common conceptions of our society and thus our actions. This is one reason that an analysis of mass-media portrayals of women is important.

The studies I have mentioned here show the importance of what the media write about, how they write, and the language they use. It is important because when the press writes less about women candidates, such candidacies are portrayed as less normative and as a result fewer women may aspire to political office. It is important because if the press always mentions what women wear, it may convey the impression that women are not serious candidates. It is important because if women are described by their emotions, it may falsely imply that women are not rational enough to lead. It is important because if women are always mentioned in relation to their families instead of their professions, they may appear less qualified for or dedicated to office, and it is important because when women are portrayed as less viable than they actually are, people might believe it and not vote for them, or women might believe it themselves and not run.

References

Berger, P. L., and T. Luckmann 1966. *The Social Construction of Reality: A Treatise in the Sociology of Knowledge.* New York: Anchor Books.

Carmichael, L. 1964. "The Early Growth of Language Capacity in the Individual." In *New Directions in the Study of Language,* ed. E. H. Lenneberg, 1–21. Cambridge, Mass.: MIT Press.

Carmichael, L., H. P. Hogan, and A. A. Walter. 1932. "An Experimental Study of the Effect of Language on the Reproduction of Visually Perceived Form." *Journal of Experimental Psych* 15:73–86.

Cohen, B. C. 1963. *The Press and Foreign Policy.* Westport, Conn.: Greenwood Press.

Darley, J. M., and P. H. Gross. 1983. "A Hypothesis-Confirming Bias in Labeling Effects." *Journal of Personality and Social Psychology* 44 (1): 20–33.

Entman, R. M. 1993. "Framing: Toward Classification of a Fractured Paradigm." *Journal of Communication* 43 (4): 51–58.

Foster, G. G., C. R. Schmidt, and D. Sabatino. 1976. "Teacher Expectancies and the Label 'Learning Disabilities.'" *Journal of Learning Disabilities* 9 (2): 58–61.

Fowler, R. 1991. *Language in the News: Discourse and Ideology in the Press.* London: Routledge.

Gerbner, G., and L. Gross. 1976. "Living with Television: The Violence Profile." *Journal of Communication* 26:172–99.

Goldenberg, E. N., and M. W. Traugott. 1987. "Mass Media in U.S. Elections." *Legislative Studies Quarterly* 12 (3): 317–39.

Hilgartner, S., and C. L. Bosk. 1988. "The Rise and Fall of Social Problems: A Public Arenas Model." *American Journal of Sociology* 94 (1): 53–78.

Iyengar, S. 1991. *Is Anyone Responsible? How Television Frames Political Issues.* Chicago: University of Chicago Press.

Iyengar, S., and D. R. Kinder. 1987. *News That Matters.* Chicago: University of Chicago Press.

Katz, P. A. 1963. "Effects of Labels on Children's Perception and Discrimination Learning." *Journal of Experimental Psychology* 66 (5): 423–28.

———. 1973. "Stimulus Predifferentiation and Modification of Children's Racial Attitudes." *Child Development* 44:232–37.

Kahneman, D., and A. Tversky. 1984. "Choices, Values, and Frames." *American Psychologist* 28:107–28.

Lakoff, G. 1987. *Women, Fire, and Dangerous Things: What Categories Reveal about the Mind.* Chicago: University of Chicago Press.

Lazarsfeld, P. F., and R. K. Merton. 1948. "Mass Communication, Popular Taste and Organized Social Action." In *The Communication of Ideas,* ed. L. Bryson, 95–118. New York: Institute for Religious and Social Studies.

Leach, E. 1964. "Anthropological Aspects of Language: Animal Categories and Verbal Abuse." In *New Directions in the Study of Language,* ed. E. H. Lenneberg, 23–63. Cambridge, Mass.: MIT Press.

Mares, L. 1996. "The Role of Source Confusions in Television's Cultivation of Social Reality Judgments." *Human Communication Research* 23 (2): 278–97.

McCombs, M. E., and D. L. Shaw. 1972. "The Agenda-Setting Function of Mass Media." *Public Opinion Quarterly* 36 (2): 176–87.

Meyrowitz, J. 1995. "The Problem of Getting on the Media Agenda: A Case Study in Competing Logics of Campaign Converge." In *Presidential Campaign Discourse: Strategic Communication Problems,* ed. K. E. Kendall, 35–67. New York: State University of New York Press.

Sapir, E. 1929. "Status of Linguistics as a Science." *Language* 5 (4): 207–14. Retrieved July 26, 2007, from Jstor.

Shrum, L. J. 1995. "Assessing the Social Influence of Television: A Social Cognition Perspective on Cultivation Effects." *Communication Research* 22 (4): 402–29.

Stephens, M. 1988. *A History of News: From the Drum to the Satellite.* New York: Viking.

St. George, A., and S. Robinson-Weber. 1983. "The Mass Media, Political Attitudes, and Behavior." *Communication Research* 10 (4): 487–508.

Vygotsky, L. S. 1962. *Thought and Language.* Cambridge, Mass.: MIT Press.

Whorf, B. L. 1956. *Language, Thought, and Reality: Selected Writings of Benjamin Lee Whorf.* Edited by J. B. Carroll. Cambridge, Mass.: MIT Press.

Unnatural,
Incapable,
and Unviable

"**S**o now women think they are capable of holding the highest office in the land. It's bad enough that we allow these female creatures to operate automobiles. Imagine what would happen if one of them became president! Let's keep the women at home where they belong" (Krasner 1964). This opinion, expressed in a letter to the editor during Margaret Chase Smith's campaign for the presidency in 1964, is just one of many articulating the idea that women do not belong in the political sphere. An analysis of the explicit arguments in the press over the last 130 years of coverage of women presidential candidates reveals three points that were consistently made: women are unnatural in politics; women are incompetent as leaders; and women are not viable as candidates. Though these arguments were rarely justified, when reasons were given it was usually that women were considered too emotional, unable to handle crises, or obsessed with trivial matters.

There were also voices in the texts that disputed these themes. The assertions of women's unsuitability and incompetence were occasionally countered by historical examples of competent and capable national leaders who were women. Understanding these arguments gives us insights into our expectations for both leaders and women. Moreover, an awareness of the rhetorical challenges women are likely to encounter can help women aspiring to lead to develop communication strategies that will overcome these hurdles.

Many scholars date the idea that women and men belong in "separate spheres" to the rise of industrialization and professionalization in the 1800s. As industrialization brought men into a *public* work space and as they became identified with an occupation, a parallel *private* sphere was created for women at home. As one observer put it, "Middle class homes were being built on the concept of men working in the public world and depending on women's labour, both conjugal and servant, in the private realm of the home" (Ross 2006, 228). The ideology suggested that not only was it proper for women to stay home and take care of the house, children, and other domestic needs, but also that such a position was natural and instinctual.

Some scholars note that although the ideology of the public/private divide is often dated to the rise of industrialization in the 1800s, in fact women have always worked (see Bose 1987). Moreover, they note that the idea that women are unnatural in the public sphere has its roots further back in social history. For example, the communications scholar Kathleen Hall Jamieson (1988) noted that from the time of Aristotle and before, women were supposed to be silent in public and their primary duties pertained to childbearing and not to public acts. As evidence she cites Paul in the Christian Bible: "I permit no woman to teach or have authority over men; she is to keep silent. For Adam was formed first, then Eve; and Adam was not deceived, but the woman was deceived and became the transgressor. Yet women will be saved through bearing children" (1 Timothy 2:9–15). Such sentiments resulted in a cultural taboo against women's public speech. This taboo persisted though much of Western history so that "it was virtually unheard-of for women outside the Quaker community to give speeches until the ante-bellum period, and then only the brave attempted this feat. Indeed, the taboo was so strong that a man chaired the famous [women's rights] meeting at Seneca Falls in 1848" (Matthews 1992, 7).

Thus political women throughout American history were considered unnatural in part because they were fighting a general belief that the appearance of women in any public sphere was inappropriate. The feminist scholar Glenna Matthews (1992) noted how this ideology has even seeped into our language. For example, "public man" has a positive connotation as one who serves society, while "public woman" is negative, connoting a prostitute.

This ideology of the separate spheres was in part based on a conceptualization of men and women as binary opposites grounded in women's ability (and men's inability) to bear children (Poovey 1988). Maternal instinct was credited with making women naturally self-sacrificing, domestic, and nurturing. At the same time a woman's "natural" talents with children and her ability to bear children were also considered the cause of her irrationality and emotionality.

Women as Unnatural

The notion that women are somehow "unnatural" in the public sphere but "natural" in the private sphere is one of the more enduring arguments against women's full participation in elective politics found in press accounts of women seeking office.

Typical of this line of argument is this example from a *New York Herald* editorial from Victoria Woodhull's race in 1872: "At present man, in his affection for and kindness toward the weaker sex, is disposed to accord her any reasonable number of privileges. Beyond that stage he pauses, because there seems to him to be something which is unnatural in permitting her to share the turmoil, the excitement, the risks of competition for the glory of governing" ("Woman's Idea of Government" 1870). Almost a hundred years later the editors of the *Bangor Daily News* similarly implied that women were unnatural in the public sphere and by nature belonged at home. After noting the dearth of women in public office the editors wrote, "Maybe the great majority of women just aren't interested in public careers. They don't have what intellectuals nowadays like to call 'motivation.' . . . Though women make up a substantial part of the nation's work force, only a relatively few hold top jobs. . . . could it be that is because women essentially are mothers and homemakers at heart?" ("Few Women" 1964).

Though rare, similar sentiments were also expressed in Elizabeth Dole's race as recently as 2000. According to one account, "'I think she's a fine woman,' Wayne Lilly, an active Republican from Chilton, N.H., said after a recent Christian Coalition event in his state. 'But I don't believe a woman ought to be in that particular place of leadership. She would be a good helpmate. But the Bible teaches us that a woman should not have authority over men. It's nothing but foolishness'" (Berke 1999a).

Remarks about the proper sphere for women were more common in 1964 than in any of the other years I studied. This may be because Chase Smith's campaign occurred during the second wave of feminism, at a time when women's roles and responsibilities were very much the subject of popular debate. One commentator noted there was a "prevalent anti-Margaret chorus" saying she is a woman; and women are not, never have been and never will be suited to an office like the presidency" (Lewis 1963). Similarly, in an article by Nellie Penley and Marie Sullivan (1964) entitled

"Ladies at Odds over Woman as President," one woman was quoted as saying, "I don't approve of a woman running for president as I think it is definitely a man's job." In a "person-on-the-street" interview known in journalism as a vox populi, one man said, "Women generally are not ready for high elective office" (Jemail 1963).

Some of the most explicitly sexist comments found in the papers were direct quotes from citizens. The sexism found in the straight news coverage tended to be more subtle. Still it is not really possible to separate the citizens' voices from the media voice because the reporters and editors selected and framed the quotations that were printed. The reader does not know if many people were interviewed to get one incendiary sexist comment to print or if all people expressed the same basic sentiment. Even though examples from vox populi represent citizen voices, they still reveal the power of the media because they represent only the citizen voices that the media choose to disseminate.

Sexist comments sometimes came from the candidates themselves. Chase Smith echoed the sentiment that women belong at home. She said, "I view the role of wife and mother as the foundation, the keystone and the basis for women to expand their activities. . . . the home is the springboard for the fight for different conditions in communities, for improvement in food, housing, school, health and recreational facilities—and that fight is best led by the women of the home. . . . Education that a degree gives to a housewife better equips her for being a good and intelligent wife . . . and informed mother" ("At Visit" 1963). Even though Chase Smith was arguing for political involvement, she was nonetheless reaffirming the notion that women's primary sphere was the home. Elizabeth Dole, too, made at least one comment that had a similar tone. According to one reporter, "The childless Dole made this observation, 'I think the most important career a woman can have is that of a mother raising fine young future citizens'" (Connolly 1999).

These cases convey the notion that public life for women is somehow against the natural human order. In these and other examples, no evidence or reasoning was provided to back up the claims. The notion that women are unnatural or defying some transcendental (godly) purpose in seeking office is not the dominant argument against women's participation, but it has cropped up consistently through the ages as a justification for limiting women's access to the presidency. Inherent in these criticisms of the women candidates is the notion that nurturing/mothering and leadership/public life are at odds. By picking up and printing such explicit comments about women's inappropriateness in the public sphere, the press amplifies and reasserts the traditional notion of separate spheres and women's unsuitability for public office.

The First Candidate (or Novelty Frame)

One subtle pattern that may contribute to the perception that women are unnatural in the political sphere emerges in the consistent way in which women candidates for president have been framed as firsts. The first woman to publicly seek the presidency was Victoria Woodhull in 1872. She was followed by Belva Lockwood in 1884. However, those facts did not stop one columnist from writing almost a century later of Chase Smith, "Even in defeat she could take solace in that great accomplishment alone and also always be proud and happy that she had the distinction of having been the *first* [emphasis added] woman in the country to bid for that office" (Arnold 1963). Penley and Sullivan (1964) also erroneously dubbed Chase Smith "the *first* [emphasis added] woman ever to stand as a candidate for nomination for the presidency," and an editorial depicted her as the "*first* [emphasis added] woman to seek nomination by a major political party" ("A Campaign Style" 1964). In fact, Chase Smith is liberally portrayed as a political pioneer throughout her campaign coverage.

Chisholm, like Chase Smith, was also framed as a first and a novelty. The *Seattle Times* wrote, "Representative Shirley Chisholm today became the *first* [emphasis added] black woman to begin a serious bid for the presidency of the United States" ("Shirley Chisholm Declares" 1972). Similarly it printed, "The eyes of the *first* [emphasis added] black woman to run for president of the United States flashed" ("People in the News" 1972). She was also described as "Mrs. Chisholm, *first* [emphasis added] black woman to seek the presidency" ("Shirley Chisholm Rejects" 1972), and as "the *first* [emphasis added] black woman to seek a major-party presidential nomination" (Lynn 1972).

Schroeder, like Chisholm and Chase Smith, was likewise cast as a first. Papers reported, "If she runs, Mrs. Schroeder would be the *first* [emphasis added] woman to seek the presidency since 1972" (Gailey 1987), and "Schroeder would be the *first* [emphasis added] woman to campaign for the presidency since Shirley Chisholm, a Democrat, in 1972" (C. Grimes 1987). It was also written, "If Schroeder gets into the race, she will be the *first* [emphasis added] woman to seek a major party presidential nomination since 1972" (Freivogel 1987).

People who are not well versed about history but read the paper may even have been led to believe that Elizabeth Dole (in 2000) was the first woman to run, as this example demonstrates: "A small army of business-women [were] angry that one of their own—and the *first* [emphasis added] to seek the presidency—was not faring better in a field of men" (Sobieraj 1999). The *New York Times* described her as "the *first* [emphasis added] woman to become a really serious candidate for President of the United States" (Collins 1999). Another report noted that "as the *first* [emphasis added] serious female candidate for president, Dole would have unique appeal" (Balz and Broder 1999). Even when the candidates preceding her were acknowledged, she was still called a first. "A woman running for president of the United States is not a breakthrough. Victoria Woodhull was a minor-party candidate . . . and elected officials like Margaret Chase Smith and Shirley Chisholm have made long-shot bids for the nomination. But Elizabeth Dole is still making history as the *first* [emphasis added] woman to enter the presidential primary season as one of the front-runners" ("Mrs. Dole Leaps" 1999).

Dole's own campaign manager participated in eradicating women's political history when he said, "There isn't any history. There isn't any barometer. There hasn't been a female candidate for the President who was serious" (Berke 1999b). Her pollster Linda DiVall said in explaining her participation in the campaign, "No one before Mrs. Dole had attempted 'a serious, viable, female candidacy for the Presidency'" (Bruni 1999). As a presidential candidate, George W. Bush also framed Dole's candidacy in that way, saying, "I think it's instructive to America that the *first* [emphasis added] viable female presidential candidate is a Republican" (Glover 1999).

Even Moseley Braun was framed as a first, though not as frequently as were previous candidates, and her coverage was more likely to mention the women who preceded her. Still, one article noted that "with the recent exception of Carol Moseley Braun, there have been 'no credible campaigns by women in the U.S. for president'" (Fitzgerald 2003).

While Moseley Braun's press coverage frequently framed her as a "first," it did so in a different way than in coverage of previous candidates. In her case the frame centered around her term in the Senate. Virtually every article described her as the "*first* [emphasis added] black woman in the Senate." The novelty frame persisted in other ways as well. Moseley Braun was frequently identified as the "only woman candidate" in the field. Future women candidates may continue to be portrayed as the first, or they just may swap the designation of first for the similarly isolating description of "only."

Many designations of the women as firsts were factually wrong, but a few were technically correct. However, even when accurate, the reporters were willing to go far to maintain the "novelty" frame. For example, it may be true that Dole was the first viable Republican woman candidate to run since 1964, but that is a highly qualified first. In real terms, she was not first at all. Whereas an experimental study of the effects of such a framing is beyond the scope of this book, it would not be surprising to find that the persistent framing of women as firsts de-normalizes them in the political field, making the proposition of a woman candidate and president seem more risky and less likely. Although the "first woman" frame may help candidates in the short term by increasing the perception of their novelty and resulting in more press coverage, the effects of reinforcing the notion of women as out of place and unnatural in the political sphere may be longer lasting and have important political consequences.

The Incompetence of Women

The notion that women can not be both competent and feminine is what Kathleen Hall Jamieson calls the double bind of femininity/competence. She argued that throughout history "those who exercised their brains and brawn in public were thought to be tough, active, analytic, decisive, competent, and masculine; those who exercised their uteruses with the attendant responsibilities in the private sphere were identified as nurturant, passive, warm, and feminine" (1995, 120). In the same work, Jamieson pointed out that in the 1800s rationality and childbearing were considered biologically incompatible because thinking drained the necessary energy for childbearing.

When an argument about incompetence was printed, the notion that women are not effective in handling crises was among the most common reasons cited. One writer opined, "How can anyone nominate a woman for President or a woman wanting to be President is beyond me. Can't you just imagine a woman being faced with a crisis (Cuba) such as president Kennedy had? The office of President or Vice President is no place for a woman" (B. Grimes 1964). In a vox populi, also from 1964, a reporter asked constituents, "Would you vote for a woman for either President or Vice President?" Among the answers given were: "No . . . nature didn't endow them [women] with dispositions to face the crises of today" (Jemail 1964). In another vox populi conducted during Chisholm's campaign, the *New York Daily News* asked, "Would you be prejudiced against a woman running for president of the United States?" One man declared, "Yes, entirely prejudiced. Women are not qualified for this high office. If one is ever elected President, she would have to depend 100% on the advice of the men she appointed to high executive positions. Heaven help us in the event of a war. She couldn't handle the awesome responsibilities" (Jemail 1972).

Another argument was that women would not be effective as international leaders. "They wouldn't have the respect of other nations," responded one person who was interviewed on the street (Jemail 1964). Another maintained, "Other countries would prefer dealing with men"; another said that "some countries would think a lot less of us"; and still another, "other countries will laugh at us" (Jemail 1963).

The notion that women are incompetent because they are emotional and irrational has often been cited as a reason for keeping women out of office. This ideological position assumes that women have a biological drive toward nurturing and child raising that makes them emotional and irrational, rendering them incapable of logic and reason (and therefore of leading and legislating). In Jamieson's (1995) words, it is the double bind of womb/brain.

Examples from recent history show a lingering belief that biological drives inhibit women's ability to reason. Edgar Berman, Senator Hubert Humphrey's physician, argued at a session of the Democratic Party Committee Meeting that "'raging hormonal influences' caused by the menstrual cycle and menopause should exclude women from executive responsibility" (Jamieson 1995, 53). Of course, there is also evidence of women's resistance to the womb/brain double bind. "In the early 1970s Representative Pat Schroeder, a Colorado Democrat, told a hostile constituent, 'Yes, I have a uterus and a brain, and they both work'" (Jamieson 1988, 69).

The notion that emotionality would render women incompetent at leadership was present in the news coverage of female presidential candidates. In one vox populi, a man put it rather bluntly: "Women are too illogical and too emotional for high elective posts" (Jemail 1963). In another, a man added, "A woman isn't emotionally or physically capable of assuming the obligations of the most powerful office in the world. . . . We'd be in mortal danger with a female President" (Jemail 1964). When asked, "Would you be prejudiced against a woman running for president of the United States?" Stephen Eisman gave a familiar reply: "Definitely! A woman is too emotional. She acts on impulse. And she's often too sensitive to criticism" (Jemail 1972). In a lone letter to the editor, a constituent of Margaret Chase Smith countered the incompetence argument and wrote, "Our time has come. We women are tired of being the brains behind some smart man. It's about time people acknowledged that women can run this country" (Velez 1964). This example aside, explicit statements about women's incompetence predominated in 1964 and 1972. However, the argument that women are incompetent because they are obsessed with triviality had peaked in 1884.

Triviality

Another argument against women's competence, often made subtly, was that women are too interested in trivial matters to undertake the serious task of governing. It was Lockwood who was most often subjected to this critique. The article "Belva in the White House: A Cabinet Meeting of the Period When Women Shall Steer the Ship of State" (1884), from the *Boston Globe,* was dedicated to just this idea. The article was intended to be a humorous, fictional look at what politics would be like if women held elected office. All the same, its content was a scathing condemnation of women in politics. For example, it described the president as being very late for a meeting with the attorney general because she was "trying on her dress." Then when the president did arrive the cabinet meeting was taken up with a lengthy discussion of the style and merits of her attire: "'It's perfectly magnificent' said the Secretary of War, 'Those fine pleatings of crepe de chine give it such a lovely finish.'" The article then described the secretary of the navy as unable to do her job because she gets seasick and other women as unwilling to serve in international posts because the climate "is so damp that your hair never stays in curl at all." The cabinet decided there was no reason to send an emissary to Germany since, as far as they knew, "Bismarck is only a color." The article continued in this vein. Though cast in a humorous tone, the message was serious. Women (and explicitly Lockwood) are uninformed, incompetent, and obsessed with their appearance and related trivial matters. The meaning was clear. No woman could be fit for higher office.

The *New York Times* also argued, albeit implicitly, that women were too vapid for leadership. The paper did not bother to cover Lockwood's nomination and acceptance. However, when she did appear in its pages for the first time, on September 14, 1884, her campaign was satirically framed around the question of whether full-length culottes should be worn by women. The editors wrote that Lockwood was considering "the divided skirt question" and stated it was depriving Mrs. Lockwood of sleep. "If Mrs. Lockwood pledges herself to support the great divided skirt reform she will receive the enthusiastic support of the divided skirt wearers, but she will lose the confidence of the wearers of ordinary skirts. . . . Mrs. Lockwood had seriously thought of extricating herself from difficultly by a sunstroke, but her friends convinced her that to do any good a sunstroke would have to last until election day, and that in such a case such a large number of women would refuse to support a candidate who had been dangerously ill for two months" ("The Way of the Candidate" 1884). The article was wholly melodramatic and framed the campaign around an inconsequential issue of fashion in order to trivialize Lockwood's campaign. Moreover it made Lockwood appear unable to cope with even minor controversy and to be wholly consumed by trifling matters.

This editorial did note that Lockwood resisted the framing of her as too banal for office. It quoted her as saying simply that what kind of skirt a woman wears is not a matter of federal politics and that she had nothing more to say on the matter. Her remark shows she was not unduly burdened by the question and that she rejected it as an issue in the campaign. However, her comment was ignored by the author of the editorial, who insisted and reasserted that Lockwood was undecided and agitated by the "controversy" and almost unable to go on with her campaign because of it. These are not the only examples of press coverage that accuse women of triviality. Other articles, no less typical, charged that Lockwood had fake hair and that she rode a bicycle, which showed off her underpants.

Similar sentiments were found in other races, though less often. One article about Chase Smith, for example, invited the assumption that women are too insipid to lead; a woman who was interviewed said, "I would hope that a woman President and the Queen of England would not vie with each other in hat or dress styles. It might result in a diplomatic break" (Jemail 1964). Ironically, Chase Smith herself made one of the more trivializing comments about her own candidacy. When asked "how she might make out in a confrontation with Soviet Premier Khrushchev . . . she said, 'If it were on making blueberry muffins, I would probably win'" ("Mrs. Smith Says" 1964).

Even in recent times there was coverage that could only trivialize a woman's campaign. For example, there were several stories about the rendering of Moseley Braun's last name. In a lead paragraph to a *Chicago Tribune* story, a reporter wrote, "A decade ago, after her election to the U.S. Senate, Carol Moseley Braun introduced a hyphen to her name after 15 years in politics. Now it's gone" (Zeleny 2003a). Though the story went on to note that Moseley Braun would "rather discuss the war with Iraq," the reporter didn't, and instead the article was filled with information about her divorce and the spelling of her name. Such coverage trivialized the campaign because it focused on personal and irrelevant material and not substantive matters of policy and character.

Another article about the Moseley Braun campaign actually suggested that women did not run for president because they would have to disclose their body fat index. A columnist wrote on page 2 of the *Chicago*

Tribune, "Someday, a woman will be president of the United States. She may be sorry. One day, she will go to the suburban National Naval Medical Center for a three-hour physical, as the current president did Aug. 2, and then the entire world will know her body fat index" (Gerhart 2003). The article went on to say that if a woman were president she might have to disclose whether she had symptoms associated with menopause, and it questioned "whether Americans need to know the state of the uterus to be sure about the state of the Union."

Women as Not Viable

The third argument against women in office—that women are not viable as candidates—was the most prevalent. In the early years, the viability argument was framed as a lack of "readiness." In later years the argument was cast in terms of poll results, and only in 2000 did the problem of discrimination and prejudice openly make its way into the newspapers.

The earliest arguments against women candidates were set out in terms of the nation's lack of readiness for women in leadership. For example, one man who was interviewed during Chase Smith's run said, "The country isn't ready for a female president" (Jemail 1963). The papers never elaborated on what "not ready" meant, why America was thus unprepared, or when it would get ready. The phrase implies that since there is much discrimination against women, they cannot be elected, but it falls short of naming the problem as prejudice.

In Victoria Woodhull's race in 1872 one paper wrote of her, "She is rather in advance of her time. The public mind is not yet educated to the pitch of universal woman's rights" ("Woman's Idea of Government" 1870). Nearly a hundred years later, in 1964, a columnist wrote, "There are a number of influential commentators here who believe that Senator Smith will thank all of her supporters . . . and say it is flattering to be considered for the high office . . . but that she is realistic to know that the country is not quite ready to elect a woman as president" ("Washington Forecast" 1964). Lorin Arnold similarly assessed the tenor of the electorate, writing that "the presidency was no place for Senator Smith or any other woman—not yet, at least" (1964a). Though the word "viability" was not used in these early races, these are essentially arguments about women's lack of viability as candidates.

In 1987, the viability argument was expressed not in terms of readiness but in terms of poll results. For example, one article reported, "Many observers have said that Schroeder, because she is a woman . . . doesn't have a serious shot at the nomination. A recent poll for the National Women's

Political Caucus found that 30% of the public believe that a man would make a better president than a woman" (Lowey 1987). A similar sentiment was expressed by a former City Council member of Ames, Iowa: "I don't think any woman can win" (Blake 1987). In these examples the press never questioned why people didn't believe the woman candidate could win or what role prejudice and discrimination played. The women were just framed as unviable as though it were an immutable truth.

Schroeder was not the last woman to be saddled with the viability argument. Both by the reporters' frames and by quoting individuals, as late as 2000 the press was still promulgating the idea that America was not ready for a woman president. "Though the idea of the first woman as president excites many voters, it also injects some risk and uncertainty in the Republican Party's headstrong quest to retake the White House. The uncertainty placed immense pressure on Mrs. Dole to demonstrate—and do so early—that hers was a campaign that could win. . . . While most Republicans say the country is ready to make a woman President, a full third say it is not, according to an NBC News/Wall Street Journal poll taken in March" (Berke 1999b).

"Readiness" in addition to viability was a theme in interviews about Dole as well. In addition to citing polling data, a press report quoted an audience member who came to hear Dole speak: "I don't know if I'm ready for a woman." Another member of the audience expressed a similar senti-ment: "My gut feeling is that she has a good chance at the Vice Presidency. My gut is that the country is not ready for a woman president" (Berke 1999b). Similarly, in a *Newark Star-Ledger* article a woman was quoted as saying, "The country is not ready for a woman president" (Sobieraj 1999).

Carol Moseley Braun was also painted as unviable though this was less frequently cast in terms of "readiness" or polling, as were the previous candidates. Instead her campaign was simply dismissed as "symbolic" or a "long shot." For example, even as Moseley Braun received an endorse-ment from the National Organization for Women, the *New York Times* noted that "there is a place in the American political system for symbolic candidacies" ("NOW's Woman Problem" 2003). Similarly, in an article that ran in the *Chicago Tribune* the reporter wrote that the campaign insists it is "not a symbolic effort," inviting the implication that in fact it was (McMahon 2003). In other places the Moseley Braun effort was simply dismissed as a "long-shot" (Zeleny and McCormick 2004). Thus, one of the dominant themes in the coverage of these women candidates was that they were simply unelectable.

Though the dominant portrayal of the women candidates maintained they were not viable because they were women, there were times when the candidates themselves challenged this framing. Chase Smith countered the viability argument at least twice. In one case when "a reporter wondered if the country were ready for a woman president, she replied, 'If this is not the time for a woman candidate, when would the time be?'" (Larabee 1964). In another article Chase Smith countered that there have always been effective women political leaders and that therefore it was silly to say the time was not right. "Summing up a woman's chances of becoming president she said: I would remind you there was once a Joan of Arc . . . once a Catherine the Great . . . once a Queen Victoria" ("Mrs. Smith Says" 1964).

Schroeder also challenged the opinion that she was not viable because she was a woman. She said, "I get the Ferraro thing, which I think is irrelevant. Nobody says Sam Nunn can't run because Carter was from Georgia" (Toner 1987a). In a similar circumstance, Schroeder said of the Mondale/Ferraro loss in 1984, "The ticket was already down 19 points when she was put on it. . . . perhaps they should not have put a man on the ticket; it was he who lost" (Brozan 1987).

From 1872 through 1972 there were cases in which the press printed rebuttals to the viability arguments, but in every instance it was the candidate herself who made the argument that she was a viable candidate. That changed by 1987. In Schroeder's race, other political women rebutted the viability argument. For example, at the National Women's Political Caucus biennial convention, Bella Abzug said about Schroeder's chances of winning, "Is America less of a nation than Iceland . . . ? Is America less of a nation than Denmark? Is America less of a nation than England? If those countries are man enough to elect a woman, I think America can do so as well" (Toner 1987b). Similarly, another paper reported Friedan's rebuttal: "Some feminists like Betty Friedan, one of the first to urge Mrs. Schroeder to run, strongly disagree. 'People say, how can the Democrats support a woman after what happened with Ferraro?' Ms. Friedan said, 'I say how can the Republicans support a man after what happened with Ollie North?'" (Dowd 1987).

Feminist voices, however, were not always used to bolster a candidate's viability. Ellen Goodman used feminists to question the candidate's viability. In "Schroeder Could Close Campaign's Pizazz Gap" she wrote, "Yet the common wisdom even among political women has been that this is 'not the year for a woman.' According to the long-term game plan of women strategists—the A Team—this was the post-Ferraro time for regrouping and planning. Says one activist bluntly and off-the-record, 'We're not interested in seeing her run and do poorly'" (1987). Similarly in another case, it is feminists who are called upon to say why Schroeder could not win: "In stark contrast to the euphoria that greeted Ms. Ferraro's nomination, Mrs. Schroeder's exploration has uncovered a deep ambivalence among Democratic officials and women activists at the idea of a woman running" (Dowd 1987). Thus, women activists did not always speak out in favor of the candidates' chances of winning.

It was not until Elizabeth Dole's 2000 campaign that newspapers seriously entertained the idea that a woman might be a viable candidate. For example, the *Newark Star-Ledger* ran an article different from all previous ones in that it clearly presented the point of view that America was ready for a woman chief executive. In "A Lady Leader? America Says It Wouldn't Mind," it was written, "A majority of Americans are more than ready for a female chief executive. . . . When the Gallup organization of Princeton asked voters in February whether they would support a woman nominated by their party who was 'generally well-qualified,' 92 percent said yes." The article then listed the advances women have made in other offices (e.g., that 56 of the 425 seats in the House were held by women) and quoted Governor Christine Todd Whitman, who said, "The public is ready for a woman president, and I've heard that from people time and time again." It also quoted Jeanne Shaheen, governor of New Hampshire, who voiced a similar sentiment: "The bottom line is that people are not going to make a decision about who the best person for the president would be based on whether the candidate is a woman or a man. . . . They are going to make their decision based on who they think can do the best job" (Hassell 1999).

It is probably not insignificant that such positive assessments of Dole's viability were made by two women governors. Such women were far scarcer in previous eras and hence would have been less available for quotation. The same article also interviewed a voter who agreed that America was ready for a woman. "We've had, what, 42 male presidents? . . . Seems to me we might try a woman for a change, don't you think?" In an interesting tacit acknowledgment of the stereotype that women are more chaste than men, another voter added, "after all the controversy surrounding President Clinton's sex life, Americans may be even more inclined to vote for a woman chief executive" (Hassell 1999). Dole's race was the first in which there were notable voices arguing that America was ready. Moreover, it is the first race where some cited the problem as prejudice.

It was during Dole's race that there first appears in the papers a suggestion that a woman candidate might be subject to discrimination. In an editorial, the *New York Times* wrote,

As a woman, she will have to put up with the kind of scrutiny that male candidates are not bothered with. Critiques of her appearance, her wardrobe and her style will go far beyond anything her male opponents will have to endure. That is unfortunate but inevitable, since she is taking the American public on a shakedown cruise, acclimating it to what will inevitably become a long line of women presidential candidates in the future. The women who are moving up the political ladder behind her may be able to enter the competition on a more even basis because Elizabeth Dole got the public used to the idea of seeing a woman running for the White House. ("Mrs. Dole Leaps" 1999)

Another commentator did some casual research on the amount of coverage that Dole was getting compared to other candidates. When she found that Dole got less than Steven Forbes and John McCain, she presented the possibility that the media might be discriminating against Dole because of her gender. "The other day, among a group of friends I came right out and did it: I asked whether the public might be taking Dole less seriously, whether she might be having more trouble raising money and getting media coverage, because she's a woman" (Overholser 1999). The next day the paper printed a letter to the editor from Bob Dole. He wrote, "Much of the stingy coverage of Elizabeth Dole's campaign has been nitpicking and negative. Is it so because she is a woman, or could it be the mainstream media cannot abide the fact that she is a qualified Republican woman running for president" (Dole 1999). In Elizabeth Dole's race we see what may be evidence of an evolution of attitudes. Prejudice, instead of gender, is named as the problem in the question of viability.

Whether it is because America is not ready or because the polling says people won't vote for a woman, the dominant portrayal in the press is that being a woman makes you unviable as a candidate. However, there is evidence that this portrayal may be changing. While America was liberally portrayed as "not ready" for Dole, there were for the first time fissures in this frame. People did name the problem as prejudice, and there were diverse voices arguing that being a woman would not de facto make a person unelectable.

Arguments for Women

When arguments were presented in favor of women presidents (and these occasions were rare) the case was often made that historically or in other parts of the world women have made competent national leaders. In one of Nellie Penley and Marie Sullivan's columns in 1964, they wrote, "History shows that some of the great leaders of the world were queens and empresses and probably their background of world affairs was not as great as Senator Smith's." A similar sentiment was expressed in a letter to the editor: "If Senator Margaret Chase Smith should win the election, although she would be the first lady to hold the title of president, she wouldn't be the first woman to run the government as some of the presidents' wives helped quite a bit. There is no physical labor to hold this office, to me a woman could indeed handle the work as well as a man" (Arey 1964). In another letter to the editor a citizen wrote, "There are many women capable of taking the place of men (which has been proven time and time again) in high office, in industry, education, science, politics and other areas. . . . When one reads history, even kings and emperors have been successful, because of their wives—and what better example of truly great leadership is there when we mention England's Queen Victoria?" (Rowe 1964).

One of the better-developed arguments in favor of women appeared in a column in the *Seattle Times* during Chisholm's race. D. J. R. Bruckner (1972) wrote, "Woman president? Why not?" and argued that men have not made such great presidents and that there have been lots of successful women heads of state from other countries throughout history. He concluded, "A woman leader . . . might teach American men not to be so afraid of women. . . . Men and women are not as essentially different as Americans pretend." The piece is notable not only because it takes up gender explicitly and argues that it is not important, but also because it provides evidence for its claims in the form of examples of historical women who have led effectively.

Women's roles during World War II were also cited occasionally as evidence of women's capabilities. In a vox populi running in the *New York Daily News* a woman said, "Women can do everything men do and do it as well. I weigh only 95 pounds but during the war I was a riveter. Some women are brilliant and they are ready for high elective office. Sen. Margaret Chase Smith would be a strong president." A similar sentiment was expressed by another woman: "Where would business be today without women? During war days how could heavy industry and other parts of the economy get along without women? Men certainly are not more intelligent than women" (Jemail 1963).

Other justifications for encouraging women to enter elected office ran the gamut. In a letter to the editor one person argued that women are tougher than men and therefore should be in office. Referring to Chase Smith, the author wrote, "Now we have a woman aspirant! One that even the late president Kennedy classified as 'formidable!' Rudyard Kipling has said that the 'female of the species is more deadly than the male'; if this is true, surely that is what the nation really needs to combat the Castros and Khrushchevs who seem to be winning on all fronts. Khrushchev called her, 'the devil in the disguise of a woman.' Perhaps it will take a woman in the White House to call all bluffs of the Communists . . . the men just haven't the 'guts'" (Smith 1964). Taking a different tack, another citizen referring to Chase Smith said, "Sure I'm going to vote for her. . . . We need a woman in the White House so we can balance the budget" (Arnold 1964b).

Moseley Braun herself argued that being a woman was an asset to the presidency. She said, "A woman can fix the mess they [the current administration] have created . . . because we are practical, we are not afraid of partnerships and we are committed to making the world better for our children" (Lee 2003).

Another argument that seemed to surface for the first time in the 2004 race was that women should run for president to be role models for other women. For example, a *Chicago Tribune* reporter interviewed a student at Howard University, where Moseley Braun was appearing. "Braun faces long odds, but that does not mean her candidacy is in vain, said Howard freshman Ciara Famble. 'That she's even coming out and trying makes her a role model for me,' Famble said. 'I hope to be a senator someday'" (Mihalopoulos 2003). Eleanor Smeal, president of the Feminist Majority, said in relation to the Moseley Braun campaign, "We are stuck at 13 percent of the seats in Congress, and yet we're bragging we're a democracy. . . . It's very important for women to see women running for office. It gives inspiration to young women" (Crary 2003). Although these arguments may seem on the surface to be in favor of a woman's running in principle, they still may undercut the specific candidate by making her campaign seem symbolic.

Conclusion

The bad news about the media coverage of women candidates for office is that arguments against women's fitness, viability, and capabilities persist. The good news is that the arguments against women's fitness for office seem to be dropping in prominence while voices articulating the idea that women are both capable and viable appear to be on the rise. Still, the next woman to run should be prepared to be painted in the press as unnatural, incompetent, and unviable. These charges will come via explicit statements as well as through the use of polls; frames that present her as a "first," "only," or "symbolic" candidate; and portrayals of her as emotional and distracted by triviality.

Though not every woman in every race is depicted as unable to handle crises, too emotional, obsessed with triviality, or unviable, at least some of these arguments were made about all of the women. Overcoming these depictions and perceptions will be an important part of the campaign strategy of any woman candidate. Traditional notions of womanhood are an enduring legacy and represent a challenge to America. The articles that present the idea that females are unfit for office are devoid of any supporting evidence or rational thought. The concept that women may not be decisive, courageous, energetic, ambitious, or tough enough is rarely explicitly stated; rather these components are usually subtly conveyed in the text in other ways.

The idea that the country is not ready for a woman is one of the more enduring and prominent arguments against women, yet it is vague and undeveloped. In no case did any reporter ask what it meant to the interviewee to say the country was not ready. In no case did this depiction result in an awareness or condemnation of prejudice and discrimination as an anti-American value. Yet decade after decade, reporters advanced the idea that America was not ready for a woman in the White House. Even in recent races where the issue was more likely to become a question of viability, it was always framed as "women's viability," thus promoting the idea that it was a problem with women and not prejudice.

On a positive note, in recent races arguments have emerged for women's competence, usually based on historical or international precedents, and in Dole's race, there was evidence that people were aware that prejudice and discrimination might have been at play. The papers treated Schroeder and Dole as much more viable than Lockwood or Woodhull ever were. As women's resumes have come to look more like men's, the arguments against them are harder to make, and as women assume other high-level elected offices, there are more official voices available to make the case for them. After 130 years, some have asked when women candidates will stop being the "first" to run. The answer may lie in the woman's campaign that occurs after one wins.

References

Arey, S. 1964. "Has Been Done Before." *Bangor Daily News,* February 3, 10.

Arnold, L. 1963. "Maine's Political Whirl: Vote Boost for Republicans Seen behind V-P Move by Mrs. Smith." *Bangor Daily News,* November 16, 10.

———. 1964a. "Can She Win? Sen. Smith's Chances in N.H. Seem Slim." *Bangor Daily News,* February 15, 1.

———. 1964b. "Low-key Campaign: Senator Starts Drive in N.H." *Bangor Daily News,* February 11, 1.

"At Visit to U-M: Sen. Smith Mum on Candidacy." 1963. *Bangor Daily News,* November 11, 1

Balz, D., and D. S. Broder. 1999. "Elizabeth Dole Hints at Presidential Bid; Analysts Predict Effect on 2000 GOP Contest." *Washington Post,* January 5, A1.

"Belva in the White House: A Cabinet Meeting of the Period When Women Shall Steer the Ship of State." 1884. *Boston Globe,* October 24, 2.

Berke, R. L. 1999a. "Dole Presents Herself as Both Nonpolitician and an Insider." *New York Times,* March 11, A28.

———. 1999b. "Running toward 2000: Dole Fights to Recapture Her Early Star Status." *New York Times,* August 10, A1.

Blake, P. 1987. "Schroeder Is Scornful of 'Wingtip' Moderates: Colorado Dem Vows Spirited Attacks on GOP." *Rocky Mountain News,* July 4, 10.

Bose, C. E. 1987. "Dual Spheres." In *Analyzing Gender: A Handbook of Social Science Research,* ed. B. B. Hess and M. M. Feree, 267–85. Newbury Park, Calif.: Sage.

Brozan, N. 1987. "Schroeder Can Qualify for U.S. Funds after Donations at NOW Convention." *New York Times,* July 19, 22.

Bruckner, D. J. R. 1972. "Woman President? Why Not?" *Seattle Times,* January 5, A12.

Bruni, F. 1999. "One Republican Trailblazer Joins Forces with Another." *New York Times,* August 23, A10.

"A Campaign Style All Her Own." 1964. *Bangor Daily News,* January 30, 14.

Collins, G. 1999. "Editorial Observer: Mrs. Dole Takes a Leap into the Gender Gap." *New York Times,* February 10, A24.

Connolly, C. 1999. "The Dole Mystique: Strategy Aims to Capitalize, But Not Rely, on Gender." *Washington Post,* April 11, A1.

Crary, D. 2003. "Feminist Groups Feeling Targeted." *Chicago Tribune,* September 24, 3A.

Dole, B. 1999. "Stingy Coverage." *Washington Post,* September 15, A24.

Dowd, M. 1987. "Schroeder: At Ease with Femininity and Issues." *New York Times,* August 23, A24.

"Few Women in High Office." 1964. *Bangor Daily News,* February 6, 14.

Fitzgerald, J. 2003. "Women Encouraged to Raise Their Voices." *Chicago Tribune,* April 9, 2.

Freivogel, M. W. 1987. "Schroeder Rejects Idea of Running as 'Symbolic' Candidate." *St. Louis Post-Dispatch,* September 27, B1.

Gailey, P. 1987. "Schroeder Considers Running for President." *New York Times,* June 6, 33.

Gerhart, A. 2003. "Let's Examine a Woman President's Physical." *Chicago Tribune,* August 20, 2.

Glover, M. 1999. "Elizabeth Dole Steps toward 2000 Race to 'Rekindle Spirit.'" *Newark Star-Ledger,* March 11, 3.

Goodman, E. 1987. "Schroeder Could Close Campaign's Pizazz Gap." *Rocky Mountain News,* June 13, 55.

Grimes, B. 1964. "No Place for a Woman." *Bangor Daily News,* February 14, 16.

Grimes, C. 1987. "NOW Delegates Give Schroeder Cheers, Money." *St. Louis Post-Dispatch,* July 19, 1.

Hassell, J. 1999. "A Lady Leader? America Says It Wouldn't Mind." *Newark Star-Ledger,* August 8, 1.

Jamieson, K. H. 1988. *Eloquence in an Electronic Age: The Transformation of Political Speechmaking.* Oxford: Oxford University Press.

———. 1995. *Beyond the Double Bind: Women and Leadership.* Oxford: Oxford University Press.

Jemail, J. 1963. "The Inquiring Fotographer." *New York Daily News,* December 11, 53.

———. 1964. "The Inquiring Fotographer." *New York Daily News,* January 30, 35.

———. 1972. "The Inquiring Fotographer." *New York Daily News,* January 28, 45.

Krasner, J. 1964. "Valley Stream." *New York Daily News,* January 31, 31.

Larrabee, D. R. 1964. "Cheers Greet Sen. Smith." *Bangor Daily News,* July 13, 1.

Lee, J. 2003. "Ex-senator Announces for the Presidency." *New York Times,* September 23, A22.

Lewis, T. 1963. "Capitol Stuff." *New York Daily News,* November 13, 4.

Lowey, J. 1987. "Futurist Likes Schroeder's Odds." *Rocky Mountain News,* September 20, 42.

Lynn, F. 1972. "New Hat in Ring: Mrs. Chisholm's." *New York Times,* January 26, 1.

Matthews, G. 1992. *The Rise of Public Woman: Woman's Power and Woman's Place in the United States, 1630–1970.* Oxford: Oxford University Press.

McMahon, S. 2003. "Braun Bid Getting New Life, NOW's Ex-chief Says." *Chicago Tribune,* November 19, 16.

Mihalopoulos, D. 2003. "Presidential Contender Braun Makes Bid Official." *Chicago Tribune,* September 23, 9.

"Mrs. Dole Leaps into the Gap." 1999. *New York Times,* March 11, A30.

"Mrs. Smith Says She'll Have Austerity Campaign." 1964. *Bangor Daily News,* February 3, 4.

"NOW's Woman Problem." 2003. *New York Times,* September 14, 10.

Overholser, G. 1999. "More Press for Elizabeth Dole." *Washington Post,* September 14, A29.

Penley, N., and M. Sullivan. 1964. "Ladies at Odds over Woman as President." *Bangor Daily News,* January 28, 1.

"People in the News: Dark Horse Literally and Figuratively." 1972. *Seattle Times,* January 25, 2.

Poovey, M. 1988. *Uneven Development: The Ideological Work of Gender in Mid-Victorian England.* Chicago: University of Chicago Press.

Ross, C. 2006. "Separate Spheres or Shared Dominions?" *Transformation* 23 (4): 228–35.

Rowe, E. 1964. "'Good Luck, Margaret.'" *Bangor Daily News,* February 7, 10.

"Shirley Chisholm Declares Her Candidacy for President." 1972. *Seattle Times,* January 25, 2.

"Shirley Chisholm Rejects 'Lame Token.'" 1972. *Seattle Times,* February 20, 22.

Smith, E. R. 1964. "Smiths Speak Up." *Bangor Daily News,* February 6, 14.

Sobieraj, S. 1999. "Women Compelled to Help Dole Succeed." *Newark Star-Ledger,* August 1, 3.

Toner, R. 1987a. "Democrats and Women: Party Shifts Approach." *New York Times,* July 11, 10.

———. 1987b. "Schroeder's Potential Candidacy Is Dominating Women's Political Caucus." *New York Times,* August 22, 6.

Velez, M. 1964. "Manhattan." *New York Daily News,* January 31, 31.

"Washington Forecast: Fantastic Guessing Game over Sen. Smith's Plans." 1964. *Bangor Daily News,* January 23, 16.

"The Way of the Candidate." 1884. *New York Times,* September 14, 8.

"Woman's Idea of Government." 1870. *New York Herald,* May 27, 6.

Zeleny, J. 2003a. "Candidate Moseley Braun Gives Headline Writers a Break." *Chicago Tribune,* March 4, 8.

———. 2003b. "Moseley-Braun to Seek White House: Ex-Senator Says She'll Run on a Peace Platform." *Chicago Tribune,* February 13, 12.

Zeleny, J., and J. McCormick. 2004. "Braun to End Her Campaign, Endorse Dean." *Chicago Tribune,* January 15, 10.

Baking Muffins and Bombing Countries

I n 1984 when Geraldine Ferraro was running for vice president on the Democratic Party ticket, she was asked by Agriculture and Commerce Commissioner Jim Buck Ross, "Can you bake a blueberry muffin?" (Braden 1996, 109). On *Meet the Press,* she was asked, "Do you think that in any way the Soviets might be tempted to take advantage of you simply because you are a woman?" (Jamieson 1995, 107), and "Are you strong enough to push the button?" (Cohn 2002, 18). Over twenty years earlier, when Margaret Chase Smith was first elected to the Senate, the *Saturday Evening Post* published a photo essay showing her wearing an apron and baking in the kitchen (Schmidt 1996).

Not only does the press ask women candidates different types of questions than it poses to men, but it often uses words to describe women that are not used to describe men. Each of these can be a subtle way of conveying stereotypes. Maria Braden (1996), a journalism professor, argued that when Representative Susan Molinari (R–NY) was described as "perky" by the *Village Voice,* Senator Nancy Kassebaum (R–KA) as "demure" by the *Washington Post,* and Governor Madeleine Kunin of Vermont as "hysterical," they all were being described in ways that no man candidate would be. Kathleen Hall Jamieson of the Annenberg School for Communication made the same argument with regard to a *Washington Post* description of Canadian Prime Minister Kim Campbell as "haughty" and Golda Meir, former prime minister of Israel, as a "grandmother." In fact, Senator Kassebaum reportedly became so tired of being called "diminutive" and "soft-spoken" that she said if she heard it again she would "hit someone over the head" (Jamieson 1995, 129). Reporters ask these types of questions or choose these types of words because they are following stereotypes that associate women with domestic spheres and nurturing instead of public life and leading. These stereotypes inform their writing and interviewing of the candidates, which in turn may influence readers, often subtly conveying that the women candidates are unsuited to politics. According to Dianne Feinstein's campaign staff in her 1990 run for governor of California, "The hardest task they faced during the campaign was the need to establish Feinstein's credibility as a leader over and over and over again, despite her credentials as mayor of San Francisco and her charisma. Yet the public had no trouble seeing her mild-mannered Republican opponent, Pete Wilson, as a leader, for as a white male he fit the public's most comfortable leader image" (qtd. in Jamieson 1995, 123).

This chapter examines some stereotypes about men and women to learn to what degree the press coverage reinforced or challenged these traditional conceptions and how coverage changed over time. Specifically, I examine the treatment of emotion, family, profession, naming, and character descriptions. Such patterns are important to scholars of media bias, elections, and discrimination because they help describe the systematic forces at play in society.

Stereotypes

One reason for the difficulties women face in the press is that Western culture associates leadership with stereotypically masculine characteristics. Evidence for such an argument is found throughout the social sciences. For example, Sandra Bem (1987), a research psychologist, found that when subjects were asked to choose traits that were more desirable in men, those mentioned included: leader, aggressive, ambitious, analytical, makes decisions easily, willing to take a stand, dominant, and forceful. This same list could have been derived from descriptions of good leadership. The list of attributes that were more desirable in women were decidedly not associated with leadership: compassionate, childlike, yielding, soft-spoken, gullible, and shy. Kathleen Hall Jamieson (1995) noted that this dichotomy in traits grew out of the separate-sphere philosophy. Masculine traits tend to be associated with work and rationality (the public sphere). Feminine traits are associated with mothering, reproduction, and emotion (the private sphere).

Given this, it is noteworthy that when two researchers, Shirley Miller

Rosenwasser and Norma Dean (1989), asked college students to describe the qualities of a good president, they found 61 percent of the descriptions for a good president were categorized as masculine; none of the students described a good president as feminine. They found that masculine traits were considered more important for all offices from local to national. The political scientist Leonie Huddy (1994) concluded from this and similar research that "a female candidate stereotyped as a typical *feminine* woman would most certainly lose electoral support because she would be seen to lack typical male traits and expertise in policy areas thought most necessary for effective national leadership" (177).

If stereotypically masculine traits are associated with leadership in our culture, it makes sense for candidates to highlight these qualities when running for office. In fact, both men and women are more likely to stress stereotypically masculine traits in their ads; nonetheless, press reports diminish the number of masculine characteristics in women while exaggerating them in men. Kim Fridkin Kahn (1996), a political scientist, found that when the media reported on men candidates they covered stereotypically masculine traits 72 percent of the time, despite the fact that the men candidates themselves mentioned such traits only 67 percent of the time. By contrast, stereotypically masculine traits were mentioned in less than half (41 percent) of discussions about women candidates, despite the fact that in their ads women emphasized stereotypically masculine traits 91 percent of the time. The media, therefore, painted men as more masculine and leaderlike than the candidates did themselves and the women as less masculine and leaderlike than the women characterized themselves.

Similarly, in a study of newspapers and news magazines conducted in 1994, researchers found that men were more likely to be described as "leaders" than were women. Men leaders were featured in 85 percent of the articles whereas women leaders were featured in only 26 percent (Bridge 1994). Thus, the media may actually promote stereotypes by describing women as having more stereotypically feminine traits even when the candidates do not present themselves in such ways.

Stereotypes can be better understood by looking at what many modern cognitive theorists call cognitive schemata. Cognitive schemata are conceptualized as knowledge structures in memory. Ideas are represented as nodes that are connected by pathways. The more use a pathway receives in connecting concepts and ideas, and the more recently a link between ideas has been made, the stronger the link will be. More strongly linked concepts are more readily and quickly recalled. When one concept or idea is activated (also called primed), ideas that are linked to it become easier to access and more quickly recalled than thoughts not similarly linked. Hence, when news articles use words or frames to cue certain ideas, readers are more likely to think of related concepts more quickly and easily.

Stereotypes in this model can be conceptualized as "widely shared assumptions about certain types of people that are represented cognitively as extensive, well-organized categories or schemata" (Andersen, Klatzky, and Murray 1990, 192). According to this theory, the activation of a stereotype increases the likelihood that the same category and its associated knowledge will be used in subsequent judgments. After identifying a candidate as a woman, a reporter should find that the words and concepts associated with women will be more accessible than others. Given this, we might expect that mentions of family, emotions, and physical appearance would be found more often in the coverage of women. In other words, traits, attributes, and concepts stereotypically associated with women will be more likely to appear in articles about women candidates than in articles about men candidates. The fact that people are more likely to recall information consonant with extant stereotypes suggests that there may be an additional amplification effect when the press covers women in stereotypical ways. To the degree that the mental associations we have with women have changed over the last 130 years, we would also expect to see a commensurate change in the way authors write about women. However, for the most part this was not the case, suggesting that our traditional assumptions about women and men are still very much a part of our culture. When it comes to public service, one stereotype that has dogged women is the idea that they are too emotional to lead.

Stereotypes about Emotion

The assumptions that women are emotional and men rational is part of conventional stereotyping (e.g., Brody and Hall 1993; Wood 1994). Such stereotyping also has its basis in the separate-spheres philosophy, which held that natural sexual differences included the irrationality of women and the rationality of men. Two professors of psychology, Janice Kelly and Sarah Hutson-Comeaux, described the belief that women are more emotional and men rational as one of the most common findings in gender stereotype research (1999). In fact, as discussed in the previous chapter, the idea that women are irrational and therefore unable to lead is one of the explicit arguments found in newspaper coverage of women's campaigns. Plant, Hyde, Keltner, and Devine (2000) found that women were *believed* to experience more sadness and less anger than men, and that when subjects saw pictures of ambiguous facial expressions they were likely to say that the women were sadder and less angry than the men. However, an extensive literature review on women and anger was conducted by the Correctional Service of Canada, and the authors concluded that it was a myth that women express less anger than do men (see Crump 1995). When popular attitudes that attribute emotionality to women and rationality to men are applied to the arena of political judgments, they have often been used as the premise for an argument for keeping women out of the political sphere.

To determine if women were portrayed as more emotional than men, I counted any emotional descriptions of the candidates in press accounts. For example, the words or phrases "alarmed" ("Mrs. Lockwood in New York: Disappointed" 1884), "delighted" ("Butler in New York" 1884), "was moved to wipe away tears" ("GOP Picks" 1964), and "showed a flash of temper" ("Sen. Goldwater" 1964) would each have been counted as one emotional description. When I examined the number of emotional descriptions in the presidential campaign press coverage of women compared to that of the men, in every case except one there were more for women. The campaign of Lenora Fulani was the exception to the trend. Very few articles were written about her and so results from her race should be treated with caution. Otherwise the trend is quite stable with women receiving more than twice as many emotional descriptions per 10,000 words written about them. On average, women received 4 emotional descriptions per 10,000 words whereas men received just 1.8. By using more emotional descriptions in the coverage of women than men, the press may have reinforced and amplified the stereotype that women are emotional and irrational and therefore unfit for leadership while creating a contrasting picture of men as less emotional, more rational, and more leaderlike.

Moreover, women candidates in this century were no less likely to be described emotionally than were women candidates from the nineteenth and twentieth centuries. Elizabeth Dole in 2000 and Carol Moseley Braun in 2004 received as many emotional descriptions as did Victoria Woodhull in 1872. The most notable score for the difference between men and women came with the Schroeder-Gephardt matchup in 1987. Pat Schroeder was described emotionally eleven times per 10,000 words written about her whereas less than one emotional description was used for Representative Richard Gephardt in an equivalent amount of coverage. Despite the advances in women's rights, there is no noticeable trend toward decreasing emotional descriptions over time. This is surprising given the dramatic change in the number of women in leadership positions over the period covered and suggests that such stereotypes are deeply ingrained in the culture.

Types of Emotion

Not only do people believe that women are more emotional than men, but they are also more likely to ascribe different emotions to women than to men. Fear and sadness are associated with females and anger with males (Kelly and Hutson-Comeaux 1999). In the six races in which there were emotional descriptions for both candidates, women were on average more likely to be described as feeling more fear and sadness and less anger than men. On average 27 percent of the emotional descriptions for men described anger whereas just 14 percent did so for women. In contrast 10 percent of emotional descriptions of women ascribed sadness to women whereas just 2 percent did so for the men. Similarly 9 percent of emotional descriptions for women singled out fear whereas just 4 percent did so for men. Shirley Chisholm and Henry Jackson were the only candidates who did not fit this pattern. In that race Chisholm was more likely to be described as angry and Jackson as fearful.

Emotions played a particularly interesting role in the coverage of Victoria Woodhull's 1872 campaign. Early in her campaign she was described as different from other women precisely because she was taking action. Notice how emotional women in general were portrayed in this first editorial about Woodhull to appear in the *New York Herald:* "The sorrowful sisterhood 'Sorosis' [A woman's club] has pined itself into melancholy over strong tea at Delmonico's because of the obstinacy or neglect of their autocratic husbands in not allowing them to organize among themselves coteries of female repeaters, ballot stuffers and primary strikers. And this waste and emaciation of womanly tears and womanly beauty has as yet achieved no results whatever beyond its corollary of miseries." In these two sentences women are described five times as experiencing sad emotions. They are "sorrowful," "pining," "melancholy," have "tears," and experience "misery." Woodhull is then described in contrast to the other women. She is said to describe herself as having the "means, courage, energy, and ability necessary" for the presidency ("The Coming Woman" 1870). Woodhull works while other women weep.

Ironically, the press at one point suggested that she become more emotional and less rational in order to accomplish her goals. After the press covered a particularly strong, intellectual, and rational argument by Woodhull concerning why women should have the right to vote, the *Herald* counseled her to be more emotional and stereotypical. A *Herald* editorial suggested that Woodhull's written response was utterly ineffective, but that she might be able to change minds if she would cry instead of argue. Referring to Judge John Bingham, who had commented adversely about Woodhull's suffrage petition, the *Herald* wrote, "We do not feel that eloquent peroration, however, will affect him at all. If it were a tearful appeal or a heart-rendering wail from the crushed sex we might have some hope" ("Mrs. Woodhull" 1871). Thus the *Herald* publicly encouraged Woodhull to act in a more stereotypical and emotional way.

In general, Lockwood was portrayed with more negative emotions than was her opponent, General Benjamin Butler. She was described as "alarmed" ("Mrs. Lockwood in New York: Disappointed" 1884) and apprehensive ("Belva in the White House" 1884). Butler in contrast was much more likely to be described with positive emotions. For example, he was described as appreciative ("Accepting the Nomination" 1884), in excellent spirits, and delighted ("Butler in New York" 1884). The emotional descriptors used for Butler are all more socially acceptable for people in leadership positions than those describing Lockwood.

In the case of Chase Smith, positive emotions such as "enjoying" predominated, with "hopeful" being the most common. Consistent with gender-role stereotypes, Chase Smith was twice described as sad, as in "was moved to wipe away tears" ("GOP Picks" 1964). Nelson Rockefeller never was portrayed as sad, though he was described as angry, as when he "showed a flash of temper" ("Sen. Goldwater" 1964). Conversely, Chase Smith never was described as angry.

Coverage of Shirley Chisholm's emotions was notable, and counter to the general trend, because she was so often described as angry whereas her opponent Henry Jackson was described as fearful. She was described as experiencing "scathing anger" (O'Neill 1972), as "fiery" (Narvaez 1972, 37), ranting and raving (Maggi 1972), and having a "temper" ("Dark Horse" 1972). Jackson was described as "filled with anxiety" (Larsen 1972b), fearing deals ("Summit Questioned" 1972), and "worried" (Larsen 1972a). The reason that the stereotypical patterns were reversed for Chisholm and Jackson is not apparent. Chisholm may have invoked the stereotype of the "angry feminist" and hence made her anger more salient to reporters.

As mentioned before, Schroeder was far more likely than the other candidates to be portrayed as having emotions. Throughout her coverage she was portrayed as both angry and sad. She was described as "fuming" and "upset" (Lowy 1987a), "irked" and "angry" (P. Brown 1987). Even before her withdrawal Schroeder's emotions were already attracting a lot of coverage. However, much press attention was given to the fact that Schroeder cried when she announced that she would not continue to pursue the presidency. Fully 32 percent of her emotional descriptions appeared when the press reported that she would not run for office. These depictions almost all mentioned that she was sad, using words such as "disappointment" (Amole 1987), "tearful" (Blake 1987c), and "fought back tears" (Freivogel 1987a).

As with many of the men, Elizabeth Dole was most likely to be described as having hope, as when the press described her as "optimistic" (Neal 1999) and "hoping" (Balz 1999b). She received a smattering of other emotional descriptions, including those mentioning love ("Elizabeth Dole Exiles" 1999), "trepidation" (Purdum 1999), and her being "upbeat" (Connolly 1999).

Carol Moseley Braun in 2004 had a wide variety of emotions attributed to her. They included positive emotions, as suggested by words such as "encouraged" (Zeleny and Mihalopoulos 2003), "happy" (Wilgoren 2003), and "passionately" (Mihalopoulos 2003a). She was also described as "ashamed" (Wilgoren 2003), aggravated (Mihalopoulos 2003b), and "outraged" (Davey 2003). As in earlier races, expressions of anger dominated the emotional descriptions of her competitor for the Democratic nomination, Robert Graham. He was frequently described as "outraged" (e.g., Adair 2003) and occasionally as proud (Zeleny 2003). Though the candidates were described as exhibiting varying emotions, the broadest trend was to describe women as more emotional than men and with emotions less appropriate for leadership. This pattern demonstrates one way in which social stereotypes were projected onto the women, and it was these stereotypical depictions that then created the mediated visions of these candidates in the minds of the electorate.

Family and Profession

Another of the common stereotypes that we carry in American culture is that women's marital status and role as mother are important whereas men's private roles are not. When Kathleen Hall Jamieson (1995) analyzed headlines in 1990, 1992, and 1993 from the *New York Times, Washington Post,* and major state newspapers covering the federal elections in which women ran, she found that political women were identified in spousal or parental roles more often than were men. For example, Carol Moseley Braun was described as "divorced and the mother of a 15-year-old son" (170). Men who similarly won a Senate seat were more likely to be described according to profession; for example, Robert Bennett was described as a "59-year-old Republican businessman" (170). Jamieson did not find any man candidate who was described by his marital status. Similarly, when the press did mention the spouse of a candidate, the spouse's profession was given if the spouse was a man, but not necessarily if the spouse was a woman (see also, Foreit et al. 1980).

Family

I noted any reference (aside from courtesy titles) that would indicate that the candidate had a spouse or a child (or was childless) as "family mentions." The following examples all qualified as family mentions: "Dole who is married to 1996 Republican presidential nominee Robert J. Dole" (Balz 1999a); "Gov. Rockefeller and his wife Happy" (Holeman 1963); "Margaret Chase Smith, prior to her marriage to Clyde H. Smith" ("Skowhegan Plans" 1964).

Although on average women were more likely to have their families mentioned in an article than were men, on closer inspection the pattern is more complex. Women had their families mentioned on average once in every five articles. Men's families were mentioned about half as often, or in one in every ten articles. Overall there was no trend toward decreasing family mentions for women over time. Women candidates were as likely to have their families mentioned in the nineteenth century as they were in the twentieth and twenty-first centuries. For example, the woman whose family was most frequently mentioned was the Republican primary candidate in 2000, Elizabeth Dole. Her rate was high due to frequent mentions of Bob Dole (who had received the Republican nomination in the previous presidential election). Elizabeth Dole was frequently defined by her relationship to her husband—as in "Bob Dole's wife"—and this accounted for her family-mention rate being high.

She was followed in the number of family mentions by Victoria Woodhull, in 1872. The press was obsessed with coverage of Woodhull's home and family life. It interviewed her sister, who opposed her campaign; it covered her relationships with her current and ex-husbands; it covered a family squabble between her ex-husband and mother. Her family was mentioned about four times in every ten articles.

In five of the eight races, women's families were mentioned at a higher rate than were the men's. In 1964, 1972, and 2004, men outpaced the women, but there were several factors that could explain this pattern. The three women whose families were rarely mentioned (Chase Smith, Chisholm, and Moseley Braun) did not campaign with their spouses or relatives. In fact, their family members played no role in the campaigns. Chase Smith and Moseley Braun were not married at the time of their campaigns; and according to their biographers, Chase Smith and Chisholm were not very close to their respective families. In other words, for these three candidates there just wasn't much opportunity for family to be mentioned. In contrast the three men who ran against these women chose to have their families play a prominent role in their campaigns.

Rockefeller (1964 campaign), who had tied for the highest rate of family mentions of the men, had a home life that was very public. In 1962 Rockefeller divorced his first wife, and he married his second wife fourteen months later. His pregnant new wife accompanied him on the campaign trail, and later both his wife and the wife of his son from his earlier marriage had babies during the campaign. This accounted for many of the mentions of his family in the articles. Jackson (1972 campaign), like Rockefeller, campaigned with his wife and this accounted for most of his family mentions. The same was true of Bob Graham in 2004. He was accompanied by his wife and children at many campaign events. In fact, one of the major events of his campaign was a "family vacation" they took in Iowa in order to gather support for his run. Virtually all of the references to Graham's family came from mentions of his relatives who attended campaign events.

It is interesting that three of the seven women in this study had no children, including the two with the lowest rate of family mentions (Chase Smith in 1964 and Chisholm in 1972). Candidate Dole was the third woman without children but her rate of family mentions was high because of frequent references to her husband, Bob Dole. The overall pattern for family mentions may be that, all things being equal, women are more likely to have their families mentioned, but that when men bring family members on the campaign trail with them, they are likely to receive increased references.

Profession

When I coded if an article referred to a candidate's profession, including using titles like "Representative" and "Governor" (if that was the candidate's job when running), I found that men were slightly more likely to have their professions mentioned than were women. However, in this case there is a clear temporal pattern. Women who ran in the earliest period I studied were more likely than later women to have their professions mentioned relative to the men in the same race. In the first three races (1872, 1884, and 1964) the women were more likely than the men to have their professions mentioned. In all of the subsequent races the men were more likely than the women to have their professions mentioned.

It is notable that in the races from the nineteenth century the women were more likely to have their professions mentioned than were the equivalent men running in the same race. One reason for this may have been because these women held positions that were atypical for women at that time. Woodhull was a stockbroker and publisher and Lockwood was an attorney. Even into 1964 it was very rare to be a woman in the Senate, as Chase Smith was.

The fact that women had overall more family mentions and fewer professional mentions is again instructive in understanding the way stereotypes affect what reporters choose to write about. Though the ideology of separate spheres may be far from dominant in the present era, the cognitive associations of women with home and men with work are still part of our thinking and affect how women candidates are framed, and of course those frames work to reinforce and reiterate our stereotypes in society.

Naming

When I looked more closely at professional references another interesting pattern appeared. Of the four women who had held national elected offices (Chase Smith, Chisholm, Schroeder, and Moseley Braun), three were more likely to have their honorary titles diminished than were the equivalent men. When I counted the percentage of times senators, representatives, and governors were referred to as "Mr.," "Mrs.," or "Ms.," I found that Chisholm, Chase Smith, and Moseley Braun were more likely to be referred to as "Mrs." or "Ms." than Rockefeller, Jackson, and Graham were referred to as "Mr." This is a mistake, according to standard etiquette rules, which call for the use of a person's highest-status identification. By reducing "Senator Smith" to "Mrs. Smith" and "Representative Chisholm" to "Mrs. Chisholm" the press reduced the stature and experience of these women and reframed them by marital status.

On average, women's honorary titles were dropped in 32 percent of the references in these four races. The rate for men was just 11 percent. Chisholm was the most likely member of Congress to have her honorary title dropped (63 percent of the time). Schroeder was the least likely of the women to experience this. She lost her title just 10 percent of time, making her more like the other men studied. She was actually the only woman to be less likely to lose her title relative to the equivalent man. Four data points are not sufficient to justify hypotheses about trends. As more women incumbents run, more data will have to be collected to see if there is a pattern wherein women's stature is diminished more than men's.

The women in this study were also slightly more likely to be referred to using only their first name than were the men (4 percent compared with 3 percent). The only exception to this rule came in 1988 when the presidential race included Lenora Fulani and Ron Paul, both of whom had too few articles upon which to base generalizations. If this race is excluded, about 5 percent of references to women used their first name and less than 1 percent of references to men did. The pattern for the men was quite stable with all (except Paul) having 2 percent or fewer of the references to them on a first-name basis. The women ran the gamut from a low of less than 1 percent for Chase Smith to a high of 12 percent for Lockwood.

Although many of the references to women candidates' first names came from quotations, columns, and letters to the editor, those first names also made their way into the headlines. For example, a headline in 1872 about Victoria Woodhull read, "Vic says 'I will stump the states with Tennie C.'" ("A Piebald Presidency" 1872). In 1884 the *New York Times* headlined, "Belva Frees her Mind." In 1964 the *Bangor Daily News* headed a letter to the editor with, "Good Luck, Margaret," and the *New York Daily News* was similarly familiar in 1972 with "Shirley vs. Saigon." An analysis piece run in 1987 headlined "Will It Be 'Run, Pat, Run' or 'No, Pat, No'?" (Blake 1987d). "Elizabeth" and "Carol" did not end up in the headlines in the same way, but a columnist wrote in 1999, "Dump Bob, Bring on Elizabeth!" (Overholser), and another wrote in 2003, "For a moment Carol the Real and Carol the Ideal were one in the same" (Mihalopoulos 2003b). By referring more often to women by their first names I suspect the papers may have subtly cued the readers that women were less deserving of honor and respect than the men. When the press prints such diminutives in the headlines it amplifies and stresses that disrespect.

The Vice Presidency

Thomas Marshall, Woodrow Wilson's vice president, reportedly said, "Once there were two brothers. One ran away to sea; the other was elected vice president of the United States. Nothing was heard of either of them again" ("Vice President of" n.d.). Similarly, John Adams, the first vice president of the United States, once said, "My country has in its wisdom contrived for me the most insignificant office that ever the invention of man contrived or his imagination conceived" (Bostdorff 1991). Given this conception of the vice presidency as a powerless, dead-end position, it is not unexpected that the job is also often depicted as suitable for women and the object of their desire. This is because vice presidents have no real power and they take their place behind and gain their importance from the president. In fact, Denise Bostdorff, a communications professor, wrote, "Just as women traditionally have been controlled by the men around them, vice presidents . . . have been completely subordinate to the more powerful man around them: the president" (2).

In the cases of the five women who ran for the presidential nomination of the major parties, the vice presidency was mentioned as a desired goal of each of their bids, and four were more likely to be mentioned for the vice presidency than were their male counterparts. The women were regularly framed as though the vice presidency (and not the presidency) was their true ambition. Margaret Chase Smith's 1964 campaign was the one most frequently framed as a bid for the vice presidency. Such a sentiment was expressed once in every five articles about her. Pat Schroeder's 1987 bid attracted the next most frequent expression of this idea. Interestingly the two black candidates out of these five were less likely to be cast as vice presidential candidates than were the white women. None of the candidates from third parties was ever mentioned as a prospective vice presidential candidate.

In contrast, only two of the eight men were even mentioned for vice presidential office. There was a single reference to that position in regard to Henry Jackson in 1972, and Bob Graham in 2004 was only man who, like the women, was the subject of frequent speculating about his possible suitability for the vice presidency.

At face value the frequency with which women were mentioned as potential vice presidents may seem like a boon to the women candidates, but in fact, my impression is that this was a way of making them seem as though they were not really running or suited for the presidency. The redirection of the women from the presidency to the vice presidency was particularly noticeable in Margaret Chase Smith's race. Even though she repeatedly told the press that she was not running for, nor was she interested in, the vice presidency, the press framed that as her ambition.

Typical of these mentions is the comment from the *New York Daily News* referring to "Sen. Margaret Chase Smith of Maine—who said she'd like to run for President, period, but is believed willing to settle for the Vice Presidential nomination" ("New Hampshire Free" 1964). More outrageous, however, is this example from the *Bangor Daily News:* "If Mrs. Smith made a good showing in the primaries, she would be in a position to seek the second spot on the Republican ticket" ("She May Test" 1963). Thus, even in the scenario under which Chase Smith did well, the papers funneled her to the vice presidency. These examples are not anomalies. In fact, mentions of Chase Smith as a vice presidential candidate occurred in

21 percent of the articles that referred to her. Although it was Rockefeller who would later hold the position, he was never mentioned as a potential candidate for vice president.

Mentions of Chisholm as a potential vice presidential candidate were much less frequent, as in, "A black civil-rights activist says a group has been formed to push a Democratic national ticket that would offer something for everyone—Alabama Gov. George C. Wallace for President and black United States Representative Shirley Chisholm of New York for vice president" ("Ticket of" 1972).

The next time a light-skinned woman candidate ran for the Democratic nomination (Schroeder), there were many suggestions that she seek the vice presidency. Unlike the references regarding Chase Smith that often framed her "real" ambition as the second slot, vice presidential mentions for Schroeder were more likely to suggest that it was an option even though Schroeder repeatedly said she was not interested in the position. In an early article in the *Rocky Mountain News* the reporter built the story around the suggestion that Schroeder may seek the vice presidency. His lead sentence said, "U.S. Representative Pat Schroeder of Denver, saying she was no 'cheerleader,' dismissed the suggestion that a possible long-shot presidential campaign might at least be useful in getting her the second spot on the next years' Democratic ticket" (Blake 1987b). Here the news was that she was *not* seeking the vice presidency. In fact, there were many jobs that Schroeder was not seeking, but the headline for that story was "Schroeder Doubts No. 2 Role: Lawmaker Not Eager to Be 'Cheerleading' Vice President." That kind of information makes news only if there is some reason to think Schroeder is seeking or would be appropriate for the vice presidential position. In no cases was it considered news that men candidates were not seeking the vice presidency. Despite the fact that this reporter devoted a whole article to reasons why Schroeder was interested in the presidency and *not* the vice presidency, three days later he wrote, "She wouldn't have to resign her House candidacy until nominated for president or vice president" (Blake 1987a). Here again he suggests that the vice presidency may be where Schroeder is headed. The vice presidency was also mentioned as the best possible outcome of Schroeder's race, as in, "Rep. Pat Schroeder will seek the Democratic presidential nomination and probably end up on the ticket as a vice presidential candidate." Later in the same article a similar comment appeared: "Schroeder, D–Colo., probably will do well enough to land the spot as vice-presidential candidate on the Democratic ticket" (Johnson 1987).

Dole, like Schroeder and Chase Smith, was asked repeatedly about the vice presidency and consistently denied that was her goal, as these examples show:

> [She] deflected questions about becoming her party's vice-presidential nominee. "I haven't really thought about it because I've been focused on running for president and running to win." (Cohen 1999)

> Until now Dole has been seen more as a prospective vice presidential candidate in 2000, and some analysts said they believed that still might be her ultimate goal. But Dole associates said she would run to win the nomination if she decides to become a candidate. (Balz and Broder 1999b)

> Despite suggestions that Dole's realistic target is the vice presidency, DiVall said, "Her goal is the presidency. No one on her team is looking at settling for No. 2." (Broder 1999)

> Mrs. Dole and Mr. Bush had exchanged what seemed a significantly warm greeting, but both said afterward that they were just good friends with high opinions of each other, and assiduously avoided playing into speculation that Mrs. Dole might serve well as Mr. Bush's running mate. (Goldberg 1999)

Carol Moseley Braun, like Shirley Chisholm, was less frequently mentioned as a vice presidential candidate; in fact she was the only woman running for a major party nomination who was mentioned less frequently for the position than the most equivalent man running in the same race. Still in her case there was much pontificating about her "real" ambitions since the presidency was dismissed as a possibility. She was more frequently slated for even lesser offices than the vice presidency, such as mayor. In one of the few references made about Moseley Braun and the vice presidency, she was even paired with Bob Graham. It is interesting to note the order of the members of this suggested ticket (even though Moseley Braun and Graham polled at the same level). "I propose the following slate: Bob Graham for president and Carol Moseley Braun for vice president," wrote one reader in a letter to the editor (Rapp 2003).

Unlike the other major party women candidates, Moseley Braun was not pestered repeatedly about the vice presidency, presumably because she was not taken seriously enough for even that position. However, she was frequently portrayed as not "really" seeking the presidency. For example, several articles suggested she was just trying to rehabilitate her reputation, which suffered after several scandals during her term as senator in the 1990s. For example, one reporter wrote, "Hers seems more a personal crusade for rehabilitating her image than a substantive campaign for the public office" (Mihalopoulos 2003b). Other articles suggested she was just a spoiler for the Reverend Al Sharpton. For example, one report in the *New York Times* noted, "Some see Ms. Moseley Braun as a spoiler, recruited by national Democratic operatives and the Rev. Jesse L. Jackson ... to siphon black support from the Rev. Al Sharpton" (Wilgoren 2003). Still other articles suggested her real ambitions were for offices lower than the vice presidency. One article hinted her campaign "wasn't about the presidency at all" but was about giving her "buzz in the Democratic party" and could help her in a race for mayor of Chicago ("Back to Reality" 2003).

By repeatedly mentioning the women for vice president instead of president the press may have promoted the idea that it is not proper for a woman to have access to the kind of power afforded the presidency. The press may have transposed its stereotypical notions of the appropriate place for women from the home to the political arena by viewing and therefore portraying the women candidates as vice presidential and not presidential hopefuls.

Character

Increasingly, evidence has shown that the character and personality of a candidate have as much, if not more, influence on voting decisions as have the candidate's stands on issues (Glass 1985; Keeter 1987). Moreover, stereotypical traits for women in our culture have not been associated with leadership. The women in this study were consistently described with stereotypically feminine traits, but they were also portrayed in ways usually reserved for men and for people in leadership positions.

I examined how the women were described with regard to their personality and character. I did this regardless of who did the describing. In many cases the women themselves were responsible for the most favorable descriptions. In other cases it was citizen voices or quoted notables, rather than the reporters, who provided the descriptions that appeared in the press. Though the issue of whether different voices (citizen, reporter, candidate, notable other) provide different descriptions is undoubtedly worthy of investigation, the goal of my research was to give a gestalt impression of who the women were and what they were like, based on what a citizen might learn from the papers.

In her germinal essay "The Cult of True Womanhood: 1820–1860" (1966), Barbara Welter noted that women in the mid-1800s were judged by four cardinal virtues: "piety, purity, submissiveness, and domesticity" (152). Traces of these values are not hard to find in writings about Woodhull in the 1870s. For example, Woodhull was described as spiritual, "modest" ("The Wonderful Woman" 1871), "good," "pure," "virtuous" ("The Claflin

Clan" 1871), "reserved" ("The Woodhull War" 1871), honest ("Victoria on the Rampage" 1872), and timorous ("Victoria and Theodore" 1871). Aside from timidity, these characteristics alone would not have made Woodhull appear unfit for office, though they may have made her appear atypical of someone seeking an elected position.

However, Woodhull was also described as not living up to the standards of the cult of true womanhood, as when she was called seductive ("The Highly Colored" 1872), "soiled" ("Mrs. Woodhull's Side" 1871), "naughty" ("Female Financing" 1871), and "notorious" ("The Courts" 1872). The cult of pure womanhood was clearly a benchmark against which Woodhull was judged, and reporters felt it relevant to write about the ways in which she did or did not live up to that ideal.

Woodhull was also portrayed consistently as though she were unintelligent. She was described as "silly" ("Frantic Females" 1871), "shallow-headed" ("Victoria C. Woodhull" 1872), "foolish" and "without the light of reason" ("A Lamp" 1872), and as not having written her own lectures ("Opposition to Free Love" 1872). In fact, in no place was she characterized as intelligent though her biographies make clear that she was a very smart woman. Woodhull was also never described as capable, decisive, or aggressive.

However, there were other ways in which she was described in counter-stereotypical terms that may have made her appear fit for office. She was described as "strong minded" ("Female Financing" 1871), "independent" ("The Coming Woman" 1870), "commanding power" ("Covington's Great Poet" 1871), and even as "ambitious" ("Woman's Idea" 1870) and "energetic" ("The Wonderful Woman" 1871). In several cases she was called a "leader" (e.g., "A Woman for President," 1871), bold (e.g., "Woman's Idea" 1870), and courageous (e.g., "The Coming Woman" 1870). Similarly, an early *New York Herald* editorial described Woodhull's platform as "short, sharp, decisive, and [having] a true ring in it" ("The Coming Woman" 1870). These descriptions were atypical for women of the nineteenth century and are characterizations that Western culture has tended to associate with leadership.

During her campaign, Woodhull wrote a series of essays, published in the *New York Herald,* about her political philosophy. In addition to the counter-stereotypical descriptions used in some of the articles, the essays themselves stood as counter-stereotypical testimony. The essays were complex, intellectual, historical, and political. They presented a different view of a woman from the dominant one portrayed by others in the papers (that of women as victims or perpetrators of accidents or crimes).

On one hand, Woodhull was described as capable, competent, and qualified for the presidency, which contrasted with the portrayal of women in general as emotional and incapable of action. This latter view is especially clear in one *Herald* editorial. Although endorsing Woodhull, the paper made clear that it viewed her as an exception and that it was not endorsing the principle of women in politics. In fact, it specifically characterized its support for Woodhull as a "just for once" occurrence ("The Coming Woman" 1870). The *Herald* made clear that it supported Woodhull's candidacy as a vehicle for suffrage, not wider political or social reform or as a referendum on women's capacity to lead.

Lockwood was also described in stereotypical ways, though less often counter-stereotypically. Some examples of traditional depictions were those saying she was "courteous" ("Mrs. Lockwood in New York: The Fair" 1884), "fair," "pure" ("To Belva Dear" 1884), and "honest" ("The Way of" 1884). However, critical depictions based on her gender were not used in the same way as they were for Woodhull. Lockwood was not "soiled," "notorious," or "seductive," but neither was she "leaderlike," "bold," "courageous," "intelligent," or "ambitious." So although she was not portrayed with the negative stereotypes of a "public" woman, she was also not described as having qualities stereotypically masculine or stereotypically leaderlike.

Still, Lockwood was described as capable. For example, although the *New York Times* carried only two serious articles about Lockwood's campaign, one of them was a lengthy and substantive retelling of her short biography. The article began with humor and hyperbole by describing her as having "merciless sarcasm and pitiless verbal brutality when she was approached by ignorant and impudent reporters." One reporter was described as "drooping" and falling on a "divan" as he exited her interview ("Belva Frees Her Mind" 1884); however, he also gave a serious airing to her experience in a way that speaks volumes about the capabilities of women in general. She is described as working with her first husband in their sawmill and taking care of the farm and business in his absence. The article described her college education, her professional experience as a teacher and school administrator, and her success at law school. It also described her thriving law practice. These all paint a picture of a strong woman with unusual capabilities that she could translate into skills necessary for a head of state. However, the words "capable" or "leaderlike" were never used.

Lockwood's male counterpart, General Butler, was never described in such counter-stereotypical ways. He was usually described in typically masculine terms, for example, as a "hero" ("Going to Chicago" 1884), brave

("The Butler Sentiment" 1884), shrewd ("The Appearance of Butler" 1884), and ambitious ("Gen. Butler" 1884). He was not portrayed as nurturing or pure or as a good father.

By the time Chase Smith ran, women were no longer judged by standards of the cult of true womanhood. Instead, a new standard of femininity had emerged. Chase Smith was frequently described as "charming" (e.g., "She Is Running" 1964), gracious (e.g., Arnold 1964a), "poised" (e.g., Larrabee 1964), and honest (e.g., "Proclamation Supports" 1964). She was also characterized as devoted (Brough 1964) and as a "valentine" ("Goldwater Man" 1964). Again, most of these would not harm Chase Smith's reputation, but they are words that would not be used to describe a typical man politician.

As with Woodhull, Chase Smith was described in ways that were not stereotypically feminine and instead were typical of men politicians. For example, she was regularly tagged as "formidable" (e.g., Fernald 1964), "strong" (e.g., Jemail 1964), "courageous" (e.g., Arnold 1964b), "intelligent" (e.g., Penley and Sullivan 1964), and "capable" (Arnold 1964a). In addition, her years of political experience were often highlighted. For example, it was said she "headed a Senate investigation of the munitions shortage at the time of the Korean War" ("Sen. Smith Considers" 1964), or held "the all time record for consecutive roll call voting" ("Sen. Smith to Keynote" 1964), had "23 Years in Congress" (Penton 1964), and "served . . . on the Senate Appropriations Committee, the Defense Appropriations subcommittee, the Senate Armed Services Committee, the Senate Preparedness subcommittee, and the Senate Space Committee" (Larrabee 1963a). Thus, Chase Smith is depicted in stereotypically feminine but also in stereotypically masculine terms. She was not condemned for being a "public" woman in the way Woodhull was.

For Rockefeller, who also ran in 1964, none of the traits stereotypically associated with femininity were used. He was never depicted as "charming," "gracious," "pious," or even "honest." He was frequently described according to his political experience and job positions. He "served as Undersecretary in the Department of Health, Education and Welfare" (Shumway 1964) and had "experience with the State Department" (Phelps 1964a). He was described as "liberal" (Barkdoll 1964), "executive-minded" (White 1964), and "well informed" (Phelps 196ba), with "great administrative ability" and "superb qualifications for the presidency" ("Gov. Reed Hedges" 1963). These all imply both intelligence and leadership ability.

Stereotypes of traditional women from the 1800s and of the domesticated wife of the 1950s are simply not represented in the character depictions of Shirley Chisholm as they were for earlier women. She was neither "charming" nor "poised," neither "pure" nor "pious," though she was depicted as honest. On the other hand, Chisholm was presented in congruence with a new stereotype of women of the 1960s, that of an angry feminist. Chisholm was described as "fiery" (Narvaez 1972), as having "lung power" (Fraser 1972), as a "militant feminist" ("What Makes Shirley" 1972), and as a "crusader" ("Symbolic Candidacy" 1972).

Equally dominant, however, were depictions of Chisholm (like those of Chase Smith) that emphasized her experience in Congress. She was described as a "second term Congresswoman" ("Symbolic Candidacy" 1972), as having twenty-two years in politics (Fraser 1972), and as being the "first black woman elected to Congress" ("Mrs. Chisholm" 1972). Like many of the candidates before her, Chisholm was also described in stereotypically masculine ways, such as self-confident (Robertson 1972), "forceful" (L. Brown 1972), and having "energy" ("Spock Would" 1971). These are just some of the many examples in which Chisholm was described in political, leaderlike, and counter-stereotypical ways.

Henry Jackson, like the other men, was frequently described according to his political bent, as in "middle-of-the-roader" (Delaney 1971); according to his resume, as "Chairman of the Senate Interior Committee" (Bernstein 1972); and in terms of his capabilities, as having "outstanding ability and high competence" ("Stennis Backs" 1971). Also like the other men, he was never called "charming," "gracious," "pious," or "devoted." Nor was he ever depicted in terms such as "crusader" or having "lung power," as was Chisholm.

Schroeder, like Chisholm, was described as a "feminist" (Grimes 1987), "outspoken" (Lowy 1987b), and "having a special relationship with the feminist movement" (Brozan 1987), but these types of descriptions were exceptions to the rule. What was most commonly mentioned about Schroeder was her political experience. For example, it was pointed out that she was an "eight-term Congresswoman" (Blake 1987b), served "15 years on the armed services committee" ("Schroeder Warns" 1987), had been co-chair of Hart's 1984 campaign ("O'Neill Says" 1987), and was "sponsor of the Family and Medical Leave Act" (Lowy 1987c). She was also described in other non-stereotypical ways, as when she was called a "leader" ("Schroeder Has" 1987), "competent" (Moen 1987), and having a "sharp wit" (Freivogel 1987a). Gephardt was never described as "outspoken," "charming," "honest," "gracious," or "humble." As with the other men, he was primarily depicted according to his ideological approach or his political experience.

For Dole, too, there are traces in her character descriptions that reveal our cultural conceptions of women's ideal characteristics. For example, although she was depicted as having "no aptitude for sewing" (Von Drehle 1999), she was termed a "healer" (Broder 1999), a "Christian" (Rosin 1999), "good-hearted" (Berke 1999), a cheerleader (Collins 1999), "easy to love" (Balz 1999b), having a sugary flourish (Bruni 1999), and having "charm" ("Elizabeth Dole's New" 1999). The single most common depiction of Dole was that of "wife."

However, like virtually all of the other women she was liberally described in non-stereotypical ways as well. For example, she was termed "a lieutenant in Reagan's army" (Neal 1999), a "tough executive" (Balz and Broder 1999a), having "confident leadership" (Babcock and Havermann 1999), and as taking a "courageously tough stand" (Dionne 1999). She was portrayed as a "bold reformer" (Babcock and Havermann 1999), "intelligent" (Schemo 1999), "qualified" (Mann 1999), and a "capable manager" ("The GOP's Gain" 1999). As with the other women with political experience, her professional track record was often mentioned. It was reported that she "served in the cabinets of Ronald Reagan and George Bush" (Hassell 1999), "worked for five presidents" (Glover 1999), was a "two-time cabinet Secretary" (Sobieraj 1999), and "worked to resolve [a] devastating strike in the coalfields of Southwest Virginia" (Melton 1999). We never find out whether or not her opponent, Steve Forbes, can sew, and the reports don't mention if he is easy to love. He is never described as "gracious," "sugary," or "charming." Like the other men, he is predominantly described according to his political experience and ideology.

Unlike Dole's coverage, media reports about Carol Moseley Braun bore no traces of the cult of true womanhood, nor were there depictions of her as an angry feminist as there were for Chisholm and Schroeder. Moseley Braun was largely treated like a typical male. She was most frequently described as a former senator and former ambassador and frequently as the first black woman senator. Although she was not described as particularly leaderlike, courageous, bold, or ambitious, she was also not characterized as pious, lovely, or graceful.

Conclusion

There was evidence that depictions of women candidates for president were driven by traditional stereotypes. Even when women held higher public office, their families were more likely to be mentioned and they were depicted more emotionally (and with different emotions) than men. Women were likely to have their campaigns framed as though they were seeking the vice presidency even when that was not the case, and they were more likely to be referred to by their first names. There were also remnants of the cult of true womanhood in the depictions of the women candidates as late as 2000. At the same time, however, the data showed that many of the women were also portrayed in counter-stereotypical ways.

Character depictions of the women candidates are remarkably tenacious in reminding us of our traditional notions of femininity. It appears that our culture has not forgotten that women are supposed to be gracious, pious, and fine seamstresses, but we have learned that women are also capable of other things. Traces of traditional values are found in the descriptions of female candidates from Woodhull to Dole, but throughout the decades these political women have *also* been depicted in ways that were not stereotypical for women and were typical of the ways (political) men were depicted. By contrast, the depictions of the men were much more consistently stereotypically masculine.

Research on stereotypes has suggested that people are more likely to remember stereotypical over counter-stereotypical information. If this is the case, it may be of little consequence that counter-stereotypical characterizations are included for the women since they are often presented side by side with stereotypical ones. On the other hand, counter-stereotypes may affect perceptions of the women candidates by making them look more complex, or they may affect the way in which people generalize about what qualities women are assumed to have.

Judging from the way gender was persistently marked in the texts, it appears that society remains firmly committed to the idea of the fundamental differences between men and women. At the same time, women's spheres of competence appear to be ever expanding. If so, it might suggest a movement toward a more complex cognitive structure of gender roles, in which women in traditionally men's fields are associated with different stereotypes. More androgynous archetypes may be developing in the culture, which ultimately could help women appear more competent in the political sphere.

Considering the changes in women's political, professional, and social engagement that occurred during the period I studied, one might have expected that the texts of the 1800s would have been dominated by stereotypes and that such ideas would be absent (or nearly absent) from accounts in the twenty-first century. This was definitely not the case. In fact, I found no clear trends that showed diminishing stereotypes over time. Conversely, there were a rather high number of counter-stereotypical depictions present in the early period.

This raises the question why so little has changed in the last 130 years of press coverage despite dramatic changes in women's roles and rights. One possibility is that although women are moving increasingly into spheres formerly reserved for men, there has not been a correspondingly dramatic change in what most people believe about men and women, or in the concepts they associate with each. The public may increasingly accept women in men's spheres, but they may still believe that men and women are different or that women should take care of family and be objects of visual attention. That is, the social change may be confined to attitudes about work or politics and has not bled into a more radical adjustment in our stereotypes.

Put another way, it is possible that we have not come as far as we think we have in terms of women's liberation from traditional stereotypes. Whereas there are more women in political office now than there were 130 years ago and whereas women now vote, women are still vastly underrepresented in political positions of power. Even in 2004, when Carol Moseley Braun ran, there was a dearth of women governors, members of the House and Senate, and executives of major companies. Women in society continue to do most of the child rearing and make less money than men for comparable work. These realities remind us that many of the cultural forces at play in 1872 continue to exert influence today. The major paradigms through which people view and act in society are still in place. Men and women candidates for president are not treated comparably in the press because men and women are not treated comparably in society.

Another explanation may lie in the motivation of editors and reporters in covering women candidates. All of the races I studied occurred after the initial phases of the first wave of feminism. Even in 1872 the press was regularly looking at society through the lens of gender or, in the parlance of the 1800s, tackling the "woman question." The notion of looking at society by analyzing the roles and rights of women was firmly embedded in the social dialogue. In addition, women were and still are rare as candidates for political office. Today, women still account for only 8 percent of candidates for Congress, and this number was much lower during much of the period studied. Given that women candidates are rare, that society tends to look through a gendered lens, and that news norms put a premium on novelty, it is very likely that when a reporter or assignment editor approaches a race in which there is a woman candidate, the contest is viewed through the lens of gender. The reporters are likely to view any candidate qua woman. That is to say, the motivating force by which the reporter writes the story is one of gender. Once the notion of gender is activated in memory, reporters are more likely to write about that which they associate with gender, and in the case of women, that may mean their emotions, families, and, as we will see in the next chapter, their appearance.

Although an analysis of the effects of such differences in coverage is beyond the scope of this study, it is possible that depictions of women as more emotional and linked to family may be deleterious to their campaigns. Such portrayals are unlikely to correspond with the widespread conceptions of leadership and authority that Americans are apt to hold when selecting a political leader. The fact that information about emotions and family seldom appeared in press accounts of the men in this study suggests that the negative impact on women candidates may be compounded. Women considering vying for the Oval Office should take these patterns into serious consideration when developing their communication strategy.

Such campaign coverage poses challenges not just for candidates. Women and girls who read the coverage may have their own stereotypes of women reinforced, which can divert or suppress their political ambitions. When public positions held by political women are ignored and when these women are referred to disrespectfully by their first names; when their private lives are accentuated by mentions of their families; when women seeking the presidency are portrayed as though that can't possibly be their true ambition; and when they are portrayed as emotional, and with emotions not typically tolerated in leaders, these actions reinforce traditional notions of femininity that place the proper role of women in the home, not in public office. The emphasis on such attitudes does not provide women with new and alternative scripts and instead reinforces the idea that they belong at home. Such amplification and reassertion of traditional stereotypes may dissuade some potential candidates from running and may simply fail to inspire others.

References

"Accepting the Nomination: General Butler's Letter to the Anti-monopolists: A Clear Expression of His Appreciation of the Honor Bestowed by Them: His Determination to Work for the People and for Reform." 1884. *Boston Globe,* May 23, 3.

Adair, B. 2003. "As National Democrats Meet, Graham Considers Options." *St. Petersburg Times,* October 5, A3.

Amole, G. 1987. "Pat Schroeder: She Quits, We Lose." *Rocky Mountain News,* September 29, 4.

Andersen, S., R. Klatzky, and J. Murray. 1990. "Traits and Social Stereotypes: Efficiency Differences in Social Information Processing." *Journal of Personality and Social Psychology* 59 (2): 192–201.

"The Appearance of Butler: Why He Has Been Delaying and Yet Gaining Nothing." 1884. *New York Times,* August 8, 2.

Arnold, L. 1964a. "Campaign Trails May Cross." *Bangor Daily News,* February 13, 1.

———. 1964b. "Can She Win in N.H.? Sen. Smith's Chances: Maine GOP Sees 'Ifs.'" *Bangor Daily News,* January 28, 1.

Babcock, C. R., and J. Havermann. 1999. "Managing an Agency and Image: Red Cross Tenure Offers Insights to Dole's Style." *Washington Post,* February 16, A1.

"Back to Reality." 2004. *Chicago Tribune,* January 16, 22.

Balz, D. 1999a. "Elizabeth Dole Set to Leave the Red Cross: Move Spurs Talk of White House Run." *Washington Post,* January 4, A9.

———. 1999b. "Hoping to Be 'Part of History': Elizabeth Dole Is Wowing Women Voters, but Her Bid to Overtake George W. Bush for the GOP Remains an Uphill Struggle." *Washington Post,* July 15, A3.

Balz, D., and D. S. Broder. 1999a. "Bush Wins Iowa Poll: Forbes 2nd: Quayle, Alexander Lag as Dole Captures Third: Turnout Is Record." *Washington Post,* August 15, A1.

———. 1999b. "Elizabeth Dole Hints at Presidential Bid: Analysts Predict Effects on 2000 GOP Contest." *Washington Post,* January 5, A1.

Barkdoll, R. 1964. "Sen. Goldwater, Rocky Locked in Close Race." *Bangor Daily News,* March 10, 1.

"Belva Frees Her Mind: She Doesn't Expect to Be Elected This Year: But Is Confident That She Will Be President Some Time, When She Will Turn Things over Generally." 1884. *New York Times,* October 19, 3.

"Belva in the White House: A Cabinet Meeting of the Period When Women Shall Steer the Ship of State." 1884. *Boston Globe,* October 24, 2.

Bem, S. L. 1987. "Probing the Promise of Androgyny." In *The Psychology of Women,* ed. M. R. Walsh, 206–25. New Haven: Yale University Press.

Berke, R. L. 1999. "Eye on 2000: Elizabeth Dole Talks of a Race for President." *New York Times,* February 9, A12.

Bernstein, P. J. 1972. "Jackson to Hold Hearing on Atlantic Seaboard Oil." *Seattle Times,* January 9, B5.

Blake, P. 1987a. "Schroeder Could Run for House and Presidency." *Rocky Mountain News,* June 9, 8.

———. 1987b. "Schroeder Doubts No. 2 Role: Lawmaker Not Eager to Be Cheerleading Vice President." *Rocky Mountain News,* June 6, 26.

———. 1987c. Schroeder Won't Seek Presidency. *Rocky Mountain News,* September 29, 7.

———. 1987d. "Will It Be 'Run, Pat, Run' or 'No, Pat, No'?' *Rocky Mountain News,* September 27, 8.

Bostdorff, D. M. 1991. "Vice-presidential Comedy and the Traditional Female Role: An Examination of the Rhetorical Characteristics of the Vice Presidency." *Western Journal of Speech Communication* 55:1–27.

Braden, M. 1996. *Women Politicians and the Media.* Lexington: University Press of Kentucky.

Bridge, J. 1994. "Do Media Identify a Leader with Stereotypes?: How We Define a Leader May Be Based on Race and Gender." *The Quill* 82 (9): 16.

Broder, D. S. 1999. "Dole to Take First Campaign Steps: Announcement of Exploratory Panel Will Be Made in Iowa." *Washington Post,* March 5, A20.

Brody, L. R., and J. Hall. 1993. "Gender and Emotion." In *Handbook of Emotions,* ed. M. Lewis and J. Haviland, 447–60. New York: Guilford.

Brough, D. 1964. "Skowhegan Proud of Sen. Smith." *Bangor Daily News,* January 28, 4.

Brown, L. 1972. "Mrs. Chisholm Calls for Humanized Law." *Seattle Times,* May 2, 5.

Brown, P. 1987. "Schroeder Labels Debate a 'Stag' Event." *Rocky Mountain News,* July 2, 2.

Brozan, N. 1987. "Schroeder Can Qualify for U.S. Funds after Donations at NOW Convention." *New York Times,* July 19, 22.

Bruni, F. 1999. "One Republican Trailblazer Joins Forces with Another." *New York Times,* August 23, A10.

"Butler in New York." 1884. *Boston Globe,* September 14, 3.

"The Butler Sentiment: Represented at the Revere House Yesterday: By Half a Hundred Gentleman from All over the State: Minor Political Tremors That Are Agitating New England." 1884. *Boston Globe,* August 21, 1.

"The Claflin Clan: A Lively Morning in Thirty-eighth Street: The Fair Financiers' Family Feuds—the Irrepressible Old Lady—Calling for Blood's Blood—Both Sides of the Story: Another Chapter in the Affair—a Brother-in-law Found Dead." 1871. *New York Herald,* June 8, 6.

Cohen, R. 1999. "Shy on Cash, Dole Drops Out." *Newark Star Ledger,* October 21, 1.

Cohn, J. 2002. "Gender Bender." *New Republic,* October 14, 16–20.

Collins, G. 1999. "Editorial Observer: Politics: Taking the 'Help' out of 'Helpmate.'" *New York Times,* May 18, A22.

"The Coming Woman." 1870. *New York Herald,* April 2, 6.

Connolly, C. 1999. "Resurgent Dole Muffles Stances on Social Issues in N.H. Visit: Third-place 'Winner' in Iowa Woos Alexander Backers." *Washington Post,* August 17, A4.

"The Courts: Woodhull—Beecher—Claflin—Tilton: Tennie C. Claflin and Victoria Woodhull Arrested." 1872. *New York Herald,* November 3, 6.

"Covington's Great Poet: Woodhull and Claflin's Intimacy with the Grant Family: Government Secrets Exposed by the Woman's Rights Candidate for the Presidency—the Secessionist in the Cabinet—Grant's Utter Unfitness for His Place." 1871. *New York Sun,* June 23, 2.

Crump, J. 1995. *Literature Review on Women's Anger and Other Emotions.* FSW N°-22. Federally Sentenced Women Program. Nova Scotia. Retrieved October 18, 2006, from http://www.csc-scc.gc.ca/text/prgrm/fsw/fsw22/toce_e.shtml.

"Dark Horse, Literally and Figuratively." 1972. *Seattle Times,* January 25, 2.

Davey, M. 2003. "Challenging Bush—Sixth Article in a Series: Carol Moseley Braun." *New York Times,* December 18, A40.

Delaney, P. 1971. "Jackson in Race: He Asserts Nixon Fails to Win Trust." *New York Times,* November 20, 1.

Dionne, J. 1999. "A McCain Surprise." *Washington Post,* July 30, A29.

"Elizabeth Dole Exiles Mate to Woodshed." 1999. *New York Times,* May 19, A20.

"Elizabeth Dole's 'New Path.'" 1999. *Washington Post,* January 10, C6.

"Female Financing: Woodhull & Claflin in a 'Corner': Rich Scene in the Marine Court—the Aspirant for the Presidency Charged with Being Naughty—Woman's Wrongs versus Woman's Rights." 1871. *New York Herald,* February 2, 8.

Fernald, R. H. 1964. "In Defense of Senator." *Bangor Daily News,* January 1, 8.

Foreit, K. G., T. Agor, J. Byers, J. Larue, H. Lokey, M. Pallazzini, M. Patterson, and L. Smith. 1980. "Sex Bias in the Newspaper Treatment of Male-centered and Female-centered News Stories." *Sex Roles* 6 (3): 475–80.

"Frantic Females in a Flutter." 1871. *New York Times,* February 2, 1.

Fraser, C. G. 1972. "Mrs. Chisholm Completes 3-day Campaign in Florida." *New York Times,* February 28, 26.

Freivogel, M. W. 1987a. "Schroeder Decides Against '88 Race." *St. Louis Post-Dispatch,* September 29, 1.

——. 1987b. "Schroeder Rejects Idea of Running as 'Symbolic' Candidate." *St. Louis Post-Dispatch,* September 27, B1.

"Gen. Butler." 1884. *New York Times,* October 14, 4.

Glass, D. P. 1985. "Evaluating Presidential Candidates: Who Focuses on Their Personal Attributes?" *Public Opinion Quarterly* 49 (4): 517–34.

Glover, M. 1999. "Elizabeth Dole Steps toward 2000 Race to 'Rekindle Spirit.'" *Newark Star-Ledger,* March 11, 3.

"Going to Chicago: The Party of General Butler's Friends Who Are to Attend the Convention." 1884. *Boston Globe,* June 27, 4.

Goldberg, C. 1999. "Bush and Dole Lead Parade in New Hampshire Town." *New York Times,* July 5, A8.

"Goldwater Man Says Maggie Is a Valentine." 1964. *New York Daily News,* February 13, 6.

"Good Luck, Margaret." 1964. *Bangor Daily News,* February 7, 10.

"GOP Picks 'Moderate' Delegation: Goldwater Forces Win Only Two Spots on Panel of 14." 1964. *Bangor Daily News,* Mary 4, 1.

"The GOP's Gain." 1999. *Newark Star-Ledger,* January 7, 14.

"Gov. Reed Hedges on Rocky, Awaits Sen. Smith's Plans." 1963. *Bangor Daily News,* November 8, 4.

Grimes, C. 1987. "NOW Delegates Give Schroeder Cheers, Money." *St. Louis Post-Dispatch,* July 19, 1.

Hassell, J. 1999. "Forbes' Presidential Bid Receives a Lift: Ashcroft Withdrawal Likely Will Aid Publisher." *Newark Star-Ledger,* January 6, 6.

"The Highly Colored Human Ticket for the Presidency—the Free Love Communist Candidates in the Field." 1872. *New York Herald,* May 12, 8.

Holeman, F. 1963. "Rocky Woos GOP's Who's Who." *New York Daily News,* November 19, 5.

Huddy, L. 1994. "The Political Significance of Voters' Gender Stereotypes." *Research in Micropolitics* 4:169–93.

Jamieson, K. H. 1995. *Beyond the Double Bind: Women and Leadership.* New York: Oxford University Press.

Jemail, J. 1963. "The Inquiring Fotographer." *New York Daily News,* December 11, 53.

——. 1964. "The Inquiring Fotographer." *New York Daily News,* January 30, 35.

Johnson, C. 1987. "Armstrong Sees Schroeder in No. 2 Spot." *Rocky Mountain News,* August 31, 8.

Kahn, K. F. 1996. *The Political Consequences of Being a Woman: How Stereotypes Influence the Conduct and Consequences of Political Campaigns.* New York: Columbia University Press.

Keeter, S. 1987. "The Illusion of Intimacy: Television and the Role of Candidate Personal Qualities in Voter Choice." *Public Opinion Quarterly* 51 (3): 344–58.

Kelly, J. R., and S. Hutson-Comeaux. 1999. "Gender-Emotion Stereotypes Are Context Specific." *Sex Roles: A Journal of Research* 40 (1/2): 107.

"A Lamp without Oil." 1872. *New York Times,* February 22, 4.

Larrabee, D. R. 1963. "Sen. Muskie's Party Won't Hurt, Either: Sen. Smith: Maine's Pipeline to the White House." *Bangor Daily News,* December 23, 1.

——. 1964. "Sen. Smith as Running Mate? 'Yes!': Scranton." *Bangor Daily News,* July 15, 1.

Larsen, R. W. 1972a. "Jackson Hits Party 'Leftists' and Says He'll Keep Fighting." *Seattle Times,* May 4, F7.

——. 1972b. "Was Jackson Right on New Hampshire?" *Seattle Times,* March 5, 21.

Lowy, J. 1987a. "Limit on Mailing AIDS Report Upsets Schroeder.' *Rocky Mountain News,* June 2, 7.

——. 1987b. "Schroeder Camp Hails Grass-roots Support." *Rocky Mountain News,* August 9, 42.

——. 1987c. "Schroeder Gets Firsthand Look at Parental Leave." *Rocky Mountain News,* June 7, 69.

Maggi, J. 1972. "Shirley vs. Saigon." *New York Daily News,* May 6, 17.

Mann, J. 1999. "For Elizabeth Dole: Time Will Tell." *Washington Post,* January 8, E3.

Melton, R. H. 1999. "Dole Preaches Values in Motivational Forum." *Washington Post,* March 19, A16.

Mihalopoulos, D. 2003a. "Chance for 2nd Act on National Stage." *Chicago Tribune,* February 14, 8.

——. 2003b. "Crusading for a Second Chance: The Former U. S. Senator Strives to Revitalize Her Tarnished Political Image. But Her Campaign Has Little Money and She Left behind a Trail of Disillusioned Supporters." *Chicago Tribune,* October 23, 1.

Moen, T. 1987. "Patricia Schroeder Is the Real Thing." *Rocky Mountain News,* August 5, 32.

"Mrs. Chisholm to Speak Here on Law Day.' 1972. *Seattle Times,* April 2, 8.

"Mrs. Lockwood in New York: Disappointed." 1884. *Boston Globe,* October 20, 1.

"Mrs. Lockwood in New York: The Fair Presidential Aspirant Talks to Reporters and Has Her Picture Taken." 1884. *Boston Globe,* October 19, 3.

"Mrs. Woodhull." 1871. *New York Herald,* February 5, 7.

"Mrs. Woodhull's Side of the Question." 1871. *New York Times,* May 24, 2.

Narvaez, A. 1972. "Mrs. Chisholm Pressing for Key Convention Role." *New York Times,* June 15, 37.

Neal, T. M. 1999. "Dole Evokes Reagan's Legacy: New Hampshire Speech Tests Her Themes for Presidential Run." *Washington Post,* February 9, A2.

"New Hampshire Free-for-All." 1964. *New York Daily News,* January 29, 33.

O'Neill, E. 1972. "There's No Biz Like Political Biz." *New York Daily News,* February 6, 76.

"O'Neill Says His OK of Ferraro Upset Schroeder." 1987. *Rocky Mountain News,* August 27, 42.

"Opposition to Free Love—Lecture by Mrs. Booker." 1872. *New York Times,* March 8, 8.

Overholser, G. 1999. "More Press for Elizabeth Dole." *Washington Post,* September 14, A29.

Penley, N., and M. Sullivan. 1964. "Ladies at Odds over Woman as President." *Bangor Daily News,* January 28, 1.

Penton, J. H. 1964. "Senator Smith on Campaign Trail." *New York Times,* February 11, 1.

Phelps, R. H. 1964a. "Rockefeller Gains among Undecided." *New York Times,* March 8, 76.

——. 1964b. "Rockefeller Gets Warm Response." *New York Times,* January 25, 9.

"A Piebald Presidency." 1872. *New York Herald,* May 11, 10.

Plant, A. E., J. S. Hyde, D. Keltner, and P. G. Devine. 2000. "The Gender Stereotyping of Emotions." *Psychology of Women Quarterly* 24 (1): 81–93.

"Proclamation Supports Sen. Smith at Skowhegan." 1964. *Bangor Daily News,* January 28, 4.

Purdum, T. S. 1999. "Elizabeth Dole Is Shunning 'Dead End' Abortion Fight." *New York Times,* April 10, A10.

Rapp, E. 2003. "Showing Leadership." *St. Petersburg Times,* May 11, D2.

Robertson, N. 1972. "Tracking Florida Voters along the Chisholm Trail: The Route Is Uphill, Tough but Very Well Defined." *New York Times,* February 14, 19.

Rosenwasser, S. M., and N. G. Dean. 1989. "Gender Role and Political Office: Effects of Perceived Masculinity/femininity of Candidate and Political Office." *Psychology of Women Quarterly* 13:77–85.

Rosin, H. 1999. "Wooing the Right with Personal Faith, Not Policy." *Washington Post,* June 2, A1.

Schemo, D. J. 1999. "Curiosity in Dole Exceeds Support." *New York Times,* October 7, 28.

Schmidt, P. 1996. *Margaret Chase Smith: Beyond Convention.* Orono: University of Maine Press.

"Schroeder Has Shot at Ballot, Poll-taker Says." 1987. *Rocky Mountain News,* August 9, 10.

"Schroeder Warns of 'Irangate' Pitfall." 1987. *Rocky Mountain News,* August 6, 7.

"Sen. Goldwater, Rocky Locked in Close Race." 1964. *Bangor Daily News,* March 10, 1.

"Sen. Smith Considers Viet Trip." 1964. *Bangor Daily News,* May 19, 1.

"Sen. Smith to Keynote GOP Women's Conference." 1964. *Bangor Daily News,* February 24, 4.

"She Is Running for President." 1964. *New York Daily News,* January 28, 1.

"She May Test Vote-getting Power: Sen. Smith in Race?" 1963. *Bangor Daily News,* November 8, 1

"Shirley vs. Saigon." 1972. *New York Daily News,* May 6, 17.

Shumway, D. V. L. 1964. "Rockefeller, Ike Concludes Pleasant Chat." *Bangor Daily News,* April 20, 16.

"Skowhegan Plans Sen. Smith 'Day.'" 1964. *Bangor Daily News,* January 23, 16.

Sobieraj, S. 1999. "Women Compelled to Help Dole Succeed." *Newark Star-Ledger,* August 1, 3.

"Spock Would End Candidacy if Rep. Chisholm Would Run." 1971. *New York Times,* December 5, 78.

"Stennis Backs Jackson." 1971. *New York Daily News,* December 21, 8.

"Summit Questioned: Jackson Fears 'Deals.'" 1972. *Seattle Times,* May 31, 1.

"Symbolic Candidacy." 1972. *New York Times,* January 27, 36.

"Ticket of Wallace, Chisholm Proposed." 1972. *Seattle Times,* March 3, 11.

"To Belva Dear." 1884. *Boston Globe,* October 22, 4.

"Vice President of the United States." (n.d.). Wikipedia. Retrieved October 18, 2006, from http://en.wikipedia.org/wiki/Vice_President_of_the_United_States.

"Victoria and Theodore: Free Love, Passional Attraction and Celestial Affinities at Steinway Hall: Mrs. Woodhull Quotes the Bible in Favor of Promiscuity and Claims the Right to Change Her Husband Every Day in the Presence of Three Thousand People." 1871. *New York Herald,* November 21, 10.

"Victoria C. Woodhull." 1872. *Lancaster Express,* February 20, 2.

"Victoria on the Rampage." 1872. *New York Sun,* August 24, 4.

Von Drehle, D. 1999. "Dole's Role: Bridging the Past and the Future: Pioneering Candidate's Popularity Reflects Traditional Roots." *Washington Post,* October 13, A1.

"The Way of the Candidate." 1884. *New York Times,* September 14, 8.

Welter, B. 1966. "The Cult of True Womanhood: 1820–1860." *American Quarterly* 18 (2): 151–74.

"What Makes Shirley Run?" 1972. *New York Times,* January 30, 2.

White, W. S. 1964. "Rockefeller People Have Two Main Objectives." *Bangor Daily News,* January 11, 10.

Wilgoren, J. 2003. "Leaping Past Triumphs and Debacles." *New York Times,* March 14, A19.

"A Woman for President." 1871. *New York Sun,* August 18, 3.

"Woman's Idea of Government." 1870. *New York Herald,* May 27, 6.

"The Wonderful Woman: Theodore Tilton's Great American Romance." 1871. *New York Sun,* September 11, 3.

Wood, J. T. 1994. *Gendered Lives: Communication, Gender, and Culture.* Belmont, Calif.: Wadsworth.

"The Woodhull War: The Blood of the Broad Street Brokers Aroused: Continuation of the Claflin Scandal Case—a Very Happy and Unique Family—Spicy Revelations—the Gay Tennessee Celeste and the Woman's Rights Woodhull on the Stand." 1871. *New York Herald,* May 17, 10.

Zeleny, J. 2003. "Graham Spoils Rivals' Dream of Florida Windfall." *Chicago Tribune,* February 28, 14.

Zeleny, J., and D. Mihalopoulos. 2003. "Braun's Quiet Campaign Stirs Questions, Criticism." *Chicago Tribune,* May 19, 1.

Victoria C. Woodhull was nominated for the presidency of the United States by the Equal Rights Party on May 10, 1872, at Apollo Hall, New York City. From a pamphlet called "One Moral Standard for All," by M. F. Darwin.

The Equal Rights Party nominated Belva Lockwood for the U.S. presidency in 1884.

Representative Shirley Chisholm sought the presidential nomination of the Democratic Party in 1972. AP Images/Wide World Photos.

Senator Margaret Chase Smith waves to the crowd at the
Republican National Convention in California. She tried
for the nomination of the Republican Party in 1964.

In 1987 Representative Pat Schroeder ran for the nomination of the Democratic Party. Courtesy of Pat Schroeder.

Elizabeth Dole, shown here at a fundraiser in North Carolina, sought the nomination of the Republican Party in 2000. AP Images/Alan Marler/Wide World Photos.

Carol Moseley Braun greets supporters before giving an address in Chicago during her run for the nomination of the Democratic Party in 2004.
AP Images/Brian Kersey/Wide World Photos.

High-Heeled Boots
and Violet Suits

In 1980 a (man) reporter for the *New York Times Sunday Magazine* wrote a story about three candidates for Democratic senator in the New York State primary. Two were women (Representative Elizabeth Holtzman and former New York City Consumer Affairs Commissioner Bess Myerson). In it he noted,

> Miss Holtzman was dining in a Chinese restaurant on the East Side, and she was wearing a cardigan sweater over a blouse with a round collar. It is difficult to imagine her wearing a plunging neckline or a skirt slit to the thigh. Miss Myerson became famous when she was named Miss America in 1945, stretching a size 34 bathing suit the night before her coronation and then getting sewn into it the next day. Miss Holtzman became famous on the House Judiciary Committee in 1974, peering intently through horn-rimmed glasses and asking questions about Richard Nixon and Watergate. (Corry 1980)

Such observations about the appearance of the candidates are not limited to lower-level races. In 1872 a *New York Times* editorial noted that Victoria Woodhull wore "dainty high-heeled boots" ("A Lamp without Oil" 1872), and in 1999 a reporter wrote that Elizabeth Dole was "clad in a violet suit" (Dowd 1999b). It is not surprising that these reports mentioned the candidates' appearance. Many anecdotal analyses of the press coverage of women candidates condemn the press for focusing on how the women look while leaving out such observations in reporting about men candidates. However, few systematic studies have investigated whether objective differences in reporting really exist, and none has explored the question of how reporting on the appearance of candidates has changed over time.

Feminist theory has long noted that traditional philosophy separated the mind from the body and associated men with thought and the rational, while associating women with their bodies and the irrational. In fact, according to the feminist author Marianne Thesander (1997), women throughout history have been considered "synonymous with their bodies" (9). Nancy Mandell (1995), a women's studies professor, has similarly noted that women tend to be judged by how they look in a way that men are not. She writes, "For the female child, to be assessed as 'pretty' or 'beautiful' is the highest accolade. . . . Notably, these evaluative terms that focus on the girl's façade are rarely applied to boys" (107).

Part of this association of women with their bodies is what Naomi Wolf (1991) calls the beauty myth. Women, she argues, are always told they must strive for ideal beauty while men are to judge women on the basis of it; Wolf says the beauty myth defines a woman's cultural value in terms of her beauty. Feminist philosophy would predict that press reports of women candidates would tend to focus on how they look and what they wear, more so than would reports of men candidates. Moreover, such a focus on the bodies of women may have deleterious effects. Wolf writes, "Since the media routinely give accounts of women's appearance in a way that trivializes or discredits what they say, women reading or watching are routinely dissuaded from identifying with women in the public eye—the ultimate anti-feminist goal of the beauty myth. Whenever we dismiss or do not hear a woman on television or in print because our attention had been drawn to her size or makeup or clothing or hairstyle, the beauty myth is working with optimum efficiency" (274).

Mandell (1995) has similarly noted other ways in which a cultural focus on the appearance of women can have negative effects. She argues that beauty norms can be proscriptive because telling women how they should look can determine the activities in which women are willing to engage. She notes that "when women . . . want to stay home because of a 'bad hair day' . . . these behavior patterns reflect massively powerful controls over behavior, with a proportional impact on definitions of self and career opportunities" (107). Similarly if women expect their bodies and beauty to be the subject of news and scrutiny, they may be less willing to put themselves forward as political candidates.

Several researchers have documented anecdotal evidence of a heightened press attention to the appearance of women candidates. For example, Braden (1996) noted that during Roxanne Conlin's unsuccessful bid for governor of Iowa in 1982, the *Des Moines Register* published photos of the candidate with the six different hairstyles that she had worn over the previous eleven years. Such a spread was never done about her (male) opponent.

Similar anecdotes have been documented at the presidential level. When Geraldine Ferraro stood before the Democratic convention in which she was nominated as vice president, Tom Brokaw commented, "Geraldine Ferraro . . . The first woman to be nominated for Vice President. . . . Size six!" (qtd. in Braden 1996, 15). Similarly Heith noted that during Dole's 2000 race for the presidency one reporter speculated that "she looks great naked" (2003, 127). The same types of observations have been made for international women heads of state. Norris noted that President Violeta Chamorro (of Nicaragua) was described as having "silver hair" and Prime Minister Kim Campbell (Canada) was called "glamorous," but overall she concluded that "these sorts of remarks are highly exceptional and do not reflect the vast bulk of the coverage" (1997, 159)

More systematic (but noncomparative) studies have resulted in somewhat contradictory findings. Heith (2003, 126) found in her study of Ferraro's run for the vice presidency and Dole's race for the presidency that almost 30 percent of Ferarro's and over 40 percent of Dole's coverage referred to "clothing, make-up, hair, and other distinctly feminine categorizations." By contrast, Carroll and Schreiber (1997, 139) in their study of press coverage of women in the 103rd Congress found that "only three percent of articles with significant content on women in Congress made explicit reference to how women members looked or dressed."

However, these studies were either anecdotal or did not offer comparisons with the coverage of candidates who were men. The systematic studies tend to find the press more occupied with the appearance of women than that of men. When Devitt (2002) looked at men and women candidates for governor in 1998 he found the press was more likely to focus on the age, personality, and appearance of a female candidate than a male candidate. Similarly, Heldman, Carroll, and Olson (2005, 324) compared the coverage of Elizabeth Dole's presidential campaign with the coverage of the other men in the race and found that "her appearance was mentioned significantly more often than that of any of the other candidates." Finally, Schonker-Schreck (2004, 171) in a study of coverage of a 1996 primary in Israel found that reporting on women candidates more often than coverage for men included "irrelevant details related to the female candidate's physical appearance, clothing, age, marital status, and other gender-specific characteristics and behavior patterns." Even the least compelling of the evidence for different treatment of men and women candidates, a study by Bystrom, Robertson, and Banwart (2001), found women's appearance was mentioned more than men's in coverage of primary races for governor and U.S. senator in 2000. However, the results were not statistically significant (24 percent of articles about women compared with 21 percent of articles about men).

Gender Marking

One way in which the physical attributes of women have been emphasized in press reports is by gender markers. This occurs when the press explicitly mentions the gender of a candidate. When Margaret Chase Smith was running for president she was asked in a television interview how she, as a "woman president," would handle other world leaders. Cleverly she replied, "A woman president would probably do as well as Joan of Arc, Catherine the Great, and Queen Victoria" (Braden 1996, 187). Dexterous answers to such questions do not, however, change the fact that men candidates are not subjected to them. A man candidate would not be asked how as a "man president" he would handle world leaders. When women are asked such questions, reporters not only waste the precious time and column inches that the candidates could use for discussing substantive policy issues, but they also subtly cue the audience that doubt lingers about how women candidates would act on the world stage.

The press coverage makes it clear that women candidates are subject to questions about how their gender affects them whereas men are not. Women are portrayed as though they are hampered by their gender, whereas men are portrayed as gender-free. For example, women who were already in office received questions such as "What was it like to be a woman in Congress?" (Braden 1996, 1), which was asked of Representative Marjorie Margolies-Mezvinsky (D–PA). Similarly, reporters asked Governor Christine Todd Whitman, "What's it like to be a woman Governor?" (Braden 1996, 2). By asking women to answer questions "as females," the press consistently portrays women as gendered beings. Reporters imply that gender is important, and women must act qua women. Men are never asked, "What is it like to be a man in office?" because men are the norm and as such are free to be individuals or political beings. Their gender is assumed to be irrelevant.

Systematic studies have found gender marking for women quite common. Heith (2003) discovered in the coverage of Ferraro and Dole that 27 percent of articles about Ferraro contained gendered language whereas 42 percent of articles about Dole did. Heldman, Carroll, and Olson (2005) found an even greater percentage of gender marking in the coverage of

Elizabeth Dole's presidential campaign. Of the substantive stories about Dole, 63.9 percent commented on her gender. In a comparative test to see if women were more likely to have their gender marked, Bystrom, Robertson, and Banwart (2001) studied primary races for governor and senator in 2000 and found that the sex of the female candidate was mentioned in almost 12.7 percent of the articles predominantly about the women candidates, whereas it was never mentioned in any of the articles predominantly about the men.

Quantity of Physical Descriptions

In examining the physical descriptions of the candidates, I counted every description of the body of each candidate. In all of the presidential races examined in the present study, the women were more likely to be described physically than were the men. On average, per word written about them, women received close to four physical descriptions for every one applied to men. The women were described physically about 18 times per 10,000 words. The men were so described just 4.7 times per 10,000 words.

There was not a substantial change in the pattern over time, and the total number of physical descriptions of women does not appear to be dropping. The Democratic candidate Carol Moseley Braun was described physically more often per 10,000 words in 2004 than was the Equal Rights Party candidate Victoria Woodhull in 1872. In 2000, the Republican candidate Elizabeth Dole was described physically about as often as the Republican Margaret Chase Smith had been in 1964.

On a per article basis, Margaret Chase Smith (1964) was the least likely to be described physically, with reporters mentioning her appearance just once in about every five articles. One reason may be that Chase Smith was the most qualified candidate of those studied. She was the only one running for president from the Senate and had the greatest amount of elected political experience. Perhaps this caused her to be seen as more viable and therefore less worthy of coverage about her appearance. This could also explain why Nelson Rockefeller's rate was lower than that of any other male candidate except James Black in the nineteenth century. Rockefeller was described physically just once in twenty articles. He was the only candidate in this study running from the position of governor, traditionally one of the more successful routes to the Oval Office. Perhaps both Chase Smith's and Rockefeller's political experience and the fact that they were incumbents in high office cued reporters to provide more substantive coverage.

Belva Lockwood (1884 campaign) was the candidate described most frequently in physical terms on a per article basis. The amount of physical coverage in her race was high because the *New York Times* ran articles framing her race in terms of false scandals. These articles noted her hair was of "fine quality" or her "back hair was not her own original hair" ("The Way of the Candidate" 1884), and that her underpants were "cardinal red" ("Another Scandal" 1884). These physical descriptions came in addition to more typical mentions of her attire and appearance, such as one that said she was "attired in black silk" ("A Woman Can Be President" 1884) or another that noted she was a "pleasant-featured lady" (Belva Frees Her Mind" 1884).

These findings are consistent with the idea that women are judged against a cultural feminine ideal. Though the details of this ideal tend to change, the primary components—motherhood and beauty—tend to be enduring. Women have traditionally been valued for their ability to find a good husband, and appearance has been assumed to be a primary measure of a woman's value in that regard. Though few in contemporary American society would agree with this, the persistence with which the press has tended to comment on women's appearance reveals the enduring legacies and unconscious ideologies of this value system. It is noteworthy that there is no clear pattern indicating that women candidates are less likely to be described physically today compared with a century ago, given the changes in women rights and roles over time. It suggests that women today are still judged (and valued) by how they look.

Quality of Physical Descriptions

Not only was the quantity of physically descriptive information greater for women candidates, but also newspaper reports seem to gravitate toward different types of information for men than for women. In addition to counting all of the physical descriptions of the candidates, I recorded and categorized the first four physical descriptions of each candidate that appeared in each article. The descriptions were characterized as appearance (e.g., "hair was parted"), attire (e.g., "blue silk stockings"), gender (e.g., "woman politician"), attractiveness (e.g., "beautiful"), age (e.g., "young"), stature (e.g., "little woman"), facial expression (e.g., "smiling"), and strength (e.g., "strong").

When I analyzed the first four physical descriptions in any one article, I found that attire was the first or second most frequently described physical characteristic for women in four of the eight races, but it made the top two in type of observations for men only once in eight. Similarly, mentioning the candidate's gender was in the top two for types of physical observations for women in seven of the eight races, but for men it never reached this threshold. Age was one of the top two physical descriptors for men in six of the eight races, but it made the top two for only one of the women's races. Note, however, that age was still overall more likely to be mentioned for women than for men.

Overall, women with light skin color were most likely to be described according to their sex and what they were wearing. For example, Woodhull (and her sister) were described as "female brokers" dressed "in high tyrolese hats, green and blue cloaks and gorgeous front finery" ("Female Financing" 1872). Women with dark skin color were most likely to be described according to their skin color and sex. Chisholm, for example, was described as "the only black and the only female seeking the 1972 presidential nomination" (Perry 1972). These patterns reveal our social understanding about what is a politician. Clearly, two unstated components are that a politician is both male and white. When a candidate does not fit this profile, reporters feel compelled to comment on it. We learn from this pattern that the race and sex of a candidate are important to our culture and the way we view and evaluate candidates. We also learn that what women wear is important in our evaluation of them. Unless voters are relying on stereotypes, however, the sex, the race, or the clothing of the candidate is unlikely to tell a citizen anything about the policy positions or character of the candidate.

Since politicians are assumed to be white and male, there is no reason to comment on these aspects of men candidates. Such aspects of their identity are already communicated by using the term "politician." In addition, in a society that does not put a paramount value on how men dress, reporters are unlikely to comment on the attire of men candidates. When men were described, they were most likely to be described by their age and either facial expressions or appearance (not including clothing). For example, Forbes was regularly described as a "51-year-old" (Hassell 1999b) and Graham as "66" (Hundley 2003). Jackson had a "beaming, effervescent Norwegian face" (Prochnau 1972), whereas Rockefeller "flashed his biggest grin" (Mazza and Moberley 1964). These patterns suggest that what is important in evaluating the physical aspects of men who run for office is how old they are, an aspect that may reflect the substantive character issue of experience, or their facial expressions, which also may give insight into the character of the candidate.

However, this pattern may be changing over time. The appearance (other than clothing) of men was not mentioned as one of the top two descriptors until 1988. Prior to that the most common physical descriptions of male candidates were limited to age, health, and facial expressions. Thus, the frequency with which men's appearance is mentioned in news articles may be growing. In fact, appearance made up 41 percent of Forbes's physical descriptions (2000) and 33 percent of Paul's (1988). These are both higher than the percentage for men who ran in the 1960s and 1970s (Rockefeller, 0 percent and Jackson, 18 percent). Similarly, the attire of Rockefeller (in 1964) and Jackson (in 1972) was never mentioned, yet attire accounted for 45 percent of the physical descriptors for Gephardt (in 1987) and 16 percent of those for Forbes (in 2000). Still, it is important to keep in mind that overall the men were far less likely to be described physically than were women.

The trend in types of physical descriptions was the opposite for women. Attire and appearance may be dropping as a percentage of total physical descriptions over time. Forty-three percent of Woodhull's physical descriptors were about attire or appearance, with 62 percent for Lockwood, 14 percent for Schroeder, and 11 percent for Moseley Braun. The flip side to decreasing mentions of attire and appearance is that gender descriptions may be increasing in prominence. Thirty-two percent of Woodhull's and 14 percent of Lockwood's physical descriptors identified gender, whereas 53 percent of Schroeder's and 61 percent of Dole's did so. Thus it appears that while society may be trending toward judging women less on their appearance, it is still fundamentally convinced that differences between men and women exist and are important.

Some of the types of physical descriptions used for women, such as mentions of their attire, have remained remarkably stable over time. For example, in 1872 Woodhull was described this way: "The lady was arrayed in a plain black dress" ("Mrs. Woodhull's Lecture" 1872); in 1884 Lockwood was described as "Attired in figured black silk" ("Belva Frees Her Mind" 1884). The trend continued in 1964 when the newspapers said Chase Smith "wore a black suit" (Hunter 1964), and in 1972 when Chisholm "wore a black and white block print suit" (Turner 1972). These are all strikingly similar to descriptions of Schroeder in 1987, when she wore a "breezy blue outfit" (Dowd 1987); of Dole, when she was "dressed in a bright red suit" (Melton 1999); and of Moseley Braun, who was "resplendent in a dark suit" (Halbfinger 2003). Aside from the fact that the recent candidates wore colors other than black, it might be impossible to tell which description came from which year. The similarity in these descriptions suggests that it is not the fact that women wear different outfits, in contrast to the monotony of men's attire, that makes their clothing worthy of mention in news articles, but rather some underlying value about what aspects of women are important.

A similar list of examples could be generated from what the newspapers said of the candidates' beauty. Woodhull was in several places described as "attractive" (e.g., "Covington's Great Poet" 1871), Lockwood as a "pleasant-featured lady" ("Belva Frees Her Mind" 1884), Chase Smith as an "attractive lady" ("The Wrong Reasons" 1964), and Schroeder as an "attractive woman" (Blake and Lowy 1987). Moreover, many of the women were depicted as smiling. Woodhull had a "charmingly polite smile" ("The Modern Amazons" 1870), whereas Chisholm was simply "smiling" (O'Neill 1972b). Schroeder was "smiling stiffly" (Blake and Lowy 1987) and Dole had a "seamless smile" (Dowd 1999a), whereas Moseley Braun had a "million-dollar smile" (Zeleny 2003b). The similarity in these descriptions heightens the question why they were considered worthy of comment.

Marking Gender

One of the more interesting patterns in the press coverage of these women is the particular way that they have been categorized and identified as females through the decades. Some of the more explicit and pronounced gender marking occurred in Victoria Woodhull's 1872 and Belva Lockwood's 1884 campaigns. In these races it was common to mark the candidate's gender in the headline, a practice that was very uncommon in the twentieth century. Twenty-four percent of the headlines that mentioned Woodhull highlighted her gender in some way, as did 28 percent of those referencing Lockwood. We know from research in the social sciences that labels and categorizations such as these can have an important effect on how we think about and judge people.

In almost all cases Woodhull's gender was marked by using "woman" or "female" as an adjective to separate her activities and creations from those of males. For example, we find headlines (emphasis added in all cases) with the phrases "A *Female* Philippic: Victoria C. Woodhull on the Tendencies of Government" (1870) and "The *Women* Bankers' Home" (1870), and "*Female* Financing: Woodhull & Claflin in a 'Corner'" (1871). Similarly, gender was highlighted in the headline "The *Petticoat* Politician: Mrs. Woodhull's Latest Epistle to the Americans—The Limits and Sphere of Government' Considered from a *Female* Point of View" (1870). In other articles Woodhull and/or her sister are described in the headlines as "*Women* Brokers" (e.g., "The Death of Dr. Woodhull" 1872), "The *Women* Slanderers" (1872), and "A *Woman* for President" (1871). Gender was also marked consistently within the text of the articles. The typical gender identifiers were "female broker," "woman broker," and "lady broker."

As in the press coverage of Woodhull's campaign, Lockwood's gender was regularly marked, for example, in the following headlines (emphasis added in all cases): "Mrs. Lockwood and Her Campaign: A Talk with the *Female* Candidate for President" (1884); "Mrs. Lockwood Explains the Mystery of *Woman* Politics" (1884); and "Ratifying Mrs. Lockwood's Nomination: A Meeting at the *Female* Candidate's House" (1884). Similar descriptions were used in the body of the texts as well. The *Washington Evening Star,* for example, mentioned "Belva Lockwood, the well-known *woman* lawyer" ("A Woman's Candidate for President" 1884). In the *Boston Globe* she was described as the future "presidentess" ("Mrs. Lockwood in New York: Disappointed" 1884).

Such gender markings were less frequent in the headlines about women who ran in the twentieth century. Only three headlines explicitly marked Chase Smith's gender in a way comparable to the treatment of Lockwood and Woodhull: "Ladies at Odds Over *Woman* as President" (Penley and Sullivan 1964); "Skowhegan Honors its Noted *Lady* Politician" (Brough 1964); "A Chic *Lady* Who Fights: Margaret Chase Smith" (1964) (emphasis added in all cases). Such gender markers were also rarer in the body of the story in 1964 than they were in the previous century. Nonetheless, they were still present and still represented the dominant type of physical description for Chase Smith. Descriptions such as this one from a *Bangor Daily News* editorial were common: "Not just a woman candidate, but a woman with credentials" ("Enter Margaret Chase Smith" 1963). Similarly she was liberally referred to as "lady Senator," "lady law maker," "lady politician," and "woman candidate."

None of the headlines for Chisholm, Fulani, Schroeder, or Moseley Braun marked gender in the explicit way used for Lockwood and Woodhull, and only one headline about Elizabeth Dole did so: "A *Lady* Leader? America Says It Wouldn't Mind" (Hassell 1999a). In the text, however, the rate of gender marking remained high. Chisholm was described as a "lady politician" (Perry 1972) and a "woman official" (Johnson 1971). Schroeder was depicted as a "woman member" (Grimes 1987) and "woman candidate" (Freivogel 1987); Dole was repeatedly described as a "female presidential aspirant" (Broder 1999) and "female candidate" (Cohen 1999). Although Moseley Braun was more frequently described as the "black" candidate, she was regularly described in the articles as the "first black female senator" (Zeleny 2003a).

Even when the articles did not explicitly mark gender, the candidate's sex was nonetheless clear. For example, sex may be clear from the inclusion of a gendered courtesy title as in : "The Tendencies of Government: *Mrs.* Woodhull's Third Letter" (1870), and "*Mrs.* Lockwood's First Gun" (1884); "Admirer of *Mrs.* Smith, Rocky Says" (1963); "*Mrs.* Chisholm Chides

Black Caucus" (Johnson 1971); and "*Mrs.* Dole and Money" (1999) (emphasis added in all cases). Inclusion of the candidate's first name (which occurs in virtually all articles) would also reveal the gender of all of the candidates in this study except Pat Schroeder. This is, of course, in addition to the fact that the article makes the sex of the candidate clear through the pronouns used. There were other cues, some subtle, others direct, about the candidates' gender in the following headlines (emphasis added in all cases):

"The Modern *Amazons* . . . *Mesdames* Woodhull and Claflin, Mrs. Stanton, and Sister Norton All Up for Sentence" (1870).

"A *Woman* Can Be President: Mrs. Lockwood Defines the Position of the Equal Righters" (1884.

"GOP's *Sweetheart* Lands & the Maggie Mania Is On" (Wilson 1964).

"Shirley Tosses *Chapeau* in Ring" (O'Neill 1972a).

"Schroeder: At Ease with *Femininity* and Issues" (Dowd 1987).

"One Small Step for *Womankind;* Elizabeth Dole's Candidacy Becomes Merely the Symbol She Avoided" (Givhan 1999).

In these cases gender was not explicitly marked but would be clear nonetheless. References to Amazons, sweethearts, femininity, womankind, and chapeaus highlight that a woman and not a man is running. Though there is virtually no way that gender could be occluded, given English language structure and naming conventions, reporters still felt it necessary to explicitly and implicitly mark the gender of the candidates. This pattern is both enduring and prominent in the coverage and reveals not only the fundamental belief that women and men are different, but more important, that they are different in ways that are believed to be relevant to politics and the decisions citizens must make as voters.

Implications for Gender Marking

In each of these cases throughout the decades, by including an adjective or noun that mentions the candidate's gender along with a political noun or action, the authors put the women into a different category than they did the men. The women were not candidates but female candidates; they were not politicians but women politicians. The implications of this are intriguing.

First, this practice gives light to the unspoken cultural understanding that politicians, senators, and candidates must be men. The reporters who covered these women must have consistently felt that the words "candidate" and "politician" contained maleness as a necessary component. If that were not the case there would be no need to modify the noun with a gendered adjective. That is not surprising given our political history, but such use of "women" to modify gender-neutral nouns may nonetheless reinforce the idea that women are acting in an unnatural sphere or that men are more appropriate in these positions. With the addition of the adjective "female" to various political positions, the text may subtly read "woman doing man-activity" or "woman doing male job." In this way the mass media reflected the dominant social attitudes and structure, while simultaneously reinforcing them.

The tendency for reporters to point out the sex of women (and not men) may originate in the fact that since most candidates were male the reporters felt it was necessary to indicate a difference from the norm. Nevertheless reporters felt this "difference" from the norm was important to mention precisely because the culture contains the belief that men and women are different in important ways (relevant to politics). It may be that there are very few blue-eyed members of Congress, but because our culture believes that differences in eye color are not important, reporters don't notice or care and as a result don't write about the eye color of the candidates.

Second, the mere use of gender-marked nouns emphasizes that sex is important and relevant to politics. By stating in the headline that Woodhull is female rather than mentioning her age, education, or height, the paper indicates that Woodhull's gender has importance. Perhaps in a patriarchal society where the relative value of individuals is determined in part by their gender, it is important to communicate to the public the gender of a candidate. Such designations contain important information on the credibility, seriousness, and value of the individual in question. In a highly sex-differentiated society, gender also connotes spheres of competence and authority.

Social scientists have documented that information about one's gender affects receivers' judgments about an individual. For example, when an article contained a byline of a man, those reading the article rated it more highly than when the same article contained a byline of a woman (Goldberg 1968). Similarly, when subjects believed a candidate profile was that of a man, they made different assessments of the strengths of the politician than when they believed the same profile was that of a woman (Kahn 1996). These contemporary studies are likely to underestimate the ways in which highlighting gender was a cue to an individual's qualities over a century ago, when sex segregation and discrimination were more institutionalized and commonplace. Thus, it is likely that by highlighting the gender of the candidates in the headline, these articles framed women's candidacies as less significant and serious.

Third, by regularly gendering nouns, papers promote the link between women and their biology. Similarly, by asking a woman to answer questions "as a female," the press portrays her as a gendered being. Reporters show women acting as women and as representatives of women (instead of as party members, for example). Men are never asked, "What is it like to be a man in office?" because men are the norm and as such are free to be individuals or political beings. Their gender is assumed to be of no consequence to their conduct. Highlighting women's gender and asking about it may tacitly suggest that they are influenced by it. There may be another effect of highlighting women's gender. Many feminist authors have noted the way in which our culture associates biology with the destiny of women. In other words, women are believed to be affected by their physical being, more so than men. Women are not candidates unto themselves but are portrayed qua female.

Finally, a gendered lexicon helps maintain the division between men and women in our society. Using the term "female politician" implies that a female politician is different from a male politician, perhaps even different from a "real" politician. The newspapers present this claim without ever explicitly making it. Such terminology prevents women from fully entering the male political sphere. The closest they can get to being a politician is to be a female politician.

Despite the thousands of decisions that led to a pattern of marking gender, there is a progressive note. The women are portrayed with widening areas of capabilities (president, politician, fighter, candidate). After all, newspapers are calling attention to the fact that the person is female and doing something that we as a culture usually associate with males. There remains a duality in this prevalence of gender markers. On the one hand, the basic premise of gender differentiation is solidly and simultaneously reasserted by a paper's qualifying women's actions with gendered modifiers and putting them into different categories. On the other, the paper is publicizing the ability of women to operate (competently) in traditionally male spheres. In other words, whereas the papers simultaneously expand and reinforce the basic premise that men and women are different by lexicalizing the stereotypically masculine actions and behaviors of the female candidates, they also present an expanding area of competence for women.

Nevertheless, I would argue that the net impact of the way gender was (and continues to be) marked in reports about women candidates promotes the fundamental belief that women and men are different in ways related to political leadership. This occurs despite the slow change by which women have been able to enter ever-expanding realms previously off limits due to sex roles. Today, over a hundred years after the first woman ran for president, the language is still based on a fundamental separation of men and women. Though few people may agree on how men and women are different, almost all believe they are. It may be true that as long as we have separate concepts and categories for men and women there cannot be cultural equality. At the same time, the domains of men and women have become less clearly defined and the spheres for women have broadened. Perhaps, to some extent, this is a result of the publicity received by women candidates in this study. Taking this theory to its logical extreme, we may find ourselves in a society where the spheres are ultimately equivalent, but where we nonetheless remain firmly and faithfully convinced that men and women are different.

Conclusion

Physical descriptions of all kinds are more common in press accounts of women candidates than in the accounts of equivalent men candidates. Furthermore, the types of physical descriptions differ between men and women. Women are most likely to have their attire and gender mentioned and men are most likely to have their age and appearance (other than clothing) noted; women are still more likely to have their age and appearance mentioned than are men. By including more physical descriptions of women candidates, the press may reinforce the conception that women are objects of beauty as opposed to political actors; it may trivialize women's campaigns by including irrelevant information such as comments about attire and appearance, and it reveals the unconscious ideology that women are valued by their appearance.

Women may be less likely to run if they feel that their appearance will become the subject of public dialogue, and voters may conclude that candidates with more physical descriptions should not be taken seriously. Perhaps more coverage of appearance reinforces the prejudiced view that women are first and foremost objects whereas men are actors. Additional research needs to be conducted to learn whether these or other consequences result from coverage about a candidate's physical being.

Over the last hundred years, gender has remained a persistent and predominant part of news articles about women candidates for president. Such categorizing of the candidates may link women with their biology and promote the association that men are natural and women unnatural in the political sphere. It may also reinforce the social division between men and women, while at the same time disseminating the idea that women can operate successfully in traditionally male spheres thereby expanding and changing the public's notion of women's sex roles and capabilities.

References

"Admirer of Mrs. Smith, Rocky Says." 1963. *Bangor Daily News,* November 19, 17.

"Another Scandal." 1884. *New York Times,* October 12, 8.

"Belva Frees Her Mind: She Doesn't Expect to Be Elected This Year: But Is Confident That She Will Be President Some Time, When She Will Turn Things over Generally." 1884. *New York Times,* October 19, 3.

Blake, P., and J. Lowy. 1987. "'Run, Pat, Run'—Parties Test Political Waters." *Rocky Mountain News,* September 21, 6.

Braden, M. 1996. *Women Politicians and the Media.* Lexington: University Press of Kentucky.

Broder, D. S. 1999. "Elizabeth Dole Takes a Step toward Republican Presidential Bid." *Newark Star-Ledger,* March 5, 11.

Brough, D. 1964. "Skowhegan Honors Its Noted Lady Politician." *Bangor Daily News,* January 28, 1.

Bystrom, D., T. A. Robertson, and M. C. Banwart. 2001. "Framing the Fight." *American Behavioral Scientist* 44 (12): 1999–2013.

Carroll, S. J., and R. Schreiber. 1997. "Media Coverage of Women in the 103rd Congress." In *Women, Media, and Politics,* ed. P. Norris, 131–48. New York: Oxford University Press.

"A Chic Lady Who Fights: Margaret Chase Smith." 1964. *New York Times,* January 28, 1.

Cohen, R. 1999. "Dole Bolsters War Chest but Still Trails Bush." *Newark Star-Ledger,* April 28, 19.

Corry, J. 1980. "The All-Star Race." *New York Times Magazine,* June 22, 16.

"Covington's Great Poet: Woodhull and Claflin's Intimacy with the Grant Family: Government Secrets Exposed by the Woman's Rights Candidate for the Presidency—The Secessionist in the Cabinet—Grant's Utter Unfitness for His Place." 1871. *New York Sun,* June 22, 2.

"The Death of Dr. Woodhull: A Scene in the Home of the Women Brokers—The Sisters' Recent Troubles—The Doctor's Intemperance in the West." 1872. *New York Sun,* April 9, 1.

Devitt, J. 2002. "Framing Gender on the Campaign Trail: Female Gubernatorial Candidates and the Press." *Journalism and Mass Communication Quarterly* 79 (2): 445–63.

Dowd, M. 1987. "Schroeder: At Ease with Femininity and Issues." *New York Times,* August 23, A24.

———. 1999a. "Liberties: Discipline Us Please." *New York Times,* January 6, A23.

———. 1999b. "Liberties: Sugar Lips Rips N.R.A." *New York Times,* May 5, A25.

"Enter Margaret Chase Smith." 1963. *Bangor Daily News,* November 14, 14.

"Female Financing: Woodhull & Claflin in a 'Corner': Rich Scene in the Marine Court—Aspirant for the Presidency Charged with Being Naughty—Woman's Wrongs versus Woman's Rights." 1871. *New York Herald,* February 2, 8.

"A Female Philippic: Victoria C. Woodhull on the 'Tendencies of Government': The Balmoral Brokers 'Bull' on Social Laws—God in Creation, in History and in Government—a Philosophical Preface to a Philosophical Discourse." 1870. *New York Herald,* April 16, 5.

Freivogel, M. W. 1987. "Schroeder Rejects Idea of Running as 'Symbolic' Candidate." *St. Louis Post-Dispatch,* September 27, B1.

Givhan, R. 1999. "One Small Step for Womankind: Elizabeth Dole's Candidacy Became Merely the Symbol She Avoided." *Washington Post,* October 21, C1.

Goldberg, P. 1968. "Are Women Prejudiced against Women?" *Trans-Action* 5:28–30.

Grimes, C. 1987. "Alliance Broken: Schroeder Separating Herself from Hart Debacle." *St. Louis Post-Dispatch,* June 18, B1.

Halbfinger, D. M. 2003. "The 2004 Campaign: The Scene; A New Episode of 'Friends'? No, Just the Democrats Debating." *New York Times,* January 5, A15.

Hassell, J. 1999a. "Forbes Runs Again, Using Fortune and New Friends: White House Bid Has Conservatives' Blessing." *Newark Star-Ledger,* March 16, 1.

———. 1999b. "A Lady Leader? America Says It Wouldn't Mind." *Newark Star-Ledger,* August 8, 1.

Heith, D. J. 2003. "The Lipstick Watch: Media Coverage, Gender, and Presidential Campaigns." In *Anticipating Madam President,* ed. R. P. Watson and A. Gordon, 123–30. Boulder, Colo.: Lynne Rienner.

Heldman, C., S. J. Carroll, and S. Olson. 2005. "'She Brought Only a Skirt': Print Media Coverage of Elizabeth Dole's Bid for the Republican Presidential Nomination." *Political Communication* 22 (3): 315–35.

Hundley, K. 2003. "Graham Profits from a Modest Image." *St. Petersburg Times,* July 13, A1.

Hunter, M. 1964. "Margaret Chase Smith Seeks Presidency." *New York Times,* January 28, 1.

Johnson, T. A. 1971. "Mrs. Chisholm Chides Black Caucus." *New York Times,* November 20, 18.

Kahn, K. F. 1996. *The Political Consequences of Being a Woman: How Stereotypes Influence the Conduct and Consequences of Political Campaigns.* New York: Columbia University Press.

"A Lamp without Oil." 1872. *New York Times,* February 22, 4.

Mandell, N., ed. 1995. *Feminist Issues: Race, Class, and Sexuality.* Scarborough, Ont.: Prentice-Hall Canada.

Mazza, F., and L. Moberley. 1964. "Grinning Rocky: 'I'm Still in It.'" *New York Daily News,* March 11, 3.

Melton, R. H. 1999. "Dole Preaches Values in Motivational Forum." *Washington Post,* March 19, A16.

"The Modern Amazons: The Woman's Rights Movement in a Row: The Crinoline Stockjobbers Denounced: The Princess Edith's 'Crown Diamonds': Matilda

Heron, Mesdames Woodhull and Claflin, Mrs. Stanton, and Sister Norton All Up for Sentence." 1870. *New York Herald,* June 17, 5.

"Mrs. Dole and Money." 1999. *Washington Post,* October 22, A32.

"Mrs. Lockwood and Her Campaign: A Talk with the Female Candidate for President—The Sinews of War—A Letter from Elizabeth Cady Stanton." 1884. *Washington Evening Star,* September 13, 1.

"Mrs. Lockwood Explains the Mystery of Woman Politics." 1884. *Washington Evening Star,* September 4, 1.

"Mrs. Lockwood in New York: Disappointed." 1884. *Boston Globe,* October 20, 1.

"Mrs. Lockwood's First Gun: The Opening of the Equal Rights Campaign at Wilson's Station—A Meeting at Mrs. Best's House." 1884. *Washington Evening Star,* September 19, 4.

"Mrs. Woodhull's Lecture: A Tremendous Jam Last Evening in Irving Place: The Academy Jammed with a Screeching Laughing Uproarious Auditory—The Lecturer's Conundrum and the Answer." 1872. *New York Sun,* February 21, 1.

Norris, P. 1997. "Women Leaders Worldwide: A Splash of Color in the Photo Op." In *Women, Media, and Politics,* ed. P. Norris, 149–65. New York: Oxford University Press.

O'Neill, E. 1972a. "Shirley Tosses Chapeau in Ring." *New York Daily News,* January 26, 5.

———. 1972b. "There's No Biz Like Political Biz." *New York Daily News,* February 6, 76.

Penley, N., and M. Sullivan. 1964. "Ladies at Odds Over Woman as President." *Bangor Daily News,* January 28, 1.

Perry, J. 1972. "Shirley Casts Mills on a Winning Ticket." *New York Daily News,* June 17, 16.

"The Petticoat Politician: Mrs. Woodhull's Latest Epistle to the Americans—'The Limits and Sphere of Government' Considered from a Female Point of View." 1870. *New York Herald,* May 27, 4.

Prochnau, W. 1972. "Jackson's Ohio Office, Campaign Both Frayed." *Seattle Times,* April 30, A24.

"Ratifying Mrs. Lockwood's Nomination: A Meeting at the Female Candidate's House—Addresses by Mrs. Myra Clark Gaines and Other Orators." 1884. *Washington Evening Star,* September 23, 1.

Schonker-Schreck, D. 2004. "Political Marketing and the Media: Women in the 1996 Israeli Elections—A Case Study." *Israel Affairs* 10 (3): 159–77.

"The Tendencies of Government: Mrs. Woodhull's Third Letter." 1870. *New York Herald,* May 2, 5.

Thesander, M. 1997. *The Feminine Ideal.* London: Reaktion Books.

Turner, W. 1972. "Democrats Firm on Prisoner Issue in Coast Debate." *New York Times,* June 5, 1.

"The Way of the Candidate." 1884. *New York Times,* September 14, 8.

Wilson, T. 1964. "GOP's Sweetheart Lands and the Maggie Mania Is On." *New York Daily News,* July 13, 14.

Wolf, N. 1991. *The Beauty Myth.* New York: Morrow.

"A Woman Can Be President: Mrs. Lockwood Defines the Position of the Equal Righters." 1884. *New York Times,* October 20, 5.

"A Woman for President." 1871. *New York Sun,* August 18, 3.

"A Woman's Candidate for President." 1884. *Washington Evening Star,* September 4, 1.

"The Women Bankers' Home: The Masculine Costume of Revolutionary Times to Be Introduced by Victoria Woodhull." 1870. *New York Sun,* September 26, 3.

"The Women Slanderers." 1872. *Philadelphia Ledger,* November 5, 8.

"The Wrong Reasons." 1964. *New York Times,* January 29, 32.

Zeleny, J. 2003a. "Moseley-Braun Encouraged to Run for White House." *Chicago Tribune,* January 17, 10.

———. 2003b. "Moseley-Braun Gauges Prospects for '04: Ex-Senator Meets with Party Chief." *Chicago Tribune,* January 28, 7.

Do Newspapers Give Equal Coverage to Men and Women Presidential Candidates?

When I set out to study the press coverage of women candidates for president I feared that I would find nothing. I thought that perhaps the press would have simply ignored the candidates and there would be no data to analyze. That proved not to be the case; the press does write about women candidates. However, I still found an interesting story in the amount of coverage that women received as compared to equivalent men. The papers wrote fewer stories and fewer words per story about women than they did about men who had similar credentials and polled about the same. On average the men had about twice as many articles written about them and the articles were 7 percent longer.

Only in 1872 did the woman candidate (Victoria Woodhull, Equal Rights Party) have more stories written about her than the equivalent man (James Black, Prohibition Party). In every other case that I analyzed, the men received substantially more coverage than the women. On average the women had about 10 articles that mentioned them per newspaper per month of their campaign whereas similarly losing men had double that, about 20 articles per newspaper month. I found this disparity in the more distant as well as the more recent races. For example, in 1884 Benjamin Black of the Prohibition Party had 23 articles written about him per newspaper per month whereas Belva Lockwood had just 5. Even in the most recent race, the Democratic primary in 2004, Bob Graham averaged 22 articles per newspaper per month whereas Carol Moseley Braun garnered about a third of that at 8 articles per newspaper per month, even though they both polled at virtually the same percentage during the period they were running.

Moreover, the difference in the amount of coverage did not diminish over time. Although the gap in the percentage of stories mentioning the man versus the woman candidate narrowed between 1884 and 1987, from 333 percent more coverage for the man to just 8 percent more, it widened again after 1987. In 2000, Steve Forbes, the man candidate for Republican nomination, received 85 percent more stories than did Elizabeth Dole (also seeking the Republican Party's nomination). Thus, Forbes had a bigger advantage in net exposure over Dole than Henry Jackson had over Shirley Chisholm more than twenty-five years earlier. Similarly, a comparison of the campaigns of 1884 and 1988 (both cases in which the women ran as third-party candidates) shows that Ron Paul in 1988 had about the same advantage over Lenora Fulani as did Benjamin Butler over Belva Lockwood in 1884 (1884, 333 percent; 1988, 325 percent), despite almost one hundred intervening years of advances in women rights. Finally, even if one compares two races in which a black woman ran against a white man in the Democratic primary, it becomes clear that the gap between Carol Moseley Braun and Bob Graham in 2004 exceeded the gap between Shirley Chisholm and Henry Jackson in 1972 (1972, 54 percent; 2004, 197 percent).

The same pattern holds true for the average number of words written per article. The average lengths of the articles were longer for the men. The average length of an article about a woman candidate was 612 words. For a man candidate the average length was 656 words, or 7 percent longer. There was no clear trend suggesting that the disparity in the average length of the articles is dropping.

Did Woodhull's Gender Give Her a Boost?

One of the interesting components of this pattern is that the coverage of the first woman to run for president in the United States (1872) appears to be different from the coverage of all subsequent women candidates in terms of the number of articles. This finding raises the question, Did Woodhull's gender benefit her by eliciting more press coverage? Several factors may have contributed to the disparity in the quantity of press coverage in that race: the *New York Herald* took a special interest in Woodhull and gave her an unusual amount of coverage; Woodhull's personal life was the subject of exceptional scandal, which generated much press attention; and Black did not actively campaign whereas Woodhull did.

One reason that the *New York Herald* gave Woodhull so much attention was that it generally gave greater coverage to financial news and community scandal. The combination of both points of interest in one candidate increased the likelihood that the *Herald* would focus on Woodhull, who was a stockbroker. Since the financial pages of the paper covered the opening of her brokerage business, it was natural for the publication to continue covering Woodhull when she decided to run for office. When Woodhull's private life became a public scandal, this too fit nicely into the *Herald's* area of specialization. It was the *Herald* that published Woodhull's announcement to run for president, in the form of a letter to the editor on April 2, 1870; it was the *Herald* that published a series of essays, written by Woodhull, in the months that followed (these essays formed one of the pillars of her campaign and contributed to the skewing of her press coverage); and it was the *Herald* that published 40 percent of the total articles about Woodhull in the five papers examined for this study. The *Herald's* particular interest in Woodhull explains some, but not all, of the disparity between Black and Woodhull. One hundred six articles mentioned Woodhull. Forty-three were from the *Herald,* with sixty-three mentioning Woodhull and three mentioning Black in the remaining four newspapers that were searched.

The remainder of the explanation for the disparity may lie in traditional news values or assessments of newsworthiness. Some of these had to do with Woodhull's gender and others did not. Journalism has a long history of determining newsworthiness according to fairly stable criteria. These generally include prominence, topicality, human interest, conflict, timeliness, and unusualness (McManus 1994). Several aspects of Woodhull's life and campaign made her more newsworthy than her opponent.

Recognizability, or how well the candidate is known, tends to influence the amount of news coverage. More prominent personalities get more news coverage than those who are less well known. It is likely that at the time that the candidates declared their intention to run, Woodhull was the more prominent. Woodhull's biographers tell us that when she opened her stock brokerage in early January 1870, she made quite a splash in the press. This coverage spurred her to public prominence and transformed her into a public figure. When Woodhull declared her campaign in March, she was already a well-recognized name in the pages of the papers. Even though Black held various local and state posts in Prohibition organizations, he had no such history of press coverage.

It is likely that Woodhull's campaign was also more topical (i.e., reflective of a topic in which the audience already had some interest) than Black's. Not only had her narrative already begun in the press (over the opening of her stock brokerage), but women's changing roles and increasing politicization were very much part of the social dialogue. In 1870, the issue of women's roles in society showed up regularly in the public discourse recorded in the newspapers, much more so than did the Prohibition movement. On any given day one could find articles, letters, or editorials that touched on the role of women. These discourses covered the role of women in marriage, under the law, in work, in pay, and at home. Discussion of women in the civil and political spheres had increased at the end of 1869 when Elizabeth Cady Stanton declared herself a nominee for Congress and Wyoming and Utah extended the vote to white women. In other words, Woodhull ran during a time of public focus on the roles and rights of women. As such, her race resonated with prominent questions and dialogues of the time, which in turn probably gave her an advantage in amount of news coverage. At the time of this campaign the Prohibition issue (with which James Black was associated) was not yet a comparably prominent part of the social dialogue.

News producers also tend to gravitate to stories high in human interest (or emotion). Though some people felt strongly about the Prohibition movement, it did not challenge the very social structure on which society rested in the same way as the women's rights movement did. The issue of equal rights questioned not only the dominant social organization of sex roles but also individual and collective identities based on gender. The women's movement challenged other basic cultural institutions as well, including marriage, the political system, and the economic system. Woodhull explicitly advocated economic equality, serial monogamy, sexual liberation for women, and marriage based on love rather than economics or law. This platform aroused more emotion than did temperance.

Perhaps more important, Woodhull not only advocated change in these areas, but she also lived according to her principles. As a stockbroker and publisher, she occupied two jobs that were within the strict domain of men. She was actively involved in federal politics through her lobbying and her presentation to Congress of several well-known arguments defending women's right to vote from a legal constitutional basis. Referred to collectively as "Woodhull's Memorial," the arguments claimed that no legal action was necessary to enfranchise women because they already had the right to vote. In addition, Woodhull's personal life was considered scandalous. She was divorced. Moreover, she remained cordial with her ex-husband, living with him, supporting him, and continuing to raise their children together while simultaneously living with her second husband. In her professional, private, and political life Woodhull managed to touch the emotions of the time.

Conflict also attracts media attention and Woodhull's life was full of it. Not only were the ideas and principles she advocated at odds with the dominant culture, but her personal and professional life was marked by discord. During the course of her campaign she was brought to court several times for various complaints against her business (e.g., for losing the money of an investor). She publicly argued with the senators who rejected her "Memorial." She was in public dispute with Susan B. Anthony over whom the women's rights movement should support in the election. During her campaign her mother filed a suit of abuse against Woodhull's husband, and one of her sisters spoke out publicly against her. Much of the news about Woodhull focused on these items. Of the articles that mentioned Woodhull, 43 percent covered her in the context of some scandal unrelated to her campaign. Moreover, only about 40 percent of the articles even mentioned that she was running for president. By contrast, nothing about Black suggests his life was plagued by conflict, and all the articles about him mentioned his campaign.

As a news value, "timeliness" is usually taken to mean simply how recently an event occurred. Both campaigns were equally timely in that they were conducted during the election season, but Black did not campaign and almost nothing was done on Black's behalf by his party. By contrast, Woodhull campaigned actively. She gave many lectures, appeared before Congress, and engaged in public acts (such as attempting to vote). These actions were event oriented. News tends to focus more on events or actions rather than ideas or issues. Since there were no "events" to cover in Black's campaign, it is easy to see why there was little to cover. Woodhull in contrast kept the newspapers supplied with a steady stream of events that garnered the attention of the press.

Unusualness (or novelty) also tends to draw news attention, and Woodhull's campaign was far more atypical than Black's. Many third-party candidates who were men had run by 1872, but no other women had done so. It is likely that Woodhull's coverage, especially that by the *Herald,* was helped by the novelty of her campaign. What is surprising is that, in all of the news articles about her, at no time was she identified or labeled as "the first woman to run for president." I believe that this is because she was not taken by the press to be a "real" candidate; rather her candidacy was seen as a publicity vehicle for the women's rights movement.

In terms of the amount of coverage, it appears that being a woman did not negatively affect Woodhull. In fact, her gender probably enhanced the novelty, topicality, and even human interest aspects of her campaign, making her a more attractive news subject. On the other hand, and for the reasons stated, it is unlikely that her gender was the sole reason for the amount of coverage she received.

Did the Men in the Other Races
Get a Boost from Their Gender?

In seven other races it was the man and not the woman candidate that benefited from more press coverage. The fact that the direction of the difference was consistent in seven different races, spanning over one hundred years and encompassing many different personalities and situations, lends credence to the argument that in general males are given a benefit in quantity of coverage over females.

This pattern is confirmed by similar findings in races for other offices. In her content analysis of twenty-six U.S. Senate races between 1982 and 1986, Kim F. Kahn (1994), a political scientist, found that the women candidates received less news coverage than did their men counterparts (see also Kahn and Goldenberg 1991). Approximately 95 paragraphs a week were written about men Senate candidates, but only 79 paragraphs a week were written about women Senate candidates.

A 1996 survey of Senate races in which a man ran against a woman also pointed to a dearth of coverage for women candidates. Martha Kropf and John Boiney found respondents less likely to be able to recognize, rate, or name something about the women candidates. They also found that respondents would shift from being unfamiliar to familiar with a candidate at lower levels of media exposure when the candidate was a man. In other words, people who received fewer media reports were more likely to be familiar with a man than a woman candidate. Kropf and Boiney noted, "If a voter read the newspaper for only one day during the election cycle, he would stand a significantly greater chance of reading something about the male candidate than the female" (14).

Pippa Norris (1997) found this pattern to hold true even for coverage of international leaders. When press coverage of women presidents and prime ministers was compared with coverage of their immediate (men) predecessors or successors, the women heads of state received less coverage than did the men.

Diane Silver (1986), a communications scholar, analyzed content of Michigan newspapers' coverage of state officials and found that even though women made up 26 percent of state officials they were mentioned in only 19 percent of news stories, and though women made up 11 percent of the legislature they were mentioned in only 7 percent of stories on state lawmakers. Stories in which a woman was the first official mentioned averaged one hundred fewer words than those in which a man was the first official named.

It is reasonable to hypothesize that in a society that historically gave men, not women, access to power, associated stereotypical masculine traits with leadership, repudiated women's capacity or inclination for politics, and legally banned women from the political arena, the press would accord men who run for political office more press coverage than women. In this context women may appear less like "real" or "serious" candidates to reporters and editors who must make gate-keeping decisions, or to party workers and pundits who provide reporters with information about which candidates to watch.

Cultural limits and denial of opportunities for women, which resulted in different life experiences, may also cause women to look less typically "presidential" than men. This was clearly the case in 1884 when Belva Lockwood (Equal Rights Party) ran for office against General Benjamin Butler (Greenback Party). Though both candidates were attorneys, there were many differences in their backgrounds that legitimately may have made Lockwood appear less qualified and, therefore, less deserving of press attention. For example, whereas Butler had served in both the Massachusetts and U.S. legislatures, as governor of Massachusetts, and as a general in the Civil War (all before running for president), Lockwood had never held elected office. In fact, prior to 1884 no women in all of U.S. history had ever been elected to public office, nor were they allowed to serve in the military. Lockwood had drafted legislation and served as a school administrator, which may have made her as qualified as Butler. However, since her resume was not typical compared to that of men candidates she may not have elicited the same quantity of press coverage. The difference in the amount of press attention may then have been indirectly the result of her gender and more directly the result of her different experiences, which were limited by gender. The number of articles about Butler was more than four times the number about Lockwood, and the articles were 60 percent longer.

Butler may have been accorded more attention for other reasons as well. His involvement in politics at the national level as well as his role in the Civil War likely made him more prominent than Lockwood. He achieved some fame early in the war when there was not yet an official policy as to what should be done with escaped slaves. Some Union generals permitted some slaves to be reclaimed by their owners while protecting others. However, Butler decided that the former slaves could remain at his fort in safety as "contraband of war." The phrase "contraband of war" caught on among Northern abolitionists and received wide publicity. Butler also received some notoriety after being assigned to hold the city of New Orleans. Since the city was forcibly occupied, the inhabitants were often hostile toward Union forces. For example, women would insult the

Union soldiers. In response to such insults, Butler passed an order saying that any woman who publicly insulted an officer would be treated as a prostitute. Afraid of being raped or prosecuted, women were instantly silenced in their public speech. Butler also gained some national prominence during his tenure in Congress, for example, by supporting Victoria Woodhull's "Memorial."

Of course, Lockwood was not entirely unknown when she ran. She too had secured a reasonable amount of prominence from her work in fighting to allow women to practice law. According to Frances A. Cook (1997), a professor of women's legal history, Lockwood had garnered previous press attention. She was recognized nationally for her role in the successful enactment of the law opening the federal courts to women. She was also one of the pioneer activists on suffrage issues in the District of Columbia after the Civil War, speaking at suffrage meetings and before Congress and participating in the 1871 attempt by a large group of suffragists to register and then vote in the District. Still, Butler's and Lockwood's respective biographies suggest he may have had greater prominence upon entering the race.

One additional factor may have contributed to Lockwood's lack of coverage: the tardiness of her announcement. The fact that she was running was not mentioned in the papers until two months before the election, when they ran her acceptance letter. This did not give much time for her to publicize her cause or gain momentum. Thus, Butler's more traditional experience and greater prominence and Lockwood's lack of time to publicize her campaign could account for the difference in the amount of coverage they received. It is not clear from this race alone that Butler's advantage was due to his sex.

Roughly eighty years later, when Margaret Chase Smith ran for president in 1964, she too would receive less press coverage—about a third of that of the most equivalent man running the same race. Unlike the earlier candidates, Chase Smith was a seasoned politician, having served in both the U.S. House and Senate before running. As in previous examples, gender may have played a role in this difference, but there may have been other factors as well.

Nelson Rockefeller ran for president as a governor and Chase Smith as a senator. It is possible that governors receive more coverage than senators. However, when I designated each article as primarily about the campaign or primarily about the candidate's job as an office holder, the difference between the two in incumbency coverage was not great enough to account for the overall difference in the campaign coverage between them. Of the articles that mentioned Rockefeller, 8.5 percent were framed around his gubernatorial role, whereas 5.8 percent of Chase Smith's articles were related to her job as a sitting senator. That is a difference of just under 3 percent, but Rockefeller was mentioned in over 200 percent more stories per newspaper per month on average than Chase Smith.

It is also possible that the difference in the amount of coverage could have come from a home-state effect. Two of the three papers I analyzed came from Rockefeller's home state of New York whereas only one came from Chase Smith's, Maine. We would expect that candidates would get more coverage in their home state than in papers farther away since the natives would have greater topicality. This is, in fact, the case with Rockefeller. Rockefeller was mentioned at least once in 258 separate *New York Times* articles (about 32 articles per month of his campaign) whereas Chase Smith was mentioned just 13 times (about three articles per month of her campaign). Similarly in the *New York Daily News* Rockefeller was mentioned in 236 articles (30 per month) whereas Chase Smith was mentioned in just 23 articles (4.6 per month). However, Chase Smith got no such boost from her home-state papers. The *Bangor Daily News* covered both candidates at about equal rates, carrying 109 articles that mentioned Rockefeller (about 14 per month) and 77 that mentioned Chase Smith (15 per month). Thus, even if some of the disparity in coverage was a home-state effect, the fact that Rockefeller gained greatly from his home state and Chase Smith gained not at all suggests that home-state advantages can be obliterated by issues of gender.

The third possibility is that Rockefeller was somehow more newsworthy. This argument could be made on two accounts. First, Rockefeller came from a wealthy family, and the wealthy in our society tend to be considered more newsworthy than those with fewer financial assets. Second, in 1962 Rockefeller divorced his wife of many years to marry a much younger woman. In addition, as mentioned earlier, his second wife and the wife of his son from the first marriage each had a baby during the campaign. The divorce and second marriage elicited bad press for Rockefeller, but the story was also sensational, high in human interest, and touched by conflict. This certainly could have increased the amount of coverage he received. On the other hand, whereas Rockefeller's home life was mentioned in the stories and accusations of his "wife swapping" were repeated, these comments were often an aside to a story about Rockefeller's candidacy and were not the main angle or central topic of his stories. This differed from Woodhull's coverage where her home-life scandal became the focus of the stories about her, with many of them failing even to mention that she was running for president. In contrast, it is interesting to note that

Chase Smith was not held to a similar standard in this case. For years, including the period in which she ran for office, she was romantically involved with her (much younger) assistant, though they never married. It is not clear if the press knew or cared about the relationship; it never appeared in her presidential campaign press accounts.

Though these sensational factors may have made Rockefeller newsworthy, Chase Smith was notable in her own right. After all, she was the first woman to run for president in almost one hundred years. Moreover, her campaign, like Woodhull's, was timely. The second wave of feminism was beginning in the 1960s. *The Second Sex,* by the French feminist writer Simone de Beauvoir, in which she coined the phrase "women's liberation," had been published in the United States in 1952. In 1961 President John F. Kennedy established the Commission on the Status of Women, and in 1963 he convened a conference on the status of women. The subsequent report, which documented widespread discrimination against women in American life, received wide publicity. Also in 1963 the best-selling book *The Feminine Mystique* by Betty Friedan was published. In it Friedan described how limited options offered to women resulted in their depression and intellectual stultification. The book became a bestseller and is credited with affecting the aspirations of many women. The emerging second wave of feminism was as resonant in the pages of the newspapers as the first wave was in 1872. The topic of women's roles was a part of the community dialogue at the time Chase Smith was running, and Chase Smith's candidacy was consonant with these larger social trends.

Whereas Rockefeller may have been noteworthy for the large amount of money he spent on his campaign, Chase Smith should have been no less newsworthy for the little that she spent. Rockefeller's money may have made him more newsworthy and more able to conduct pseudo-events when he ran, and he had been in office for only a little more than six years. Chase Smith's comparatively serious twenty years of experience at the federal level, it seems, should have balanced that. Similarly it is hard to argue that Rockefeller's scandalous home life would have produced much more news than Chase Smith's topical campaign. Aside from gender bias, there is no obvious explanation as to why Rockefeller got more coverage than Chase Smith that is not balanced by an equally compelling argument that suggests that Chase Smith should have garnered more press attention than he.

In 1972, there were 50 percent more stories written about Senator Henry Jackson than about Representative Shirley Chisholm, and the articles were 25 percent longer. The fact that Jackson received more press coverage than did Chisholm is magnified by the fact that two of the three papers I searched were from Chisholm's hometown of New York City and would be expected to give her more coverage than nonlocal papers. Of the articles I coded for this campaign, 80 percent were from New York City papers. Thus, while a candidate can normally expect more coverage from a home-state paper, this advantage is clearly mitigated by sexism. On the other hand, it is possible that Jackson could have received more coverage because he was a senator and Chisholm was merely a representative. Thirteen percent of the articles about Jackson were incumbent- (not campaign-) related, whereas only 10 percent of Chisholm's articles were. However, this difference does not make up for the overall difference in quantity of coverage between the two candidates. This occurred despite the many aspects of Chisholm's life and campaign that should have provoked extensive coverage of her campaign.

It is also unlikely that Chisholm's culture or skin color accounted for the difference. The *New York Daily News* printed just eight articles about Chisholm during her campaign, whereas in 1988, when another (black) New Yorker, Jesse Jackson, ran for the Democratic nomination, that same paper printed over two hundred articles mentioning him (and Jackson, unlike Chisholm, had never held elected office). In fact, most traditional news values would suggest that Chisholm and not Henry Jackson would get more press coverage. Because of Chisholm's skin color, she was unusual precisely because she held elected office. Moreover, because she was a congresswoman of color, she was often called upon to comment in the press about a host of national issues relating to ethnic conflict. Chisholm also invited more conflict coverage during her race because some men in the political establishment openly opposed her candidacy due to her gender. Because these news values suggest that she should have received ample coverage, one might identify sexism as the cause for the dearth of articles written about her.

Chisholm's campaign was also topical in that it followed soon after the civil rights movement, making her campaign resonate with the victories gained during that period. In addition, the women's movement was also in high gear by 1972. Kate Millett's *Sexual Politics* was published in 1970, the same year that San Diego State University founded the first women's studies degree program. In 1971, the first battered woman's shelter opened; *Ms.* magazine first appeared as an insert in *New York Magazine,* propelling its cofounder, Gloria Steinem, into prominence; and the National Women's Political Caucus, cofounded by Chisholm, was established to promote women's candidacy for office. Then in 1972, Title IX of the Education Amendment mandated that girls receive the same opportunities as boys in programs that received federal funds, and the ERA was passed by Congress and sent to the states for ratification.

Henry Jackson had none of these advantages. Though he was a senator, he was not well known outside his state of Washington. If his personal story was at all unusual, this was not made apparent by his press coverage or biography. Though he supported busing to achieve racial integration, which was controversial, he otherwise did not stir much conflict, nor did his positions on particular issues resonate with wider social movements. In fact, Jackson's campaign was rather bland, emotionless, and uneventful. Traditional news values suggest that Chisholm and not Jackson should have had more news coverage. Still, Jackson garnered 54 percent more (and 26 percent longer) articles than did Chisholm. It seems reasonable to hypothesize that Chisholm's gender might have made her seem less like a "real" candidate and therefore less worthy of news attention.

Of the races I studied, the numbers of articles written about the opposing candidates were closest in the contest between Richard Gephardt and Patricia Schroeder in 1987. Gephardt had just 8 percent more articles written about him than did Schroeder, although the articles were 40 percent longer. The similarity in numbers of articles may be attributable to the fact that in this race, more than in the others, the two candidates had similar experiences. Both were attorneys running as sitting members of the U.S. House of Representatives. According to news accounts neither was particularly prominent going into the race. Schroeder did have a national following as a women's rights activist, though women's rights were not particularly resonant in the culture of the 1980s. The failures of both the ERA in 1982 and of Geraldine Ferraro's run for vice president in 1984 were important political setbacks for women, according to Eleanor Clift and Tom Brazaitis (2000), authors of *Madam President: Shattering the Last Glass Ceiling.* Clift and Brazaitis argued that these failures caused Schroeder not to have the support of many influential figures in the women's rights movement when she ran.

Aside from Schroeder's gender, neither she nor Gephardt had any characteristics that made them stand out as candidates. Neither was plagued by scandal or news that was high in emotional conflict before or during the campaign. Schroeder had slightly more seniority and was believed by pundits to have more national name recognition. Gephardt had officially declared he was running while Schroeder ran a "testing the water" campaign in which she never "officially" declared. On the other hand, there is a long tradition of giving (sometimes extensive) news coverage to candidates who might enter the race. Maria Braden (1996) argued that potential women candidates can get more coverage than actual aspirants.

Gephardt had raised more money than did Schroeder but he also ran for a much longer period of time. In the four short months that

Schroeder considered running she raised almost $900,000. Gephardt raised $9,000,000 in thirteen months, or about $700,000 per month. Moreover, the press was rather monolithic in its favorable assessments of Schroeder's fund raising during her short campaign. In almost all the accounts, the press portrayed her as having enough money to make a viable run. This makes it unlikely that the press would have covered her less because they perceived her as unable to raise enough cash. In this race, the gender of the candidates seems to have been a clear factor in the amount and length of coverage of the candidates.

In 1988, even though both candidates received very little coverage, Ron Paul of the Libertarian Party still garnered more than three times the number of articles in the press as did the New Alliance Party's Lenora Fulani. Three factors besides gender may have contributed to Paul's greater coverage: he had previously held elected office (Congress), whereas Fulani had not; he was of light skin color whereas Fulani was of a darker complexion; and Paul ran on the ticket of the third largest political party whereas Fulani ran on the ticket of the fourth largest. While these things could have contributed to differences in coverage, the quantity and the quality of the news articles reveals that both candidates were framed as having no chance of election. Paul's previous electoral experience was rarely mentioned in the articles and both candidates tended to be portrayed as third-party "nuts" running for office. This leads me to doubt that Paul's political experience or the relative size of the two candidates' parties had much to do with the coverage. It is hard to determine how the differences in skin color might have affected the coverage, but as mentioned earlier there were more than two hundred articles written about a man with dark skin color in 1988 (Jesse Jackson), who like Fulani had no elected political experience.

As late as 2000, the men candidates were still garnering more press attention than the equivalent women who ran. Steve Forbes had 85 percent more stories than Elizabeth Dole and the stories contained 20 percent more words. According to traditional news norms, it would be very difficult to make the case that in 2000 Steve Forbes should have received more news attention than Elizabeth Dole. Dole was quite well known at the time of her campaign. She had served in two cabinet-level positions for two different administrations and had campaigned nationally with her husband, Bob Dole, on three separate occasions, including once in 1996 when he had the nomination of the Republican Party. Dole had also made a name for herself as head of the American Red Cross. Forbes was wealthy and had run before but his claims to fame pale in comparison to Dole's experience. Moreover, during the course of their campaigns they raised about the same amount of money (Dole about $5 million, Forbes about $5.7 million). Dole was clearly the more qualified even under traditional criteria for candidate experience. Aside from Forbes's personal fortune it is hard to understand why he gained much press attention at all.

The pattern of men receiving more coverage still held true in 2004. Senator Bob Graham had almost 200 percent more stories written about him than Ambassador Carol Moseley Braun. For that race it is hard to make the case that Graham deserved more coverage. Both candidates were polling very poorly (under 5 percent) during their candidacies. They had both sat in the Senate, though Graham was still serving at the time of his campaign and had served for much longer (three terms compared with Moseley Braun's one). Graham had also served as governor, which has traditionally been a more successful route to the White House than was the Congress. On the other hand, Moseley Braun had held an ambassadorship, a national post. Both candidates had political experience at the state level. She had sat in her state's legislature, even serving as assistant majority leader. He had served in the Senate of his state. She was an attorney and had served as federal prosecutor before her political career, whereas he had just an LL.B. On the basis of their experience, it is not easy to make the case that one should have been considered a significantly more serious candidate and therefore deserving of substantially more press attention.

From a financial perspective, Graham may have garnered more media attention because he raised much more money. According to CNN.com Carol Moseley Braun raised $556,000, whereas Graham raised about $4,500,000. That said, the articles coded for this study rarely focused on the fund raising of the candidates.

One final factor that might have affected the coverage was a political scandal that Moseley Braun had experienced during her term as U.S. senator. She was accused of failing to pay her staff, and the Federal Elections Commission investigated allegations of inappropriate campaign expenditures during the 1990s, though it never pursued charges. Graham did not suffer from similar past scandal. Still, it is not clear that this should have resulted in less press, since the media often give more coverage to scandals. Here again sexism appears to have affected the amount of coverage.

Conclusion

As with all historical research it is not possible to say with scientific certainty what role gender played in determining how much press coverage each candidate garnered. The doubter could clearly point to something else in each race that might explain why the man would get more press coverage than the woman. Considering the coverage collectively, however, I think it is hard to make a case that gender did not influence the quantity of press coverage. In seven out of eight races, more articles were written about the man than the woman, whether he had less experience (as was Forbes), performed more poorly in the polls (as did Gephardt), was more ordinary (as was Butler), or was just less interesting (as was Jackson). This pattern in conjunction with the fact that similar findings have been reported in studies of candidates running in other types of races leads me to suspect strongly that women candidates for president have been at a disadvantage in the amount of press coverage that they received and that sexism affects how much press coverage women candidates garner.

References

Beauvoir, S. de. 1952. *The Second Sex*. New York: Knopf.

Braden, M. 1996. *Women Politicians and the Media*. Lexington: University Press of Kentucky.

Clift, E., and T. Brazaitis. 2000. *Madam President: Shattering the Last Glass Ceiling*. New York: Scribner.

Cook, F. A. 1997. "Belva Ann Lockwood: For Peace, Justice, and President." *Women's Legal History Project*. Retrieved October 24, 2006, from http://www.stanford.edu/group/WLHP/papers/lockwood.htm#I.%20INTRODUCTION.

Friedan, B. 1963. *The Feminine Mystique*. New York: Norton.

Kahn, K. F. 1994. "The Distorted Mirror: Press Coverage of Women Candidates for Statewide Office." *Journal of Politics* 56 (1): 154–73.

Kahn, K. F., and E. N. Goldenberg. 1991. "Women Candidates in the News: An Examination of Gender Differences in U.S. Senate Campaign Coverage." *Public Opinion Quarterly* 55:180–99.

Kropf, M. E., and J. A. Boiney. 1996. "The Electoral Glass Ceiling: How the News Affects the Viability of Female Candidates." Paper presented at the meeting of the Midwest Political Science Association, Chicago, April 18–20.

McManus, J. H. 1994. *Market-Driven Journalism: Let the Citizen Beware*. Thousand Oaks, Calif.: Sage.

Millett, K. 1970. *Sexual Politics*. Garden City, N.Y.: Doubleday.

Norris, P. 1997. "Women Leaders Worldwide: A Splash of Color in the Photo Op." In *Women, Media and Politics*, ed. P. Norris, 149–65. New York: Oxford University Press.

Silver, D. 1986. "A Comparison of Newspapers Coverage of Male and Female Officials in Michigan." *Journalism Quarterly* 63 (1): 144–49.

Issues, Biography, and Chaff

A number of recent studies have shown that election coverage often lacks the kind of substantive political discussion people need to make informed decisions. Rather than reporting on the candidates' positions on the issues or the experience they bring to a job, news accounts are far more likely to reduce an election to a game, telling voters who is ahead or behind or reporting on the candidates' strategies or movements (e.g., King 1990; Patterson 1991). In short, the media tend to treat an election more like a horse race than a job interview.

Generally speaking, women fare more poorly than men in this regard. Women candidates get more horse-race coverage and less reporting on the issues, and the press paints them as less viable than competing men candidates. In a study of newspaper coverage of Senate races between 1982 and 1986, Kim Kahn and Edie Goldenberg (1991) found that the coverage of women candidates focused "more on their viability and less on their issue positions . . . [and their] viability coverage was more negative than that of their male counterparts" (180). In a similar study, Kahn (1994) examined media coverage of women running in forty-seven statewide campaigns. She found the press was more likely to characterize women as less viable than competing men and more likely to emphasize "their unlikely chances of victory" (154). In a third study, Kahn (1996) found the media reported the absence of financial resources more frequently for women than for men. Scarce resources were discussed in 10 percent of women's Senate races and 5 percent of men's.

In order to assess the effects of the different coverage that men and women garner, Kahn (1992) conducted an experiment in which she modeled prototypical articles for men and women in U.S. Senate races. Then regardless of which prototype was used, the gender of the candidate in the article was altered. She found that when subjects read an article employing "male incumbent" coverage (i.e., coverage prototypical of men candidates), the candidate—male or female—was perceived to be more viable, a stronger leader, and better able to deal with military issues. Such a candidate was also considered more likely to win the seat. The prototypical "female incumbent" coverage led the subjects to believe that the candidate was more compassionate and better able to deal with health issues.

These findings are not purely hypothetical. We know that the public generally believes that the campaign trail is harder for women than for men. The 1994 National Women's Political Caucus survey found that two-thirds of the respondents thought it was harder for women than men to get elected (Newman 1994). Similarly, the Greenberg-Lake study concluded that voters identified women of either party as less likely to win even when they planned to vote for the woman (cited by Jamieson 1995). In an experiment in 1981, Virginia Sapiro had subjects read a campaign speech. In one condition the candidate was identified as Joan; in the other condition, as John. When subjects were asked to identify the likelihood that the candidate would win, 64 percent of men and 61 percent of women identified John as "very" or "somewhat" (Sapiro 1981, 74) likely to win, whereas Joan received these designations from only 49 percent of men and 45 percent of women.

Even though people tend to believe that women have a harder time winning, research shows that women candidates raise amounts of money comparable to those of men and win as often as men do. However, many fewer women than men run. As noted in the introduction to the present book, women account for only about 8 percent of candidates for the U.S. House and Senate (see Newman 1994; Seltzer, Newman, and Leighton 1997). One of the greatest impediments to garnering equal representation is the paucity of women candidates. If the press presents women as less likely to win, this could deter women from running. The belief that women make weaker candidates may also account for the fact that women incumbents are more likely to be challenged than are men incumbents. In elections for the U.S. House, 94 percent of women representatives and 86 percent of men representatives were challenged (Seltzer, Newman, and Leighton 1997).

In this chapter I look at three types of substantive coverage: those focusing on issues (policy stands and legislative proposals), biographical information (anything about the candidate's history or experience), and quotations. I also examine four topics of nonsubstantive coverage—chaff (any type of coverage that conveys nothing that would help a voter make a decision), viability (horse-race information), money raised, and supporters' gender—to see whether there was a systematic bias for or against women. The results were mixed, with women benefiting from some types of bias and being disadvantaged by others.

Substantive Coverage

Issues

According to traditional rational models of voting behavior, citizens choose (or should choose) candidates based on the stands those individuals have taken on various issues The degree to which the media provide that information, therefore, may be important in securing support for candidates. Previous studies of presidential campaign coverage have noted that information about a candidate's character or personality dominates coverage at the expense of providing information about issue positions (Graber 1971, 1976). In my own study I used two measures to assess the extent of issue coverage. I counted the number of unique issues mentioned in each article, and I categorized each paragraph to determine if it was predominantly about issues. For example, the following brief paragraph was categorized as predominantly about issues: "Mrs. Dole did advocate tax cuts, more defense spending, a more vigorous fight against drugs and 'a return of our public schools to greatness'" (Glover 1999). It was also counted as mentioning four unique issues: taxes, defense, drugs, and schools. Similarly, the following paragraph about Forbes was coded as predominantly about issues: "In his talk, Forbes touched on many of the conservative themes expected to be the cornerstone of his campaign, including his advocacy of a single 'flat tax' rate to replace the current tax code, school choice, and opposition to abortion" (Johnson 1999). This paragraph was counted as covering three unique issues: taxes, vouchers, and abortion. When I compared the total number of unique issues mentioned and the number of paragraphs focusing on issues, I found that, in general, the men were likely to have more issues covered than the women.

When I looked at each article and coded whether or not each paragraph was predominantly about issues, in all cases except coverage of Woodhull and Black (1872) the men had more issue paragraphs written about them. There was very little coverage of Black in 1872 so the reversal in this race should be viewed with caution. Since in general the men had more (and longer) articles, I calculated the percentage of issue paragraphs accorded each candidate by dividing the number of issue paragraphs by the total number of paragraphs written about each. When I did this, the pattern held for all cases except Woodhull and Black in 1872. The average apportionment of issue paragraphs was 16 percent for the women and 27 percent for the men. In other words, the men had 68 percent more paragraphs written about issues than did the women. This pattern should be worrisome for women candidates, who may have a harder time getting their legislative and policy proposals to the voters. Moreover, if the voters have less substantive information about the candidates upon which to base their opinions, they may be more likely to rely on stereotypes in casting their ballots.

The disparity in coverage was greatest in the 1987 race with Richard Gephardt and Pat Schroeder, both Democrats. Gephardt had over 339 percent more paragraphs about issues than did Schroeder. The disparity was the smallest in 1972, but even then Henry Jackson had 17 percent more paragraphs about issues than did Shirley Chisholm. There is no indication that the disparity is diminishing over time. In 2004, when Carol Moseley Braun faced off against Bob Graham, Graham garnered 78 percent more issue paragraphs than Moseley Braun. That disparity is greater than in three of the seven races that preceded it.

It was interesting to learn that Lockwood was the most likely of the women to elicit issue paragraphs. One in every four paragraphs about her covered issues. Woodhull, the other candidate from the nineteenth century, was close behind with 23 percent of her paragraphs being about issues. All of the women running in the twentieth century had less issue coverage than their male opponents. Moreover, Chase Smith (in 1964) may have been the most viable of the candidates in terms of credentials but she had one of the lowest percentages of issue paragraphs, just 8.6 percent. Moseley Braun (in 2004) garnered coverage of issues in only eight paragraphs out of one hundred. One might hypothesize that the decline in issue paragraphs among the women in the twentieth-century contests resulted from overall declining issue coverage in the press. However, the same pattern is not present among the men. In fact, the two men with the highest percentage of issue coverage were Gephardt, in 1987, and Paul, in 1988. One in two paragraphs about Gephardt were about issues and about one in three were for Paul. All told, in regard to issue coverage, it does not appear that women candidates are being treated more seriously by the press today than a century ago.

The pattern remains basically the same for the number of distinct issues. I found that the men in all cases (except 1872) had a greater number of issues of all types mentioned, even when I took into account the fact that men have longer articles written about them and calculated the number of unique issues mentioned per 10,000 words. In all cases but 1884, men had more discrete issues mentioned per 10,000 words than did the equivalent woman running in the same race.

On average the women had about 1.5 different issues mentioned per article, whereas the men had 2.5 (about 63 percent more). There seems to be a pattern of small increases in the number of unique issues mentioned per article among the candidates running in the 1900s. Chase Smith (in 1964) represents the low with just one issue mentioned in every three articles, followed by Chisholm (in 1972), who averaged about .8 of an issue per article, then Schroeder (in 1987) at 1.6, and Dole at 2.1 (in 2000). However, the rate dropped again in 2004 when Moseley Braun had just about one issue mentioned per article on average.

There is an additionally disturbing finding in this area. In studies of other races, researchers have found that women candidates are actually more issue-driven than are men candidates. Kahn (1996) conducted an analysis of campaign advertisements and found that women candidates were slightly more likely than men candidates to talk about issues in their advertisements. Women emphasized issues in 76 percent of their commercials whereas men stressed issues 71 percent of the time. Thus, it appears that women candidates are more likely to talk about substantive issues and the press is less likely to report on them. If this pattern applies to presidential races, it suggests that the press's portrayals may play an active role in making women candidates look less serious.

When I examined the types of issues mentioned, I found fewer patterns based on the candidates' sex than modern stereotypes might suggest. Overall, women were no more or less likely than men to have health care, abortion, social problems, or education mentioned as one of the first four issues in each article. Men were no more or less likely to have defense, international affairs, or taxes mentioned in their coverage. There were about equal numbers of cases in which the women and the men had more of each of these issues mentioned. However, there were two issues that did seem to be affected by the candidates' gender: the economy and issues traditionally associated with women (e.g., women's suffrage, the Equal Rights Amendment, domestic abuse, reform of marriage laws, women in the military). Men were more likely than women to have the economy (e.g., employment, economic growth, the free enterprise system, currency) mentioned in their articles. Women were more likely to have issues traditionally associated with women mentioned in their articles.

On average, 18 percent of the first four issues raised in a story about men were about the economy, compared with just 10 percent for women. Thus stories about men were about 75 percent more likely to mention the economy as one of the first issues. In every race the economy was mentioned as an issue for the women candidates, although it was more frequently mentioned in regard to the men candidates. That is different from the pattern for women's issues.

In half of the races, the coverage of the men candidates never included issues traditionally considered "women's issues" (such as pay equity or domestic abuse) as one of the first four issues mentioned in the articles. In an additional two races, issues comprised just 1 percent each of the coverage. By contrast, they were mentioned in relation to women candidates in seven out of the eight races. For example, in 1871 the *New York Times* reported, "Victoria C. Woodhull's petition demanding the enfranchisement of women under the provisions of the Fourteenth Amendment, was a fortunate and propitious idea" ("The Women in Council" 1871). In 1972 Chisholm was reported to have said that she "saw nothing wrong with drafting women for military service" (Fraser 1972b). More recent references by women to issues traditionally associated with women included those in an article from the *Washington Post* in 1999 noting that Elizabeth Dole was frustrated with the media for focusing on other issues while ignoring "critical issues such as domestic violence, child care, sexual harassment, and women's health" (Neal 1999). Overall about 16 percent of the first four issues concerned such topics in coverage of women candidates. That is four times the rate such issues were mentioned in relation to men (4 percent). In only two races did men mention traditional women's issues with any frequency. That was in 1872 and 1884, when women's suffrage was a significant topic of debate in the political landscape.

The press's proclivity to skip issues in its coverage of women candidates is troublesome and may originate in the belief that women are not serious contenders and therefore their stances on issues are not important. More worrisome is the self-fulfilling nature of this pattern. If issues are less frequently covered in the press about women candidates, the candidates may appear as less serious to the electorate.

Biographical Information

Whereas traditional models of democratic decision making have always emphasized issues, more contemporary political models have begun to emphasize the candidates' character as an important part of the package on which voters cast their ballot. Glass (1985) has argued that basing one's choice for leader on the candidate's character may be rational, since issues change but a leader's personality and disposition will probably remain constant.

I counted biographical information as represented by the total number of discrete pieces of information about a candidate's experiences, character, or personality and also by whether or not each paragraph was primarily about a candidate's biography. For example, the following paragraph about Gephardt was classified as predominantly about his character: "He was suited to this task, some of his colleagues recalled, because of his amiability, his unfailing courtesy and his self-effacing style. Nearly everybody interviewed about Gephardt referred to his extraordinary ability to listen" (Lambrecht 1987a). In addition, this passage was coded as containing four character traits: amiability, courtesy, self-effacing, ability to listen. Similarly, a paragraph about Pat Schroeder was coded as being predominantly about her biography: "She noted that she already had a 'wonderful platform in the House.' After winning her seat in an upset in 1972, Schroeder has been re-elected six times. She also is the dean of the congressional delegation from Colorado and is the senior Democratic woman in Congress" (Freivogel 1987). In addition, this paragraph was coded as having four pieces of biographical information: won seat in an upset, reelected six times, dean of congressional delegation, senior Democratic woman in House. When I looked at the number of discrete pieces of information about a candidate's character, personality, or experience, I found that the women candidates tended to have more information printed about them than did the men.

Women in general were more likely to have their characters (including personality and experience) described. On average, women received character mentions about 37 times for every 10,000 words, whereas men received such mentions 28 times per 10,000 words (about 24 percent less frequently). The women and men who ran in the twentieth century generally had more character references than those of the nineteenth century, but otherwise there was not a clear pattern over time.

The women generally also had more paragraphs classified as predominantly about their characters than did the equivalent men. On average 16 percent of the paragraphs about the women were predominantly about their personalities or characters. Men's characters were the predominant topic of a paragraph about half as often (8 percent).

Woodhull's percentage was unusually high (45 percent), mainly because so much of her coverage focused on her home-life scandals. Interestingly,

Lockwood's 1884 race was the next highest. Character paragraphs made up 22 percent of the paragraphs about her. The percentage of character paragraphs for women candidates was notably stable for most of the twentieth century. From 1964 through 1988 it hovered at about 8 percent, and then in 2000 and 2004 it rose slightly (15 percent and 12 percent, respectively).

Even though knowing about a candidate's experience and personality may help in making voting decisions, and although women were more likely to have this information included in press accounts, these descriptions were not always exclusively flattering. For example, the *New York Times* wrote about Elizabeth Dole, "Ever professional and widely admired for what one friend calls her 'superhuman discipline,' she prepares so thoroughly for appearances that she even requires aids to count the steps she must take to the podium. Though roughly as fragile as Margaret Thatcher, she is also famously thin-skinned, and has been known to burst into tears over unflattering press" (Henneberger 1999). A similar combination of positive and negative characterizations was found in this description of Carol Moseley Braun: "Carol the Ideal is the politician with charisma, a megawatt smile and an articulate seriousness of purpose that made her the vessel for so many hopes when she became the first black woman elected to the U.S. Senate in 1992. Carol the Real has been different, a politician clouded by bad judgment, inattentiveness to detail and lack of follow-through that has left a trail of disillusioned aids and supporters" (Mihalopoulos 2003).

In contrast, this description of Pat Schroeder had a decidedly negative spin: "There's a sense that the candor and humor and down-home style that Pat has that is so terrific and attractive speaking from the House floor isn't the best way to speak as a potential candidate. Mrs. Schroeder has a tendency to call programs she does not like as 'icky,' sign her congressional mail with smiley faces and punctuate thoughts with eye-rolling exclamations like 'golly' and 'doggonit' and 'yippy-skippy'—not the perfect candidate that women hoped for, in the view of some" (Dowd 1987). Thus, the mere presence of information about the candidate does not mean he or she is advantaged, though it does suggest that the press is providing information for the electorate and not filling the articles about women solely with information about their poll standing and movements.

One reason that the press may emphasize the personalities of the women more than those of the men is that women who have run for president tend to be unusually impressive in their accomplishments and have tended to engage in work that was not stereotypical of women. For example, Woodhull was a stockbroker and newspaper owner; Lockwood was an attorney; Chisholm was a representative; and Chase Smith a career politician. The biographical information about these women, most of whom operated successfully in the traditionally male world of politics, was likely to appeal to the reporters sense of novelty and as a result may have garnered more column inches.

Quotations

Quotations are one vehicle by which the press can give voters direct information about candidates. Although quotations are selected and framed by reporters, candidates are eager to get direct access to citizens, and being quoted is one way of accomplishing this. On average, women were about as likely as the men to be quoted at least once in an article. Women were quoted in 48 percent of articles, whereas men were quoted in 44 percent. In looking at the specific races, women were quoted in more articles than men in four of the races and men more than women in three (in one the numbers were even).

When the women were quoted, however, they tended to have slightly longer quotations written about them. When I calculated the number of words quoted in all of the articles and divided that by the number of words in articles that mentioned the candidate, the women edged out the men by about 14 percent. On average, the women had 1,177 words quoted per 10,000 words written whereas the men had 1,029.

There has been an interesting decline in the length of the quotations from the nineteenth to the twenty-first century. The average length of quotations per 10,000 words for the two races in the 1800s was 2,247 words. For the four races in the 1900s the average was 845 words, and for the two races in the 2000s it was 476 words. This pattern is consistent with trends in broadcast media that indicate the length of candidate sound bites has been decreasing over time. For example, studies have shown that over a twenty-year period candidates became increasingly silent on the network evening news, with the length of candidate sound bites dwindling from an average of 43 seconds in 1968 to fewer than 9 seconds in 1988 (Hallin 1990).

Of the three substantive measures of quality news coverage discussed (issues, character depictions, and quotations), character depictions were more likely to appear in coverage of women, but issues were more likely to enter into coverage of men. The pattern and significance of the difference was less clear in regard to quotations though quotations of women appear to be longer.

Nonsubstantive Coverage

Chaff

When reporters conveyed information that was neither biographical or issue related, I coded it as chaff. Any information that would not help voters in making an informed decision received this code. Coded in this category was all coverage of the horse-race aspects of the campaign, statements about viability, and descriptions of campaign strategy, as well as mentions of the candidate's movements and how well the candidate was doing raising money. For example, this paragraph about Nelson Rockefeller was coded as chaff: "Rockefeller will be in Nashua, N.H. on Thursday. He will visit Concord on Friday, when the first official Rockefeller-for-president headquarters will be opened" ("Rocky to Jump" 1963). Similarly, this paragraph about Senator Smith was coded as chaff: "There was no inkling of how much support Mrs. Smith may have garnered in her trial run, since most of those with whom she talked appeared to give the impression that they had not made up their minds about a presidential choice" (Arnold 1964b).

According to my calculations, the percentage of paragraphs that focused on chaff was equivalent for both men and women. The women had more of such coverage on average but by a very slight margin (68 percent to 66 percent). The rate of chaff coverage of the women held fairly stable between 1964 and 2004, staying between 71 percent and 84 percent, whereas the men's varied more widely, between 42 percent and 82 percent. Thus it appears that men and women have about the same amount of chaff printed, but women have more biographical coverage whereas men have more issue coverage.

Viability

When I looked at the explicit expressions of positive viability, I found the campaigns of the women candidates were less likely to be described as viable than were those of the men. Assessments of positive viability would include, for example, this comment about Jackson: "The people up there [New Hampshire] . . . they tell us we have a shot at winning" (Apple 1971). Similarly, the *Bangor Daily News* printed this paragraph about Chase Smith: "Other Maine GOP leaders said Senator Smith's chances in a three-way battle in new Hampshire would probably be 'pretty good' because her candidacy would be a 'way out' for many not desiring to vote for either Goldwater or Rockefeller" (Arnold 1964a); I also coded this as a positive viability assessment. Examples of negative viability assessments included this comment from a *New York Times* editorial about Shirley Chisholm:

"The presidential candidacy of Representative Shirley Chisholm, the second-term Congresswoman from Brooklyn, is not a venture in practical politics. She candidly recognizes that she is not going to win" ("Symbolic Candidacy" 1972). A comment from the *Philadelphia Press* about James Black was also a negative assessment of viability: "Mr. Black will not poll a thousand votes in any one state" ("A New Party" 1872).

On average the men had about three times as many positive viability comments as the women (3.3 mentions compared with .9 per 10,000 words). The woman who was most frequently described as a viable candidate was Chase Smith (the 1964 campaign). This is notable because of all the women who have run she had the credentials that were the most similar to those of the men who have run and won. Unlike any other candidate I studied, Chase Smith had sat in both the House and the Senate. Despite her prominence among women, her rate of positive viability mentions still lagged behind those of most of the men. Of the eight men in this study, all but Ron Paul, a Libertarian, were described as viable at a greater rate than Chase Smith, including her opponent, Nelson Rockefeller; though he garnered about the same number of votes as she, Rockefeller had over three times the rate of positive viability mentions in the press.

Pat Schroeder's 1987 campaign was the second most likely to be characterized as viable on a per word basis. Although her political experience as a multiyear member of the House of Representatives does not fit the profile of recent candidates who have won the presidency, it does match the profile of many men who have run. Thus, she may have looked like a more prototypical (male) candidate than the other women. Still her opponent, Richard Gephardt, also a multiyear member of the House who polled at the same rate as Schroeder, was still 60 percent more likely to be portrayed as having a viable campaign. The 2004 campaign is also an instructive example. Although both Graham and Moseley Braun polled at about the same rate and both had experience as senators, Graham's campaign was about five times more likely to be portrayed as having positive viability than was Moseley Braun's. There is no evidence of women candidates being increasingly likely to be portrayed as viable over time.

Public opinion data do show that people believe women have a harder time getting elected than do men (even though there is no empirical information to support this position). One might expect to learn that such beliefs on the part of reporters affect the news content of their stories and result in portrayals of women as less viable than comparable men. As noted earlier, the problem with such a pattern is that these portrayals may perpetuate the myth of women's lesser viability. Moreover, women and girls may find that such beliefs diminish their own political aspirations.

The pattern for negative viability mentions is slightly less apparent. In looking simply at the number of negative mentions per 10,000 words, I did not find a clear pattern, but in looking at articles predominantly about one and not the other candidate, I discovered that women had 11 negative viability mentions per 10,000 words written about them. Men had just 7 per 10,000 words. Women had more negative viability mentions in all but two of the races.

In 1872 and 1884 men had higher rates of negative assessments about their viability printed than did the women. This is probably because the candidates from the nineteenth century were widely assumed to have no chance of winning, and reporters were likely to have figured it was too obvious to comment on their dim prospects.

Aside from Lenora Fulani, about whom very little was written, the candidate with the most frequent rate of negative assessments of viability was Margaret Chase Smith, a Republican. She had 23 such mentions for every 10,000 words written about her. This is notable because she was the most qualified of the women to run in that her credentials were the most similar to those of men who have won. Despite that, Lorin Arnold wrote, "Inside information from 'the Hill' in Washington, is that even if Maine's senior Senator, Mrs. Margaret C. Smith, does bid for the Republican nomination, 'not too many on the legislative scene will take her candidacy seriously'" (Arnold 1964d). Later he wrote, "She probably does not really expect to win" (Arnold 1964c). Another story that headlined "Rhode Island Governor Discounts Sen. Smith" noted that the governor of Rhode Island thought little of Chase Smith's campaign. "Chaffee indicated he doesn't regard Mrs. Smith as a serious candidate" ("Rhode Island Governor" 1964). Chase Smith was also the woman with the greatest number of positive viability mentions; her chances of winning were clearly an important part of the campaign debate.

The race in which the disparity was the greatest was that of 1987, when Pat Schroeder and Richard Gephardt ran. The disparity was the least in 2000, when Elizabeth Dole and Steve Forbes ran. Dole's negative assessments of viability were just 3 percent more numerous than those of Forbes. However, there was no trend toward decreasing mentions in recent years. In 2004 the negative assessments of the viability of Carol Moseley Braun were 120 percent more numerous than those of Bob Graham.

Campaign Resources

When I examined the financial assessments of the candidates I found no strong and consistent gender-based pattern. An example of an assessment of positive financial resources would be "Representative Pat Schroeder brought her undecided quest for the Democratic presidential nomination to the National Organization for Women convention here today and walked away with enough money to qualify for Federal matching funds, NOW officials said" (Brozan 1987). Similarly, when the *St. Louis Post-Dispatch* noted that "Gephardt surpassed his goal for the second quarter of this year by raising $1.1 million for his presidential campaign" (Lambrecht 1987b), I counted it too as an assessment of positive financial resources. However, when the *Washington Post* described Dole's campaign as "underfunded" and suggested that the "lack of money could cripple her efforts" (Von Drehle and Balz 1999), I coded the passage as a negative assessment of financial resources, as was a phrase from Jackson's campaign that said, "He acknowledged that money now may be a serious problem" (Larsen 1972).

There was no clear gender bias in the reporting of either positive or negative financial resources. In five of the eight races the men were described as having good financial resources in more articles than were the women, and in three of the races the reverse was true, with women having more articles that mentioned positive financial resources. With respect to negative mentions of financial resources, in five of the eight races there were more articles that made such references to women.

Supporters' Gender

On April 12, 1870, a newspaper printed the first-ever editorial about a woman who was running for president. In the course of that piece the editor noted that the only thing standing in the way of Woodhull was "the sixteenth amendment, giving to women all over the land the elective franchise" ("The Coming Woman"). The editor continued by observing, "Women always take the part of each other, and if the women can be allowed to vote, Mrs. Woodhull may rely on rolling up the heaviest majority ever polled in this or any other nation." This column said explicitly what appears implicitly in coverage throughout the decades that followed: women represent women. This example from Woodhull's coverage is not isolated. There were many other times when the papers implied that Woodhull was a woman's candidate. Another article described her as "a candidate for the presidency in 1872, should Congress legalize female suffrage" ("Enfranchisement of Women" 1871). In fact, Woodhull never made her campaign conditional on women's votes, but the papers still saw her candidacy only in terms of the women who would or would not vote for her. The *New York Sun* in one headline pronounced, "Strong Endorsements of Woodhull by the

Strong-minded Women" ("A Woman For" 1871), and the *Philadelphia Press* described her campaign tour as the "intended visit of Mrs. Woodhull to lecture the women of that city on the blessing of free love" ("A Warning" 1872), even though both men and women regularly turned out for her lectures. Collectively these comments and similar ones helped give the impression that Woodhull represented women more so than the general public, and this may have contributed to the portrayal of her as less viable.

Lockwood was framed in much the same way. The papers often gave the impression that all of Lockwood's supporters were women. In announcing her nomination, the *Washington Evening Star* headlined, "A Woman's Candidate for President," and referred to her party as the "Woman's National Equal Rights Party" (1884), instead of its correct name, which did not include the word "Woman." Similarly, an article in the *Boston Globe* reported that some women were upset because "only a handful of the ladies nominated Belva" ("Belva in Peril" 1884). In this case again, the text promoted the idea that Lockwood had been nominated only by women when, in fact, the Equal Rights Party included both men and women. The *Globe* also noted that a meeting was attended by "about 50 persons, chiefly ladies" ("Mrs. Lockwood's Party" 1884).

In "For Belva and Reform" (1884) the assumption that Lockwood's supporters were women was explicitly rebutted by the candidate herself. A reporter asked Lockwood, "Do the women who nominated you expect to appear at the polls and insist upon voting?" Lockwood challenged the premise by saying "you must remember . . . that this nomination . . . [came from] the equal rights party, a party representing men as well as women." Later, again in response to the continued framing of her supporters as women, Lockwood was compelled to set the record straight. In a letter to the editor she wrote that "fearing that some misunderstanding may arise," she wished to point out that "'The national Equal Rights Party' [is] a party composed of men and women" (Lockwood 1884).

A similar pattern was found in the coverage of Chase Smith. Articles regularly repeated the notion that Chase Smith would have the support of women, presumably because she was a woman. For example, in a commentary in the *Bangor Daily News,* Lorin Arnold wrote, "She is idolized and respected by thousands of women" and has "vote-pulling power among women of the nation" (1963). Arnold expressed a similar sentiment in a commentary on February 1, 1964, writing that Chase Smith "could no longer disappoint or let down the thousands of women in the country who for years have urged that she run for the presidency" (1964c). An article appearing soon after suggested, "She is admired by women everywhere . . . [and] Mrs. Smith would attract woman voters from both parties" ("Sen.

Smith Gets Boost" 1963). Ted Lewis, in his column, predicted, "She would pack an appeal for the feminine vote" (1964). Such observations may have been true. Women probably did respect Chase Smith, and many did vote for her, but Chase Smith was also respected by and received the votes of thousands of men. Although Rockefeller was presumably also supported by men, this was not reported. It is easy to imagine that he might appear to be a candidate of all people, whereas Chase Smith was portrayed as a candidate of an "interest group."

Unlike Lockwood, who consistently resisted the frame of running as a candidate for women, Chase Smith on at least one occasion contributed to the perception. For example, she called her showing in the Illinois primary "a victory for every woman in the United States" ("Sen. Smith Gratified" 1964). Such comments perpetuated the misperception that women cared not about Chase Smith's stands on the issues but only about her sex. On the other hand, she also pointed out that she was "a Republican" and didn't "want support from women in either party just because she is a woman" ("Sen. Smith Finally" 1964).

As this pattern would predict, Chisholm was described as "a catalyst for all . . . women" (Robertson 1972). The same article described George McGovern, John Lindsay, and Eugene McCarthy as complaining that Chisholm is "splitting away the votes of women" and that "her hidden strength is the white liberal women all over the country who are organizing like crazy." "Her main strength . . ," the *New York Times* declared, "is among the black masses, women, some Spanish-speaking groups and students" (Fraser 1972a). Even more explicitly, one reporter wrote, "Many blacks and women are supporting her because of her race and sex" (Delaney 1972). The audience of one of her addresses was described as comprised of mostly "black women" (Lynn 1972).

Like the earlier candidates, Chisholm resisted the notion that there was a monolithic woman's vote driven by the gender of candidates. In one article she said, "I don't harbor the illusion that I will get the support of all women, blacks and young people" ("What Makes Shirley Run?" 1972). In announcing her candidacy for president, she said, "I am not the candidate for the women's movement of this country, although I am a woman" (O'Neill 1972). On the other hand, she also said in the same article that she wanted to "represent all the minority forces in America; including blacks, women, the young and the Spanish speaking."

Schroeder's press coverage also implied that women would provide her main support. Ellen Goodman reported in her column that "Schroeder begins with support and name recognition among women activists" (1987).

Another writer noted that Schroeder's "audiences throughout the day were composed predominantly—and sometimes exclusively—of women" (Blake 1987). Still another described her campaign as having "already excited a lot of women" ("Voters Focus" 1987). The *New York Times* noted, "Three-quarters of the backers of Representative Pat Schroeder of Colorado were women" (Apple 1987). The *Times* also explicitly described Schroeder as a "woman's candidate" (Dowd 1987), and in explaining why she might not do too well Tom Wicker noted that "a lot of Democratic women already are committed to other candidates" (1987).

Like the candidates before her, Schroeder seemed aware of the problem of being framed as a woman's candidate. In one interview she noted that some "still saw her as 'the woman's candidate for president'" (Weaver 1987). If Schroeder had a further comment to counter that framing, it was not printed.

Many references about Dole also made it look as though women were her main constituency. These comments may have subtly conveyed the idea that she did not represent men. For example, the *Washington Post* wrote, "There may be a lot of women who would react positively to Dole but may not react so positively when they learn she is 'pro-life'" (Mann 1999). Such comments leave one wondering if men would react the same way. Similarly, when Dole's pollster was interviewed by the *Post,* she described Dole's campaign as "an historic opportunity to draw women into the party" (Broder 1999). Another reporter quoted a GOP pollster who asked Dole, "The question is can you make it through the primaries without alienating those swing female voters who may be looking for a reason to vote for you?" (Connolly 1999). Later in the same article the reporter wrote that at a campaign event "women of all ages trilled over the prospect of a President Dole." Another article noted, "She has begun to build a financial base by tapping into support from women around the country" (Berke 1999). Despite this claim the article said that less than half of her contributions actually came from women. The irony of this is that even though women made up a minority of her financial supporters, the paragraph still framed women as her main backers.

The coverage of Moseley Braun's 2004 campaign contained similar comments that explicitly mentioned the gender of her supporters. She too was portrayed as appealing especially to women voters. For example, the *Chicago Tribune* mentioned that "Moseley-Braun could energize women and black voters" (Zeleny 2003a), and the *New York Times* noted that "scores of women in the crowd stood as she stepped forward" (Wilgoren 2004). However, Moseley Braun may have contributed to this perception herself. She was reported to have said she was "target[ing] her campaign toward women voters" (Zeleny 2003b).

There were occasions in which the gender of the supporters or audience members was mentioned for the men candidates, although these were much less frequent than in the case of the women candidates. During Butler's 1884 campaign, for example, it was said he was about to address a room "filled with men and women" ("Butler's Many Troubles" 1884). Rockefeller's campaign included an incident when "soon women, many with babies, and men thronged about to shake hands" (Phelps 1964). In these examples, although there is explicit mention of the gender of the supporters in the case of the men, both men and women are portrayed as supporting the candidate.

To test whether the gender of the supporters of women was mentioned more often than that of the supporters of men, I counted every article in which the gender of supporters or audience members was mentioned for either candidate. I found in every case that the women were more likely to have the gender of their supporters noted than was the case for the most equivalent man in the same race. In Lenora Fulani's and Ron Paul's 1988 race the gender of the candidates' supporters was never mentioned for either candidate.

Not only was the gender of supporters of the women candidates more likely to be mentioned, but also there was no apparent trend indicating that such mentions diminished in number over time, nor did the disparity between the men and the women appear to be ebbing. Elizabeth Dole, who ran in 2000, had the greatest number of articles that mentioned the gender of her supporters. It was noted in one in every three articles. Excluding Dole (and Fulani), the rate of mentions was fairly stable, ranging from 14 percent to 19 percent of articles. On average the gender of the supporter was mentioned in about 16 percent of the articles. For men it was much less frequent—once in every hundred articles on average, but not once in any of the last four races.

This finding is not limited to women who run for president. Jamieson (1995) reported, for example, that when Feinstein ran for governor of California in 1992 the *Washington Post* noted that "polls show Feinstein with equal support among men and women" (167). However, the article never mentioned whether equal numbers of women supported the man she opposed. Similarly, the *San Francisco Chronicle* reported that "it was a big night for Bay Area women as Barbara Boxer and Dianne Feinstein claimed historic victories" (167). The fact that men had also voted for them and women had also voted for their opponents went unmentioned.

The penchant of the press to mention the gender of the supporters for women candidates may result in framing the women as special-interest candidates and therefore not effective representatives of the entire electorate. This is also another way to make the gender of the candidate salient. More important, it simply provides irrelevant information that does not shed light on the candidate's character or stance on issues.

Conclusion

Newspapers seem to neglect supplying issue-based content for women candidates. Women get less issue coverage than the equivalent men running in the same race. At the same time they are less likely than similar male candidates to be described as having a campaign that is likely to succeed. Finally, they are more likely to be portrayed as representing a special interest (women) than as being a candidate for all.

On the other hand, female candidates are slightly more likely to have biographical information printed, and their quotations are a little longer. It appears that the extra issue coverage garnered by men is mostly converted to character coverage for the women.

To explain the greater amount of biographical coverage of women, we may have to go no further than traditional news norms. What made many of the women in this study unique was who they were and what they had accomplished. All of them gained a certain amount of fame by being women who lived and worked in the traditionally male sphere of politics. It is precisely for these reasons that their stories were novel.

However, it is not clear that this novelty would account for the longer quotations for women. It may be that the women who reach such high degrees of success tend to be more articulate than "equivalent" men and what they say is more likely to be perceived as quotable by reporters. Alternatively, reporters could have lower expectations for women; they may be surprised at the quality of what women say and therefore quote them more. This has been referred to in other contexts as the talking platypus phenomenon. The phrase was originally used in a study by Abramson, Goldberg, Greenberg, and Abramson (1977) that found that when the same biography (of an attorney) was attributed to both a man and a woman, the woman was perceived as having greater competence. The four researchers hypothesized that if people were sensitive to the struggle of women in male-dominated fields, when they confronted a woman who was successful they would conclude that the woman must be extremely competent. These experimenters called this the talking platypus phenomenon: if one did see a platypus talk, the phenomenon would be impressive no matter what was said.

The question remains, Why do reporters provide less issue coverage for women candidates? It is possible that the perceived novelty of the personalities of women in politics may have inspired more character coverage and deterred issue coverage. Perhaps reporters were never convinced that the women were "real" candidates requiring issue coverage, but instead viewed any newsworthiness as stemming from the candidates' gender. A candidate who appears less viable but is nonetheless unique may get press, but the reporters writing those stories may regard issues as of secondary interest. These results indicate that women who run for office may want to make a special effort to get their issues into the news.

One reason reporters may feel it is more relevant to mention the gender of the supporters of women candidates is that the idea of gender is primed when women are covered. Social scientists have begun to conceptualize knowledge as being organized by cognitive schemata. According to this approach, associated concepts are linked together. When one component of a linked concept is activated, related ideas are more easily accessed. Thus, if a reporter is sent to cover women candidates qua women, it is likely that the concept of gender will be primed as the reporter approaches the story, making an analysis of gender more likely than if the reporter were covering a man.

In the end, several factors may combine to make women candidates seem less likely to succeed. They may receive less issue coverage; they may garner fewer assessments of positive viability; and they may be portrayed as appealing only to a limited and special constituency. In that context the comparisons used in this study are especially stringent. These women performed as well as the comparable men in the same race despite receiving less favorable coverage. Had women received the same kind of coverage as the men, they may have done better than the men used for comparisons in this study.

Less issue coverage may make women look less serious; poor assessments of viability could reduce support for them; and greater coverage of their character could highlight their novelty or rarity in the political sphere. All of that could make women less likely to win; more important, it may make women less likely to run. My findings on viability may be particularly important in this regard. Women will be less likely to put themselves forward as candidates if all of their role models are described as not serious, as representing a special interest, and as not having a chance of winning. In more subtle ways, less issue coverage and more personal coverage could reinforce this view.

References

Abramson, P. R., P. A. Goldberg, J. H. Greenberg, and L. M. Abramson. 1977. "The Talking Platypus Phenomenon: Competence Ratings as a Function of Sex and Professional Status." *Psychology of Women Quarterly* 2: 114–24.

Apple, R. W. 1971. "Jackson and Yorty to Run in New Hampshire Contest." *New York Times,* November 5, 26.

———. 1987. "In Democratic Field, No One Is Nearing the Winner's Circle." *New York Times,* August 23, 4.

Arnold, L. 1963. "Maine's Political Whirl: Vote Boost for Republicans Seen Behind V-P Move by Mrs. Smith." *Bangor Daily News,* November 16, 10.

———. 1964a. "Can She Win in N.H.? Sen. Smith's Chances: Maine GOP Sees 'Ifs.'" *Bangor Daily News,* January 28, 1.

———. 1964b. "Low-Key Campaign: Senator Starts Drive in N.H." *Bangor Daily News,* February 11, 1.

———. 1964c. "Maine's Political Whirl: Recalls Mrs. Smith's State House Visits When Husband in Politics." *Bangor Daily News,* February 1, 14.

———. 1964d. "Yarmouth Senator Rockefeller's Choice to Head Maine Committee." *Bangor Daily News,* January 4, 10.

"Belva in Peril: Feminine Opposition to Her Takes Shape at Buffalo in the Guise of a Suffrage Convention." 1884. *Boston Globe,* October 5, 3.

Berke, R. L. 1999. "Running toward 2000: Dole Fights to Recapture Her Early Star Status." *New York Times,* August 10, A1.

Blake, P. 1987. "Schroeder Offers Trade Plan in Iowa Visit." *Rocky Mountain News,* July 3, 10.

Broder, D. S. 1999. "Dole to Take First Campaign Step: Announcement of Exploratory Panel Will Be Made in Iowa." *Washington Post,* March 5, A20.

Brozan, N. 1987. "Schroeder Can Qualify for U.S. Funds after Donations at NOW Convention." *New York Times,* July 19, 22.

"Butler's Many Troubles: He Has to Abandon His Palace Car and Get Out of the Way of Freight Trains." 1884. *New York Times,* October 1, 1.

"The Coming Woman." 1870. *New York Herald,* April 2, 6.

Connolly, C. 1999. "The Dole Mystique: Strategy Aims to Capitalize, but Not Rely, on Gender." *Washington Post,* April 11, A1.

Delaney, P. 1972. "Chisholm Appeal Divides Blacks; Imperils Liberals in Florida Race." *New York Times,* March 14, 30.

Dowd, M. 1987. "Schroeder: At Ease with Femininity and Issues." *New York Times,* August 23, A24.

"Enfranchisement of Women: A Delegation of Fair Ones Before the House Judiciary Committee: Grand Display of Ancient and Tender Loveliness—A Female Candidate for the Presidency Expounding the Constitution—The Committee Captures—Woman's Suffrage Convention—The Movement Making Headway in Washington." 1871. *New York Herald,* January 12, 3.

"For Belva and Reform: How the Equal Rights Canvass is Progressing: Letters Received by the Candidate, etc." 1884. *Washington Evening Star,* September 17, 1.

Fraser, C. G. 1972a. "Mrs. Chisholm Completes 3-day Campaign in Florida." *New York Times,* February 28, 26.

——. 1972b. "Mrs. Chisholm Starts Campaign in State." *New York Times,* March 30, 32.

Freivogel, M. W. 1987. "Schroeder Cancels Debate Appearance." *St. Louis Post-Dispatch,* September 24, A8.

Glass, D. P. 1985. "Evaluating Presidential Candidates: Who Focuses on Their Personal Attributes?" *Public Opinion Quarterly* 49 (4): 517–34.

Glover, M. 1999. "Elizabeth Dole Steps toward 2000 Race to 'Rekindle Spirit.'" *Newark Star-Ledger,* March 11, 3.

Goodman, E. 1987. "Schroeder Could Close Campaign's Pizazz Gap." *Rocky Mountain News,* June 13, 55.

Graber, D. A. 1971. "The Press as Opinion Resource during the 1968 Presidential Campaigns." *Public Opinion Quarterly* 35 (2): 168–82.

——. 1976. "Press and TV as Opinion Resources in Presidential Campaigns." *Public Opinion Quarterly* 40 (3): 285–303.

Hallin, D. 1990. *Sound Bite News: Television Coverage of Elections 1968–1988.* Woodrow Wilson International Center for Scholars.

Henneberger, M. 1999. "Tough and Self-controlled, Dole Gets Ready to Be '00 Contender." *New York Times,* March 10, A1.

Jamieson, K. H. 1995. *Beyond the Double Bind: Women and Leadership.* New York: Oxford University Press.

Johnson, T. 1999. "Forbes Hits All the Notes of a Candidate." *Newark Star-Ledger,* March 9, 31.

Kahn, K. F. 1992. "Does Being Male Help? An Investigation of the Effects of Candidate Gender and Campaign Coverage on Evaluations of U.S. Senate Candidates." *Journal of Politics* 54:497–517.

——. 1994. "The Distorted Mirror: Press Coverage of Women Candidates for Statewide Office." *Journal of Politics* 56 (1): 154–73.

——. 1996. *The Political Consequences of Being a Woman: How Stereotypes Influence the Conduct and Consequences of Political Campaigns.* New York: Columbia University Press.

Kahn, K. F., and E. N. Goldenberg. 1991. "Women Candidates in the News: An Examination of Gender Differences in U.S. Senate Campaign Coverage." *Public Opinion Quarterly* 55:180–99.

King, E. 1990. "Thematic Coverage of the 1988 Presidential Primaries: A Comparison of *USA Today* and the *New York Times.*" *Journalism Quarterly* 67 (1): 83–87.

Lambrecht, B. 1987a. "Focus on Gephardt: Candidate Takes Center Stage after Just 10 Years in Congress." *St. Louis Post-Dispatch,* June 8, B1.

——. 1987b. "Gephardt Tops $1 Million Goal for Quarter." *St. Louis Post-Dispatch,* July 2, A16.

Larsen, R. W. 1972. "Sen. Jackson Counts His Money, Heads for Ohio." *Seattle Times,* April 5, B1.

Lewis, T. 1964. "Capitol Stuff." *New York Daily News,* January 18, 4.

Lockwood, B. 1884. "A Card from Mrs. Lockwood: She Explains the Status of Her Party." *Washington Evening Star,* September 20, 1.

Lynn, F. 1972. "New Hat in Ring: Mrs. Chisholm's." *New York Times,* January 26, 1.

Mann, J. 1999. "For Elizabeth Dole: Time Will Tell." *Washington Post,* January 8, E3.

Mihalopoulos, D. 2003. "Crusading for a Second Chance the Former U.S. Senator Strives to Revitalize Her Tarnished Political Image. But Her Campaign Has Little Money and She Left Behind a Trail of Disillusioned Supporters." *Chicago Tribune,* October 23, 1.

"Mrs. Lockwood's Party: Meets in the State of Maryland to Ratify the Ticket: The Candidate Wants to Know What the Rights of Ladies Are: And Quotes at Length from the Constitution." 1884. *Boston Globe,* September 19, 1.

Neal, T. M. 1999. "Dole Enters the 'Big Tent.'" *Washington Post,* April 10, A5.

Newman, J. 1994. *Perception and Reality: A Study Comparing the Success of Men and Women Candidates.* Washington, D.C.: National Women's Political Caucus.

"A New Party." 1872. *Philadelphia Press,* March 22, 4.

O'Neill, E. 1972. "Shirley Tosses Chapeau in Ring." *New York Daily News,* January 26, 5.

Patterson, T. E. 1991. "More Style Than Substance: Television News in U.S. National Elections." *Political Communication and Persuasion* 8 (Fall): 145–62.

Phelps, R. H. 1964. "Rockefeller Gets Warm Response." *New York Times,* January 25, 9.

"Rhode Island Governor Discounts Sen. Smith." 1964. *Bangor Daily News,* January 30, 6.

Robertson, N. 1972. "Tracking Florida Voters along the Chisholm Trail: The Route Is Uphill, Tough but Very Well Defined." *New York Times,* February 14, 19.

"Rocky to Jump into Ring Today." 1963. *Bangor Daily News,* November 7, 1.

Sapiro, V. 1981. "If U.S. Senator Baker Were a Woman: An Experimental Study of Candidate Images." *Political Psychology* 3:61–83.

Seltzer, R., J. Newman, and M. V. Leighton. 1997. *Sex as a Political Variable: Women as Candidates and Voters in U.S. Elections.* Boulder, Colo.: Lynne Rienner.

"Senator Smith Gratified by Showing." 1964. *Bangor Daily News,* April 16, 1.

"Sen. Smith Finally Gives Word: Yes, She's in Race." 1964. *Bangor Daily News,* January 28, 1.

"Sen. Smith Gets Boost." 1963. *Bangor Daily News,* November 18, 1.

"Symbolic Candidacy." 1972. *New York Times,* January 27, 36.

Von Drehle, D., and D. Balz. 1999. "Dole's Fund-raising Now a Family Affair: '96 GOP Nominee Steps Up Role in Wife's Campaign with Aggressive Money Pitch." *Washington Post,* September 25, A1.

"Voters Focus on Message, Schroeder Says." 1987. *Rocky Mountain News,* August 21, 68.

"A Warning to Mrs. Woodhull." 1872. *Philadelphia Press,* April 4, 8.

Weaver, W. 1987. "Schroeder Assailing the System: Decides Not to Run for President." *New York Times,* September 29, A1.

"What Makes Shirley Run?" 1972. *New York Times,* January 30, D2.

Wicker, T. 1987. "Pat Yes, Gary No." *New York Times,* August 24, A19.

Wilgoren, J. 2004. "The 2004 Campaign: The Former Senator; Braun Ends Campaign and Joins Dean Team." *New York Times,* January 16, A19.

"A Woman for President." 1871. *New York Sun,* August 18, 3.

"A Woman's Candidate for President." 1884. *Washington Evening Star,* September 4, 1.

"The Women in Council: A Hearing by the Judiciary Committee of the House—A Motley Assemblage—Mrs. Woodhull's Petition Advocated—The Convention in Lincoln Hall." 1871. *New York Times,* January 12, 5.

Zeleny, J. 2003a. "Moseley-Braun Gauges Prospects for '04: Ex-senator Meets with Party Chief." *Chicago Tribune,* January 28, 7.

———. 2003b. "Moseley-Braun to Seek White House: Ex-Senator Says She'll Run on a Peace Platform." *Chicago Tribune,* February 13, 12.

Is America Ready?

For as long as women have aspired to the Oval Office, citizens, pollsters, and reporters have argued that America is not ready for a woman president. When the first widely known woman candidate for president, Victoria Woodhull, declared her intention to run in 1870, the newspapers noted, "She is rather in advance of her time. The public mind is not yet educated to the pitch of universal woman's rights" ("Woman's Idea of Government" 1870). Such an attitude may seem uninteresting until one considers that over a hundred years later, similar sentiments still dominated press coverage. During Senator Margaret Chase Smith's run for the White House in 1964, a columnist wrote, "There are a number of influential commentators here who believe that Senator Smith will thank all of her supporters . . . and say it is flattering to be considered for the high office . . . but that she is realistic to know that the country is not quite ready to elect a woman as president" ("Washington Forecast" 1964). Such an attitude cannot be dismissed as a relic from the 1960s. During Elizabeth Dole's 2000 presidential campaign, the same opinion was expressed both by individuals and by pollsters. For example, an audience member at a campaign event said, "My gut is that the country is not ready for a woman president" (qtd., Berke 1999). Poll results have been used to make a similar argument. One observer reported, "While most Republicans say the country is ready to make a woman president, a full third say it is not" (ibid.).

Surveys regularly document that people say they are more likely to vote for men than for women in a presidential race. The amount of bias against women presidential candidates, however, varies from between seven and fifteen percentage points depending on the survey and the wording of the question. Despite the dire predictions of the press and pollsters, there are many reasons to think America is ready to elect a woman president.

Who Supports Women Who Run?

Most contemporary polls about generic women candidates have shown a continuing but decreasing bias against women running for the presidency. The percentage of respondents saying they would not vote for a woman moved from roughly 64 percent of the population in the 1930s to about 10 percent in the 1990s (see Kenski and Falk 2004). Since the nineties it has remained roughly in the 10 percent range, sometimes dropping a little lower and sometimes rising a bit higher. Who comprises this persistent 10 percent of the population who say they would not vote for a woman, and who are the people who consistently support women candidates?

Among the variables that have been shown to predict attitudes about women in office, the sex of the respondent has been the best documented. Most surveys show that women tend to be more favorably disposed toward a woman candidate than are men, for all kinds of offices including the presidency. The finding that women are more likely to favor women—and men to favor men—is not unexpected. Social scientists have long documented the role homophily plays in persuasion and positive opinion formation. Homophily refers to the concept that the more similar you are to people, the more likely you are to persuade them. Thus, women may be more easily persuaded by women candidates and more likely to support them.

The finding that women are more pro-women and men are more pro-men may also stem from the greater awareness generated by the women's rights movement, which has highlighted for many women the lack of female representation in government. In other words, because of the women's movement, women may be more sensitive to the fact that there are very few women in higher office; as a result women may be more inclined to support women who aspire to public service. Moreover, studies have shown that women tend to have less traditional attitudes than men and therefore may be more willing to support women in non-stereotypical roles.

The converse may also help explain the phenomenon. For example, Susan Gluck Mezey (1978), a professor of political science, found that when people were asked what disadvantages women have in holding political office, the women cited bias against them, but men pointed to inadequacies they thought women had, such as being emotional, weak, and interested in trivialities. In a similar vein, two other political scientists, Leonie Huddy and Nayda Terkildsen (1993), found that men rated warmth and expressiveness (qualities typically associated with women) as less crucial for good politicians than did women, and Marjorie Hershey (1977) found men were also more likely than women to say "women who run for political office are probably concerned mainly with women's issues" (271). All of this may contribute to men's lesser support for women candidates.

The level of education of the respondent has also been linked to support for women candidates. Susan Welch and Lee Sigelman (1982) conducted an analysis of several questions about women in government from General Social Surveys of 1972, 1974, and 1978. They found that support for women in office was stronger among the more educated. Similar results have been found by other researchers (e.g., Falk and Kenski 2006a; Huddy 1994). Kate Kenski and I (2004) found that more-educated people were more likely to say gender did not make a difference in presidential preferences than were the less educated.

We also found that younger respondents were more likely to say that gender does not make a difference for a president in the handling of the issue the respondent thought was the most important problem facing the nation. This may be because the younger people are, the more likely it is that they have been brought up in an environment shaped by the second wave of feminism, Title IX, expansion of educational opportunities, and greater familiarity and comfort with women in the work world and political office. All of this would have shaped their experiences to normalize the idea of women in political leadership roles.

Several studies show that non-whites more than whites appear to prefer women in government (Brown 1994; Dolan 1996, 1997; Kenski and Falk 2004). One reason for this may be that non-whites are more sensitive to the barriers faced by women running for political office because they face similar obstacles in achieving representation.

It is also likely that ideology affects attitudes about women and the presidency. My colleague Kenski and I (2004) found that liberals were more likely to say that a woman would do a better job as president in handling the most important problem facing the nation. Others have also found that liberals are more likely to support women for president (e.g., Dolan 1997). One reason for this is that many people believe that women are more liberal than men. Several studies document that especially under low-information voting conditions, voters stereotype women as more liberal (e.g., Koch 2000; McDermott 1997).

Stereotypical beliefs about men and women may affect attitudes about supporting a woman for president. Stereotypes can result in biased attitudes about a potential president's ability to handle issues. The Deloitte and Touche (2000) survey found a greater percentage of the public had more confidence in men's ability to handle the issues they identified as the most important. The survey reported, "On the top rated issue of law and order, a slim plurality of Americans (42%) believes that a man would do a better job as president than a woman . . . [while] only 14% expect that a female president would do a better job. On the economy—the second most important voting consideration . . . 31% believe that a male president would do a better job versus 22% who expect a woman president to perform better on the issue" (5). Men were also favored on foreign policy and balancing the budget (Deloitte and Touche 2000). In a similar study I conducted with Kate Kenski (2004), survey respondents who identified taxes as the most important issue were more inclined to say that a male president would do a better job.

Women, in contrast, were favored on issues judged as less critical. Respondents said "a woman would do a better job than a man would when it comes to social issues such as education, poverty and homelessness" (Deloitte and Touche 2000, 27). The Kenski and Falk (2004) data revealed that respondents who named health care as the most important issue facing the nation were more likely to say that a female president would do a better job than a male president, in contrast to respondents who named some other issue.

War may be a particularly important issue for women as well. My colleague Kate Kenski and I found that 25.3 percent of respondents in December 1999/January 2000 said that a woman president would do a better job in handling the issue believed most important by respondents (Kenski and Falk 2004); however, this figure decreased to 15.4 percent by September 2003 (Falk and Kenski 2006a). During that time, terrorism, homeland security, U.S. involvement in Iraq, and the strength of the economy became major concerns to the U.S. public. This drop in acceptance of a woman as president of the United States demonstrates the way current events and stereotypes interact to create a changing environment for women seeking to achieve high political office. Moreover, our study found that respondents who named terrorism, homeland security, and/or U.S. involvement in Iraq as the most important problem facing the nation were less inclined to believe that a woman president would do a better job, even when controlling for demographic and party identification variables.

The finding that perceptions of the important problems facing the nation influence whether men or women are seen as doing a better job as president has important implications for women running for political office. In times when the salient issues are ones that men are considered more competent to address, women running for the presidency may have to work harder than men. However, when issues stereotypically associated with women's competence dominate the political agenda, women should have an easier time.

The results of all of these studies suggest that a woman will have more support among younger, more-educated, liberal women in periods when issues stereotypically associated with women drive the campaign, and she will find her support toughest to garner among older, less-educated, conservative men during periods of war. However, all of these data and conclusions are based on questions posed to the electorate about a hypothetical, nonspecific, unnamed woman.

The Problem with Polling

Polling on attitudes about a woman president began in 1937. In that year, a Gallup poll asked respondents, "Would you vote for a woman for president if she were qualified in every other respect?" (Gallup 1937). Though exaggerated in format, this question is indicative of the problematic wording that has persisted for seventy years in polling about attitudes toward women and the presidency. The use of the word "other" clearly suggests to the respondent that simply being a woman makes one unqualified for the job. It is tantamount to asking whether people would vote for an unqualified person for president if he or she were qualified. Given that wording, it is not surprising that 64 percent of respondents said that they would not vote for a woman. Pollsters dropped the use of the word "other" after 1939, but the word "qualified" remains in most questions to this day. For example, a 2003 poll asked, "If your party nominated a generally well-qualified person for president who happened to be a woman, would you vote for that person?" (Gallup, CNN, and *USA Today* 2003). A more common phrasing appeared in a 2000 poll: "If your party nominated a woman for president, would you vote for her if she were qualified for the job?" (NBC News and *Wall Street Journal* 2000). Such wording clearly primes questions about a woman's qualifications.

Of course, we never ask if people would vote for a man for president if a qualified one were to be nominated by a major party. It is not at all clear that the answer to this question would be 100 percent in the affirmative. Consequently, it is hard to interpret the significance of the 7 to 10 percent of the population who currently say they would not vote for a woman. In fact, one survey found that "half or more of the public say that their vote would be positively influenced by having a woman on the ticket for the offices of the president, vice president, senator and governor" (Deloitte and Touche 2000, 3). Similar data led Darcy, Welch, and Clark (1994, 90) to conclude that "given the overall success of women who run, it appears that . . . anti-women voters are equaled by those who go out of their way to cast a vote for a woman."

Furthermore, the typically worded hypothetical question that begins "Would you vote for a woman . . ." is likely to tap attitudes that would occur in low- or no-information voting contexts that tend to be subject to mental shortcuts, such as stereotypes (Alexander and Andersen 1993; Conover and Feldman 1982; Rahn 1993). This question is tantamount to asking if you would vote for someone about whom you know nothing except his or her sex. Such a scenario is very different from the one in which people really make voting decisions, weighing comparatively the party, character, and issue positions of a candidate. Survey questions that give no information about the candidate except sex are likely to invoke heuristics (or mental shortcuts), leading people to make assumptions about a candidate's competence as a leader. By contrast, when real women run for office, knowledge about their party affiliation, experience, and issue positions, as well as those of their opponents, is likely to mitigate such attitudes.

Alexander and Andersen (1993) noted that even if extant stereotypes are applied to women who run for higher offices, one should not necessarily assume that the women will be disadvantaged by them, because helpful and unhelpful stereotypes may cancel each other out. In their study of specific real women who ran for office, they found that the different skills, traits, and issue competencies actually advantaged the woman and that "gender beliefs are associated with candidate favorability only for the least familiar candidates" (Alexander and Andersen 1993, 542). McDermott (1998) made a similar observation: "Studies have been extremely useful in establishing that voters view women candidates as different from, but not necessarily better or worse than, men candidates" (899).

Kenski and I put forth further evidence suggesting that female candidates may not necessarily be at a disadvantage. We observed (Kenski and Falk 2004) that when respondents kept in mind the national issue considered most important, the percentage of U.S. adults who contended that a man would do a better job as president was comparable to the percentage of those who said a woman would do a better job. In a survey conducted in 2000, 25.6 percent of respondents contended that a man would do a better job as president in handling the most important problem facing the nation, while 25.3 percent of respondents believed a woman would do a better job. Nearly one-half of respondents (49.1 percent) either said they did not know whether a man or woman would do a better job or said that gender would not make a difference.

There are other problems with the wording of most contemporary poll questions about women and the presidency. Questions that ask about "a woman," but not a specific woman, may downplay the role that individual characteristics and party identification play in informing citizens' political choices. Many researchers have documented the important role that individual qualities play in assessments of candidates (Glass 1985; Keeter 1987; Kinder 1986; Miller, Wattenberg, and Malanchuk 1986).

Party identification is also an important predictor of vote choice that should not be overlooked (Mann and Wolfinger 1980; Miller 1991). Generic questions such as, "Would you vote for a woman . . ." are unlikely to capture the role that partisanship plays in ballot casting. A more effective wording to capture this phenomenon might be to ask, "Would you vote for a member of another party before voting for a woman nominated by your party?" In a real-world head-to-head matchup, voters who are disinclined to vote for a woman must weigh that decision against their disinclination to vote for someone from the other party or for someone who disagrees with them on important policy issues. In fact, the Deloitte and Touche (2000) poll found that when respondents were given no information about a candidate other than gender and party, party held sway over gender.

There is a prevalent assumption that questions about women and the presidency are subject to a sizable social desirability bias (e.g., Clift and Brazaitis 2000; Kennedy 2003). In other words, many researchers think more people *say* they will vote for a woman than will actually do so. However, this may not be the case. As one report mentioned, "Some prejudice expressed to a pollster may not be carried out in actual voting when faced with the choice of a woman of one's own party or a man of the opposition party" (Darcy, Welch, and Clark 1994, 90). Moreover, surveys have shown that attitudes about women presidential candidates do not differ dramatically from attitudes toward women who run for other offices. Deloitte and Touche's poll (2000) showed little or no difference in the proportion of respondents who said that they were "much less likely to vote for a female candidate as U.S. president" (7 percent) compared to those who said they would be less likely to vote for a female for a U.S. senator (5 percent) or governor (5 percent). Studies indicate that when it comes to running for political offices other than the presidency, women are no less likely than men to be elected when incumbency is taken into account (see Burrell 1990; Darcy and Schramm 1977; Ekstrand and Eckert 1981; Gaddie and Bullock 1995; Seltzer, Newman, and Leighton 1997; Welch, Ambrosius, Clark, and Darcy 1985).

Of course, no such data are available for races for the presidency because a woman has never been nominated for U.S. president by a major party. However, as Zipp and Plutzer (1985) noted, Geraldine Ferraro, who received the vice presidential nomination from the Democratic Party, was believed to have given the Democrats a net gain of .80 percent. It is also interesting to note that the percentage of Americans who said in 1994 that they would not vote for a woman was substantially less than the percentage of those who said that they would not vote for a Catholic in 1960 (Darcy et al. 1994). Since voters in a real election did elect a Catholic (Kennedy), this suggests that the small percentage of people who say they will not vote for someone in answer to a hypothetical question does not accurately reflect the outcome of a real race.

Still, some argue that polls using head-to-head matchups between women and men would not be reliable because some respondents may say that they will vote for a woman in order not to appear to be sexist, but they will not vote for a woman when it actually comes to casting a ballot. This line of reasoning has been referred to as the "Bradley effect." It was so named after Tom Bradley (who was black), then mayor of Los Angeles, lost his 1982 bid for California governor after the final polls had him leading by 7 percent. In describing the Bradley effect, one pollster, Larry Hugick, noted that black candidates often do 10 points worse than polls show (Reddy 2003). Thus, the argument contends that a higher percentage of people will say that they will vote for a woman than will actually vote for one. However, I have found no evidence in the literature of this kind of Bradley effect for women candidates.

My colleague Kate Kenski and I conducted a study of attitudes about women and the presidency that was unique in that we asked a set of questions about how people would vote when given presidential candidate pairings of real women politicians against real men candidates (Falk and Kenski 2006b). During the Kerry/Bush race for the presidency in 2004, we set contests such that in each race a man would be running against a woman and a Democrat would be running against a Republican. The women candidates were Senator Hillary Clinton (D), Senator Elizabeth Dole (R), (then) National Security Advisor Condoleezza Rice (R), and Senator Dianne Feinstein (D), and the men were President George W. Bush (R) and Senator John Kerry (D). We hypothesized that Republicans who said they would not vote for "a woman" for president would, in fact, choose a woman candidate when we paired a specific Republican woman with a specific Democratic man. Similarly we anticipated that Democrats who said they would not support a woman would choose a Democratic woman before crossing party lines to vote for a man.

More than a majority of Republicans and Democrats who said they were *unlikely* to support a woman presidential candidate also *picked* a specific woman over a specific man when the woman candidate was from their own party. In other words, most of those who said they would not vote for a woman were more likely to pick a woman than to cross party lines in order to vote for a man when given two real names in a head-to-head matchup. The data indicated that when specific candidates were considered, partisanship mitigated sexism.

Moreover, we found that if Senator Hillary Clinton had been running against President George W. Bush, she would have done almost as well as Senator John Kerry did in May–June 2004. In the hypothetical Bush-Clinton contest, Clinton trailed by just 4.1 percent, considerably less than the 13.9 percent of respondents who initially said that they would not be inclined to vote for "a woman" for president. John Kerry polled only .5 percent less than Bush, but considering Kerry had been campaigning for the position for months at the time the poll was taken whereas Clinton had not, it is striking how well Clinton did. The results of this study suggest that most Americans, including many who say that they are unlikely to vote for "a woman," would do so depending on who is running and what party she represents. Both party identification and the specific candidates play roles in overriding gender stereotypes that affect support for a woman president.

Conclusion

Although the press coverage of women candidates persistently portrays America as "not ready" for a woman president, the polling data are dramatically at odds with that representation. Whereas women are more likely to find support among women, the young, the well educated, and liberals, even conservatives and those who say they would not vote for "a woman" still are likely to do so given real head-to-head matchups between specific women and men candidates. The press coverage that tends to portray women as less likely to win than similar men may mislead voters and potential women candidates, causing them to think that women are significantly disadvantaged in the political sweepstakes when the polling data actually do not support this conclusion.

The notion that a woman could win if she would run may seem surprising given the data from the previous chapters showing that women experience negative press bias. In considering this contradiction, it is helpful to keep in mind that studies of women candidates at lower-level races show, like this study, that the press tends to give less coverage to women and to portray them in stereotypical ways even when the women themselves do not describe themselves with such stereotypes. However, despite the bias and prejudice in the press, numerous studies show that when women run at these lower levels, they win just as often as men do. In other words, even bias in the press cannot prevent women from being elected. One reason for this may be that the select women who do run tend to be more talented and persistent than the men who also put themselves forward. That is to say, women may win despite prejudiced press coverage.

Yet, women's traditional success in the world of politics despite unfair treatment by the press should not lead to complacency about press coverage. If women think the press will portray them as weak and emotional, focus on trivialities such as what women wear instead of their policy positions, or slate them for the vice presidency instead of the presidency, they may be more hesitant to run. Moreover, if the press portrays women as less viable, women may believe that they don't have a fair chance at higher office and therefore may not aspire to such service.

Recall that just 8 percent of the candidates for Congress are women, many of whom run against incumbents and so have little chance of winning. Recall also that in the history of the United States there have been only thirty-five women with the same political and military credentials as the men who have recently won the presidency. These facts taken in conjunction with the statistics from lower-level races—which show that when women run they win just as often as men do—suggest that the real problem is that women don't run for office. Such a lack of political aspiration could only be exacerbated by the way the press covers women who do run.

References

Alexander, D., and K. Andersen. 1993. "Gender as a Factor in the Attribution of Leadership Traits." *Political Research Quarterly* 46 (3): 527–45.

Berke, R. L. 1999. "Running toward 2000: Dole Fights to Recapture Her Early Star Status." *New York Times,* August 10, A1.

Brown, C. 1994. "Judgments about the Capabilities of City Councilors and Support for Female Representation on City Council." *Social Science Journal* 31 (4): 355–73.

Burrell, B. 1990. "The Presence of Women Candidates and Role of Gender in

Campaigns for the State Legislature in an Urban Setting: The Case of Massachusetts." *Women and Politics* 10 (3): 85–102.

Clift, E., and T. Brazaitis. 2000. *Madam President: Shattering the Last Glass Ceiling.* New York: Scribner.

Conover, P. J., and S. Feldman. 1982. "Projection and the Perception of Candidates' Issue Positions." *Western Political Quarterly* 35 (2): 228–44.

Darcy, R., and S. S. Schramm. 1977. "When Women Run against Men." *Public Opinion Quarterly* 41 (1): 1–12.

Darcy, R., S. Welch, and J. Clark. 1994. "Women, Elections, and Representation." In *Different Roles, Different Voices: Women and Politics in the United States and Europe,* ed. M. Githens, P. Norris, and L. Lovenduski, 89–98. New York: HarperCollins.

Deloitte and Touche. 2000. Women in Elected Office. Survey. New York, Deloitte and Touche.

Dolan, K. 1996. "Support for Women Political Candidates: An Examination of the Role of Family." *Women and Politics* 16 (2): 45–46.

———. 1997. "Determinants of Support for Women Congressional Candidates in the 1990s." Paper presented at the meeting of the Midwest Political Science Association, Chicago, April 10–12.

Ekstrand, L. E., and W. A. Eckert. 1981. "The Impact of Candidate's Sex on Voter Choice." *Western Political Quarterly* 34 (1): 78–87.

Falk, E., and K. Kenski. 2006a. "Issue Saliency and Gender Stereotypes: Support for Women as Presidents in Times of War and Terrorism." *Social Science Quarterly* 87 (1): 1–18.

———. 2006b. "Sexism and Partisanship: A New Look at the Question of Whether America Is Ready for a Woman President." *Sex Roles* 54 (7/8): 413–28.

Gaddie, R. K., and C. S. Bullock. 1995. "Congressional Elections and the Year of the Woman: Structural and Elite Influences on Female Candidates." *Social Science Quarterly* 76 (4): 749–62.

Gallup. 1937. "Would You Vote for a Woman for President if She Were Qualified in Every Other Respect?" Question 28. ID# USGALLUP. 37–66. *Roper online.* Available through Lexis-Nexus.

Gallup, CNN, and *USA Today.* 2003. "If Your Party Nominated a Generally Well-qualified Person for President Who Happened to Be a Woman, Would You Vote for That Person?" i-Poll Databank [USGALLUP.03M0030.R06D].

Glass, D. P. 1985. "Evaluating Presidential Candidates: Who Focuses on Their Personal Attributes?" *Public Opinion Quarterly* 49 (4): 517–34.

Hershey, M. R. 1977. "The Politics of Androgyny? Sex Roles and Attitudes toward Women in Politics." *American Politics Quarterly* 5:261–87.

Huddy, L. 1994. "The Political Significance of Voters' Gender Stereotypes." *Research in Micropolitics* 4:169–93.

Huddy, L., and N. Terkildsen. 1993. "The Consequences of Gender Stereotypes for Women Candidates at Different Levels and Types of Office." *Political Research Quarterly* 46 (3): 503–25.

Keeter, S. 1987. "The Illusion of Intimacy: Television and the Role of Candidate Personal Qualities in Voter Choice." *Public Opinion Quarterly* 51 (3): 344–58.

Kennedy, C. 2003. "Is the United States Ready for a Woman President? Is the Pope Protestant?" In *Anticipating Madam President,* ed. R. P. Watson and A. Gordon, 131–43. Boulder, Colo.: Lynne Rienner.

Kenski, K., and E. Falk. 2004. "Of What Is That Glass Ceiling Made? A Study of Attitudes about Women and the Oval Office." *Women and Politics* 26 (2): 57–80.

Kinder, D. R. 1986. "Presidential Character Revisited." In *Political Cognition,* ed. R. R. Lau and D. O. Sears, 233–55. Hillsdale, N.J.: Lawrence Erlbaum.

Koch, J. 2000. "Do Citizens Apply Gender Stereotypes to Infer Candidates' Ideological Orientations?" *Journal of Politics* 62 (2): 414–29.

Mann, T. E., and R. E. Wolfinger. 1980. "Candidates and Parties in Congressional Elections." *American Political Science Review* 74 (3): 617–32.

McDermott, M. L. 1997. "Voting Cues in Low-information Elections: Candidate Gender as a Social Information Variable in Contemporary United States Elections." *American Journal of Political Science* 41 (1): 270–83.

———. 1998. "Race and Gender Cues in Low-information Elections." *Political Research Quarterly* 51 (4): 895–918.

Mezey, Susan Gluck. 1978. "Does Sex Make a Difference? A Case Study of Women in Politics." *Western Political Quarterly* 31 (4): 493–501.

Miller, A. H., M. P. Wattenberg, and O. Malanchuk. 1986. "Schematic Assessments of Presidential Candidates." *American Political Science Review* 80 (2): 521–40.

Miller, W. E. 1991. "Party Identification, Realignment, and Party Voting: Back to Basics." *American Political Science Review* 85 (2): 557–68.

NBC News and *Wall Street Journal.* 2000. "If Your Party Nominated a Woman for President, Would You Vote for Her if She Were Qualified for the Job?" i-Poll databank [USNBCWSJ.00JUNE.R09C].

Rahn, W. M. 1993. "The Role of Partisan Stereotypes in Information Processing about Political Candidates." *American Journal of Political Science* 37 (2): 472–96.

Reddy, P. 2003. "For Black Candidates, a Ceiling of Their Own." *Washington Post,* January 19, B4.

Seltzer, R., J. Newman, and M. V. Leighton. 1997. *Sex as a Political Variable: Women as Candidates and Voters in U.S. Elections.* Boulder, Colo.: Lynne Rienner.

"Washington Forecast: Fantastic Guessing Game over Sen. Smith's Plans." 1964. *Bangor Daily News,* January 23, 16.

Welch, S., and L. Sigelman. 1982. "Changes in Public Attitudes toward Women in Politics." *Social Science Quarterly* 63 (2): 312–22.

Welch, S., M. M. Ambrosius, J. Clark, and R. Darcy. 1985. "The Effect of Candidate Gender on Electoral Outcomes in State Legislative Races." *Western Political Quarterly* 38 (3): 464–75.

"Woman's Idea of Government." 1870. *New York Herald,* May 27, 6.

Zipp, J. F., and E. Plutzer. 1985. "Gender Differences in Voting for Female Candidates: Evidence from the 1982 Election." *Public Opinion Quarterly* 49 (2): 179–97.

CONCLUSION

During the mid-1800s, when Victoria Woodhull first considered running for the presidency, women could not vote and had not held state or national office. It was difficult for women to act politically at all. Walking door to door without a husband or escort was considered unwomanly, and women who engaged in this type of political activism often encountered verbal abuse. Accommodations for women traveling alone were very rare, and "respectable" restaurants would not serve women after 6:00 P.M. unless they were escorted by a man. When a woman married she suffered "civil death." This meant she was considered property, had no civil standing, lost ownership over her possessions, and legally could be beaten by her husband. With a few notable exceptions, women were not reporters, editors, or owners of newspapers. This world was very different from the one in which Carol Moseley Braun ran for president in 2004.

With the radical changes that have taken place for women in politics and journalism over the last 130 years, it is significant that the press portrayals of women candidates have not changed more. Although I found some differences in the press over time, the strongest trends did not show regular progress. Instead they suggested that women candidates from 1872 to 2004 were treated differently from their men counterparts, with women often getting the short end of the stick. The lack of progress in press coverage seems surprising until one considers that even in 2004 there was a dearth of women governors, senators, and members of the House. The glass ceiling was firmly in place in corporate America, and women continued to do most of the child rearing and made less money for comparable work than men. These facts remind us that many of the cultural forces at play in 1870 continue to exert some influence today. In the press, men and women candidates for president are not treated equivalently, because in society men and women are not treated comparably.

The Patterns

The men received more frequent and longer press coverage compared with equivalent women in the same race. On average the men candidates had twice the number of articles written about them as did the women, and these articles were on average 7 percent longer. The importance of this finding should not be overlooked. Being widely known is the sine qua non of an election, and in national races that cannot and does not happen unless the press is willing to write stories—and stories of substance—about the candidates. This trend does not seem to be abating. For example, the difference in the numbers of stories about Carol Moseley Braun versus those about Bob Graham in 2004 was greater than was the difference between the numbers of stories about Shirley Chisholm and those about Henry Jackson in 1972.

In addition, the coverage that men received was more substantive (regarding issues) and its content was less tangential (e.g., about physical appearance or family) than was the coverage of women. In the stories mentioning men candidates, 27 percent of the paragraphs were about issues. Of the stories mentioning women, just 16 percent were about issues.

In addition to shortchanging the women on substantive coverage, press reports were less likely to portray them as having viable campaigns even though the men and women were equally likely to lose. Men typically had three times the number of positive viability mentions as did the women even when the candidates were polling at the same level. In this way the press may have conveyed and exaggerated the idea that women can't win presidential contests.

There was plentiful evidence that the depictions of the women candidates were driven by long-held stereotypes. One of the persistent areas in which this pattern manifested itself was in the tendency of the media to report physical descriptions of the women candidates. The conventional association of women with their bodies and biology was aptly exhibited in these press data. Women on average had three times as many physical descriptions as their most equivalent male counterpart. These depictions often focused on the attire and appearance of the women. Their age was more likely to be reported than was the age of a man, and the gender of all of the women candidates was heavily marked in the texts. The persistent message is that gender is important and relevant to politics for women (but not for men), and what women (not men) wear and how they look are likewise important.

Women were portrayed in other stereotypical ways as well. They were depicted as more emotional, their families were more likely to be mentioned, and their professional titles were more likely to be omitted from press reports. Even though all the candidates were running for president, the women were more likely than the men to be tabbed by the press for the vice presidency instead of the presidency. In short, men and women candidates are treated differently.

Different has not *always* meant disadvantaged, however. Although it is true that the women studied here did consistently receive less press and less issue coverage, they had slightly longer quotations published than did the men and they received more coverage about their biography and character. Women garnered on average 37 character depictions for every 10,000 words, whereas men elicited just 28. On the other hand, not all of these character depictions were positive or flattering. Women's quotations were also about 14 percent longer on average than those of the equivalent man running in the same race.

Moreover, the texts show that although the press was absorbing, reflecting, and reanimating traditional gender roles in several ways, it was simultaneously highlighting and disseminating resistance and challenges to those paradigms. There were times when the women were described counter-stereotypically, for example, as bold, angry, or leader-like. In addition to this there were some early indicators (too subtle to be called trends) that the future might be brighter than the past.

The increasing number of women in office was reflected in the content of press accounts. In the early races studied, the candidates themselves were the exclusive sources for challenges to stereotypical frames or questions about their (lack of) viability. In later races, particularly in the cases of Schroeder and Dole, other political women were interviewed and quoted as speaking in favor of the candidate. In addition, in Dole's race a woman candidate was portrayed for the first time as potentially viable, and the question of whether women candidates experience discrimination was entertained (including the question of fair press treatment).

There appears to be some early evidence that the ways women and men are described will become more similar. There was no evidence of the cult of true womanhood in Moseley Braun's race, nor was she portrayed as an angry feminist; she was described much like her male opponents. Whether this is the beginning of a trend or just an unusual case, it is too early to tell. Furthermore, the propensity of the press to mention the attire and appearance of women as a percentage of their physical descriptions may be decreasing, while the same may be increasing for men. Thus, despite the dominant trend of unfair treatment and lack of historical progress, the data suggest a coming change.

On a final optimistic note, I observed that in 2000 for the first time there was reporting on the question of how prejudice affects the democratic process, and the issue of fair treatment in the press was part of the public dialogue.

It is important to point out that throughout the period I studied, the texts were never presented with a single voice. Considering the changes in women's rights and women's political participation that occurred during the time span covered, one might expect that the texts of the 1800s would have been dominated by portrayals of fragile, emotional, and dependent women, and that such ideas would be absent from accounts in the twenty-first century. This was definitely not the case. Throughout the years covered by this study there were both strong counter-stereotypical depictions of women and relics of traditional gender roles. Clearly the press is neither fully an instrument of the status quo, as many critical theorists have argued, nor wholly an agent of progress. Rather, there are ways in which the press seems to reflect simultaneously both affirmations of the status quo and challenges to it.

A Gendered Theory of Media Coverage

The view that media content is driven by news values has long been established. Theorists identify the standard news norms (or criteria by which stories are judged as being newsworthy) in different but similar ways. Typically, news norms include the following: prominence (elitism), topicality, human interest (entertainment), conflict (negativity), timeliness, unusualness, continuity, and proximity. These are useful in helping us to understand some of the patterns of women's news coverage versus that of men, for example, the greater frequency of mentions of a woman's character, personality, and experience. Since the women candidates in this study all had counter-stereotypical jobs and lives, traditional news criteria suggest that these aspects of the women would be considered more newsworthy. However, consideration of these norms tends to be less helpful in predicting why women would garner less overall coverage despite their relative infrequent appearance as contenders for the White House.

In developing a theory to explain how much and what type of press coverage was received by women seeking the presidency, it is important to incorporate two additional concepts that mediate evaluations of newsworthiness: sexism and gender stereotypes. For the purposes of this elaboration, one must differentiate these two ideas. "Sexism" refers to the way in which American society systematically overvalues men and undervalues women. For example, American society tends to pay higher salaries to those who are perceived to have greater worth, and men tend to make more money than women. Professions dominated by women tend to offer lower average incomes and less prestige than those dominated by men. As women enter traditionally male professions, average salaries and prestige tend to drop.

Gender stereotypes function slightly differently than sexism. Without making value judgments, stereotypes attribute to men and women different tendencies, characteristics, and areas of competence. Stereotypes associate men and women with different groups of traits. For example, most people believe that women are better at raising children and men are better members of the armed forces.

If notions of newsworthiness are mediated by sexism, one would expect that women candidates would receive less overall press coverage. If sexist societies systematically overvalue men and undervalue women, one would anticipate that the relative value of the candidacy of any man would be perceived as greater than the relative value of the candidacy of any woman, all else being equal. If men candidates are systematically (though probably subconsciously) afforded greater value, it is understandable that they would elicit more articles and words. To state the hypothesis simply: traditional assessments of newsworthiness will be affected by the relative value of various social classes and categories represented by the candidates; for example, classes of people with relatively lower social value will be assessed as less newsworthy (all else being equal). If this is true, then women and people with darker skin would be expected to get less press coverage (all else being equal). Though I do not have enough data to quantify how much gender affects newsworthiness, it is not difficult to conceptualize a study that could measure and test this hypothesis. Various gatekeepers (such as newspaper editors) could be given news stories about candidates with only the name and gender changed to see whether they rate stories about men as having greater news value. Such a test could also ask gatekeepers to estimate how many column inches would be allocated to different stories.

What is interesting about this hypothesis is that its inverse may also be true. Classes of people that receive less attention in the press may be perceived as having less social value. The question here is whether women candidates' relatively less prominent role in the press accounts detracts from their value in society.

Another hypothesis that could explain why women receive less press coverage than men is that perceived candidate viability is a preeminent news value when it comes to writing articles about candidates. We already know from studies that women are perceived as less viable than men even when there are no differences in actual viability. For example, when Virginia Sapiro (1981–82) asked subjects to rate the speech of a candidate with either a man's or a woman's name attached, the man candidate was consistently rated as more viable. If sexism mediates assessment of viability and viability mediates assessments of newsworthiness, this too would explain why women get less coverage overall.

The notion that press coverage is affected by sexism does not, however, explain the differences in the types of coverage men and women receive. For help in explaining that pattern we must look to gender stereotypes. If we assume that reporters hold stereotypes about women, we would expect that family, emotions, and appearance would be related to the concept of womanhood in reporters' minds and that the reporters would readily tap into these ideas when they prepare stories about a "woman candidate." As a result we would expect related concepts to seep into the words and language of the press reports. Traits, attributes, and concepts stereotypically associated with women will be more likely to appear in articles about women candidates than in articles about men candidates. This helps explain why the coverage for men and women is different.

Moreover, what reporters may find interesting about women candidates is that they are novel or defy gender-role expectations. Who the women are and not what they will accomplish in office is what gives these stories the news value of novelty. If that is the case, one would expect to find more character coverage than issue coverage in stories about women. It is the novelty of their characters that makes these women newsworthy. Their stances on issues may be less important because the reporters never expect them to assume office to implement their policies. Gender stereotypes would also make women's families, spouses, and emotions seem more relevant. The idea that stereotyping makes gender-related information more readily accessible to reporters goes a long way toward explaining the types of differences in coverage between men and women.

Gender stereotypes may also explain how much coverage men and women get. One may expect that positive viability outcomes are more closely associated in memory with men than with women, especially when higher-level elected offices are at stake. When reporters have a large field of candidates to cover but limited time and resources in which to do it, they often select and focus on the candidates they feel have the greatest chance of winning. Thus, major-party candidates receive more coverage than candidates from minor parties, as do candidates that party insiders identify as promising. The fact that women have held relatively fewer elected offices and never the presidency may make them seem to reporters (consciously or subconsciously) less likely to win, and they may, therefore, garner fewer stories and column inches.

Yet this hypothesis does not explain one additional trend identified in this study: women are quoted more than men. As mentioned earlier, this may best be explained by the talking platypus phenomenon: if one did see a platypus talk, the phenomenon would be impressive no matter what was said. Abramson, Goldberg, Greenberg, and Abramson (1977) used this analogy in proposing that if people were sensitive to women's struggles in male-dominated fields, they would conclude that a successful woman must be extremely competent. If, based on gender stereotypes, reporters have (erroneously) lower expectations for women in the political field, they may be more impressed by what women say, resulting in more quotations.

Both sexism and stereotypes have long been identified as playing a major role in American society. This study reminds us that the way news is gathered and presented is affected by gender, and that any theories that attempt to explain news content relative to men and women candidates must take sexism and stereotypes into account.

Impacts

Though biased coverage may be quite understandable given extant sex roles and sexism in American society, we should be no less concerned about its potential influences. The most important impact may not be the most obvious: current and historical coverage of women candidates (or the lack thereof) may deter women from running. By framing women candidates as not serious and not viable and by giving extra measure to their hairstyles, clothing, and general appearance, the press may dissuade potential women candidates from entering the political arena. Both men and women tend to think that women have a harder time than men in getting elected to office. The results of my study suggest that this misapprehension may come at least in part from press accounts of women candidates that portray them as less viable than equally viable men. If women have a negatively skewed impression of their chances of winning they may be less likely to run, and this may be the most important and worrisome potential outcome of press coverage of women.

The more obvious implication of biased press coverage is that it may make it harder for women to get elected. Less total coverage, less issue coverage, more physical descriptions, portrayals of women as losing candidates, and dropped titles may all make it harder for the next woman who puts herself forward for the presidency. For a society that prides itself on creating a fair and equal political playing field open to all citizens, this should be of concern.

That said, there is considerable reason for optimism. Studies of lower-level races, in which women receive similarly biased coverage, indicate that women win just as often as men do. Women are sufficiently competent to overcome any disadvantage the press creates. Similarly, actual polling about women and the presidency indicates that should a woman run for the presidency her sex is unlikely to keep her from office, even though the press tends to cover women as losers. There is good evidence that women can overcome the barriers presented by the press and run successful campaigns.

Suggestions for Candidates

Given that press coverage of women candidates has not substantially improved over the last century, women running for the Oval Office should be prepared to challenge the ways in which they are covered. Based on the finding of past coverage of candidates, female candidates and their campaign organizers may wish to consider the following recommendations:

1. *Contact the media to prevent bias.* Just before or soon after a woman announces her candidacy, she should contact the major media outlets to make them aware of this study and others that show that in the past, women candidates have not received as much coverage as men. The campaign staff should highlight the major ways in which women are treated differently than men (e.g., receiving more physical descriptions, garnering less issue coverage, being pigeonholed for the vice presidency) and should request fair and equal treatment.

2. *Prepare a grassroots organization of supporters to monitor the media.* The campaign organizers should ask supporters to write letters to the editor, call radio talk shows, and engage in Internet conversations when sexism or sex stereotyping arises. Media monitors should be aware of the typical arguments against women candidates and they should be asked to counter all such arguments they hear. These monitors should be armed with examples of women who are national leaders, data on women's rationality, anecdotes

about women's ability to handle crises, and other information. Supporters should be encouraged to make public their endorsements (based on the candidate's qualifications and issue positions, not her gender).

3. *Emphasize traditional masculine characteristics associated with leadership.* Sex stereotypes may make reporters more likely to emphasize a woman candidate's stereotypically feminine characteristics. To counter this, the campaign staff should be prepared to emphasize those stereotypically masculine characteristics of the candidate that are associated with leadership (e.g., decisiveness, boldness, courage). The campaign should avoid depictions of the candidate that are stereotypically feminine and may detract from a perception of leadership (e.g., that she is childlike, yielding, gullible, or emotional).

4. *Emphasize issues.* Women may have a more difficult time getting their issues into press coverage. The campaign organizers should make an extra effort to focus on issues in order to counter this tendency.

5. *Be prepared to counter sexist comments from the press and constituents.* The campaign should prepare answers to questions about the vice presidency, why the candidate is not home with her children, and how she will act as a "woman" leader. It should be prepared to counter portrayals of the candidate as a representative of women instead of as a representative of a broader constituency.

6. *Recast attempts to frame the candidacy as symbolic.* Many of the stories that framed the candidates as symbolic were piggybacking on things the candidates themselves said. A successful woman's campaign will have value because of the policies she promotes when she wins office. The campaign should thwart efforts by reporters to cast the candidacy as symbolic and should refocus questions and comments from gender to issues.

7. *Reframe attempts to cast the candidacy as novel.* Though campaign organizers may find it tempting to sell the candidate as "making history," voters are less likely to view women as risky when women presidents are shown to be a normal phenomenon for centuries and across countries all over the world. Deflect the novelty frame by depicting the candidate as just one in a long line of women who have been national leaders. For example, a candidate could respond, "You ask me how it feels to be the first woman nominated by a major party, but in fact women have led nations for centuries, including more than twenty-five women who have been presidents or prime ministers in the last hundred years alone. Women are tried and true national leaders." Alternatively, the campaign could counter the gender frame entirely by recasting the candidate as typical in terms of qualifications, issue stands, or experience. "You suggest that I am the first serious woman to seek nomination by a major party, but in fact I am just another

in a long line of outstanding Democratic senators (such as John F. Kennedy) who have become president."

8. *Avoid suggesting that the principal, natural, or most important role for a woman is to be a mother.* Such sentiments will just cue traditional stereotypes about women that are likely to undercut and not advance the campaign. Such sentiments also make the candidate look hypocritical and may discourage other women from seeking office. Instead, promote vivid examples that demonstrate that women have always worked and played an important role in public service.

9. *Fight the perception that women are unnatural in the political sphere.* Promote the perception that women have a long and deep history of national leadership. Mention the many, many women politicians who have served.

10. *Avoid describing the candidate as emotional. Focus on rationality.* Women's emotionality is one of the dominant reasons given in press accounts as to why people oppose women in the Oval Office. Promote the perception that women are logical and can handle crises.

In analyzing how the media portray women candidates for the presidency, I have uncovered ways that the press either advantaged or disadvantaged women. I have chronicled the historical patterns of coverage for women presidential candidates and have speculated about the possible causes and outcomes of such coverage as well as effective responses to it. Much important work still lies ahead. Research in social science should be conducted to assess more definitively the consequences of these patterns. What effect does more physical description and less issue content have on voters? What are the effects of more character coverage and more quotations? What is the result of repeatedly talking about the vice presidency, candidates' families, or emotions? How does the frame of symbolism or the trail-blazer metaphor affect perceptions of candidate viability? Moreover, what are the effects of these patterns not only on voters' assessment and voting choices, but also on women's decision to run or not run for office? These are the important questions for future research. Once these questions are tested, we can make more compelling recommendations for candidates and social activists.

One night in the winter of 1967, Shirley Chisholm answered a knock at her door. On her porch was a delegation of women from the community. They told her they wanted her to run for Congress and handed her a crumpled brown paper bag with $9.62 in it that they had raised from their welfare checks (Hicks 1971). Chisholm was so moved that she made a choice that few women do. She accepted the bag and ran for Congress. Although the race was close, Chisholm won the primary and then the general election. Four years later, she made another choice rare among women, to seek the presidency of the United States. Few women have taken similar paths, and their awareness of bias and prejudice in the media probably adds to their reluctance to run. Yet, everything we know about those who do run for office tells us that when women run, women win, despite bias in the media. Women who are aware of the media bias should take it into account in planning their campaign communications strategy; but most of all, prospective candidates should not allow press bias to affect their decision to seek office.

References

Abramson, P. R., P. A. Goldberg, J. H. Greenberg, and L. M. Abramson. 1977. "The Talking Platypus Phenomenon: Competence Ratings as a Function of Sex and Professional Status." *Psychology of Women Quarterly* 2:114–24.

Hicks, N. 1971. *Shirley Chisholm: Congresswoman from Brooklyn*. New York: Lion Books.

Sapiro, V. 1981–82. "If U.S. Senator Baker Were a Woman: An Experimental Study of Candidate Images." *Political Psychology* 3 (1/2): 61–83.

APPENDIX
HOW THE RESEARCH WAS CONDUCTED

When I decided to study how the press covers women who run for president it appeared as though there might be only one woman who would run. Since I wanted to make generalizations about how women are portrayed, that presented the problem of an inadequate sample size. The challenge of finding patterns in rare events is often solved by accumulating cases historically, hence I planned to make the added variable (time) an asset by exploring how the depictions of political women changed (or did not change) over time. To do this I selected eight women who ran in seven different decades spanning about 130 years of American history. By analyzing the races together, I was able to find over six hundred fifty newspaper articles that covered women candidates for the White House.

Of course, the historian who hopes to go beyond single case studies to theorize about the nature of culture, humanity, or institutions must confront the fact that all historical events are unique. Thus, in this study I have presented the patterns that hold true over time, those that have changed over the decades, and the unique historical events that may have affected my ability to generalize. Here, I explain how I collected my data and conducted the analysis.

Data

Data for all campaigns were drawn from the *New York Times* during a defined period: from the first day of the first month that the first candidate entered the race in each year studied to the day the last candidate withdrew or the election was held (whichever came first). In addition, I searched the largest circulating newspaper in the home state of each of the opposing candidates, from the first day of the first month when each entered the race until the election or the date the candidate exited the race. For 1872 I searched two additional papers: the largest circulating paper in each candidate's hometown.

For all newspapers except the *New York Times* in 1972, 1987, 1988, 2000, and 2004; the *Newark Daily News* in 2000; the *St. Louis Post-Dispatch* in 2000; the *Chicago Tribune* in 2004; and the *St. Petersburg Times* in 2004, I scanned the newspaper manually for headlines that might be related to the election and then copied the articles that mentioned either of the two candidates selected for study. For the papers and dates mentioned above, electronic searches were available. For the *New York Times* from 1972, I searched abstracts electronically and then manually retrieved the full articles.

I made an exception for the 1988 contest. In that race Richard Gephardt entered the race first and exited it second, but I searched the newspapers only for the four months of Pat Schroeder's "testing the waters campaign." Candidates usually get a boost in coverage when they announce, but since Schroeder never officially entered the race there was no announcement. Therefore, I felt it would be a better test not to include the early part of Gephardt's campaign since he did have a formal announcement. Nor did I include the ending of Gephardt's campaign since he did enter primaries and Schroeder did not. To include those months would have assured a finding that Gephardt had more coverage. Since I found Gephardt had more coverage, even in light of my using a method that minimized his exposure, I felt this approach assured more confident findings.

Reliable circulation information is difficult to find for 1872. The best information I was able to obtain was an 1869 publication for advertisers that lists all periodicals by city. Many, but not all, of the entries contain circulation information. According to the *American Newspaper Directory* (1869), the largest circulating daily in New York was the *New York Herald*. The paper with the second largest circulation was the *New York Sun*. According to the same source, the only local daily from James Black's hometown in 1869 was the *Lancaster Express*. The largest circulating daily in the state was the *Philadelphia Evening Telegraph*.

It was also difficult to find reliable circulation information for 1884. According to the *United States Newspaper Directory Revised* (1881), which was published just three years before the presidential race I studied, the paper with the largest circulation in the District of Columbia was the *Washington Evening Star*. The paper with the largest daily circulation in Benjamin Butler's home state was the *Boston Globe*.

According to the *Editor and Publisher International Yearbook* for 1964, the largest circulating paper in Chase Smith's home state of Maine was the *Bangor Daily News*. The paper with the largest circulation in Rockefeller's home state was the *New York Daily News*.

The Editor and Publisher International Yearbook for 1972 showed that the paper with the largest circulation in Chisholm's home state of New York was the *New York Daily News*. The paper with the largest circulation in Washington state, Jackson's home, was the *Seattle Washington Times*.

The *Gale Directory of Publications* (Gill and Boyden 1988) listed the *Rocky Mountain News* as the paper with the largest circulation in the state of Colorado, where Schroeder lived. The largest paper in Gephardt's home state of Missouri was the *St. Louis Post-Dispatch*.

Circulation data for 1988 from the *Editor and Publishers International Yearbook* indicate that the largest circulating paper in Fulani's home state of New York was the *New York Daily News*. The largest circulating paper in Paul's home state of Texas was the *Houston Chronicle*.

According to the Audit Bureau of Circulation (1999), the largest circulating paper for Dole's home state of Washington, D.C., was the *Washington Post*. The largest circulating paper for Forbes, who was from New Jersey, was the *Newark Star-Ledger.*

According to the Media InfoCenter, in 2004 the largest circulating paper in Moseley Braun's home state of Illinois was the *Chicago Tribune*. The largest circulating paper for Bob Graham's home state of Florida was the *St. Petersburg Times*.

Coding

Once the data were collected, I began reading the articles and looking for patterns. For some arguments, I analyzed the data using rhetorical analysis. For others, I collected and quantified data using content analysis. I developed a coding instrument designed to pick up and count the occurrence of various comments and words to perform the content analysis. Once the codebook was established, I trained one other coder and then conducted a reliability test with that person. We both coded the same nineteen articles. Two variables fell below a Krippendorff's Alpha of .7 and were dropped from the analysis. All of the remaining variables were reliable at Krippendorff's Alpha of .7 or better. After I coded two-thirds of the data, I conducted another reliability test with another coder and a new set of nineteen articles. This test too revealed a reliability of Krippendorff's Alpha of .7 or better for all variables. After the coding was completed for all but one race, I conducted yet another reliability test, this time with myself, since much time had passed since beginning the project. I recoded ten articles that were coded earlier in the process. All variables were reliable at Krippendorff's Alpha of .7 or better on all three tests.

References

Audit Bureau of Circulation. 1999. "Top 20 US Daily Newspapers by Circulation." *Facts about Newspapers.* September 30. Retrieved November 1, 2006, from http://www.naa.org/info/facts00/14.html.

Cook, C. A. 1881. *Newspaper Directory.* Chigago: Cook.

Editor and Publisher International Yearbook. 1964. New York: Editor and Publisher Co.

———. 1972. New York: Editor and Publisher Co.

———. 1988. New York: Editor and Publisher Co.

Gill, K., and D. P. Boyden. 1988. *Gale Directory of Publications.* Vol. 1. 12th ed. Detroit: Gale.

Media InfoCenter. 2004. "Top 50 Newspapers by Circulation, 2004." Retrieved June 30, 2005, from http://www.freep.com/legacy/jobspage/links/top100.htm.

Rowell, G. P. 1869. *American Newspaper Directory.* New York: Geo. P. Rowell.

INDEX

33–34; viability, 41, 43, 125–27; and vice presidency, 64–65; on women at home, 34

source confusion, 27

Stanton, Elizabeth Cady, 104

status conferral, 22

stereotypes: activation of, 55; in beliefs about candidates, 142; and cognitive schemata, 54–55; in coverage, 152–53, 155–56; defined, 55; emotion, 55–56; about family, 59–61; about leadership, 54; in polling, 144; recall of, 73; traits, 53–54; about women, 140–41

strategies, in an election, 116

suffrage, 58, 128

suggestions for candidates, 158–60

supporters of women candidates, 128–33, 140–48

talking platypus phenomenon, 133, 157

Thatcher, Margaret, 5

Title IX, 111, 141

titles, 62

Tversky, Amos, 26

unnatural, women's role in politics as, 33–37

Vgotsky, Lev, 18

viability, 156, 41–45, 116–17, 125–27, 152, 156

vice presidency, 63–67

Welter, Barbara, 67

Whitman, Christine Todd, 44, 86

Whorf, Benjamin Lee, 18, 20

Wolf, Naomi, 84

women candidates: age of, 89, 152; amount of coverage of, 101–2, 106, 152, 156–57; appearance of, 83–87, 153–54; arguments for, 45–47; biographical coverage of, 121–24, 153;

chances of winning, 6; character descriptions, 67–75, 153; compared to Catholic candidates, 146; crying by, 123; and emotion, 38, 56–59, 153, 160; failure to run, 4–6; 74, 117, 148, 157; family mentioned, 60–61, 153; and family responsibility, 6; first names used, 63; as incompetent, 37–41; as irrational, 38; issue competence of, 142; issue coverage of, 118–21, 152; likelihood of getting elected, 145; in lower offices, 4, 145; marking gender of, 91–96; not ready for presidency, 41–43, 139; novelty of, 36, 159; numbers who run, 3; physical descriptions of, 87–91, 152; polling on, 13; 41–44, 140–48; profession mentioned, 59, 61–62; as qualified for presidency, 45–47; quotations of, 124, 153, 157; as ready for presidency, 44, 147; and stereotypes, 53–55, 140–42, 152–61; strategies for, 158–60; supporters of, 128–33; as symbolic, 159; titles of, 62; as trivial, 39–41; as unnatural, 32–37, 160; viability of, 125–26, 152, 156

women's issues, 121

Woodhull, Victoria: about, 7, 101–5; amount of coverage of, 101–5; announcement of candidacy by, 139; attire of, 83; character described, 67–69, 121–24; compared to James Black, 10; and emotion, 56–58; and family, 60; first name used, 63; and issues, 118–21; not ready for presidency, 139; and physical descriptions, 87–91; profession, 61–62; quotations, 124; raising money, 11; supporters of, 128–29, 132; as unnatural in politics, 33; viability of, 41, 125–27; and vice presidency, 64

Woodhull's Memorial, 104, 105, 108

ERIKA FALK is associate program chair for the master's degree program in communications at Johns Hopkins University. Her articles have appeared in *Women and Politics; Sex Roles: A Journal of Research; Social Science Quarterly; Journal of Women and Language;* and other journals.

The University of Illinois Press
is a founding member of the
Association of American University Presses.

Composed in 10.5/13 Hoefler
with Meta display
at the University of Illinois Press
Designed by Copenhaver Cumpston
Manufactured by Sheridan Books, Inc.

University of Illinois Press
1325 South Oak Street
Champaign, IL 61820-6903
www.press.uillinois.edu